Chin up,
girls!

Georgia Powell

Georgia Powell read classics at University College, Oxford. She has worked on television documentaries for the BBC and Channel Four and joined the Daily Telegraph obituaries desk in 2000. She is married with two children.

Katharine Ramsay

Katharine Ramsay read history at Cambridge and worked as a member of the Number 10 Policy Unit under John Major. She joined the Daily Telegraph obituaries desk in 1997 and is married with two children.

Contents

Acknowledgements   vi

Introduction   1
Heroines   7
Trailblazers   27
Battleaxes   65
Sportswomen   111
Matriarchs and Muses   135
Adventuresses   161
Bluestockings   191
Entertainers   217
Upstairs, Downstairs   255
Writers and Artists   287
Low-life and the Afterlife   339

Index   355

Acknowledgements

We would like to pay tribute to obituarists, past and present, who have contributed to this collection – in alphabetical order: Johnny Acton, Sandra Barwick, the late Chaim Bermant, the late Ted Bishop, Alan Blyth, David Bowman, Tim Bullamore, Aurea Carpenter, Will Cohu, James Delingpole, Philip Eade, Claudia Fitzherbert, Bob Francis, Tim de Lisle, Stan Gebler Davies, Dean Godson, Robert Gray, Edward Hart, Lady Selina Hastings, Jay Iliff, George Ireland, Patrick Jourdain, Anthony Lejeune, Quentin Letts, Andro Linklater, the late Midge Mackenzie, Patrick Marnham, Adam McEwen, Sheena Morgan, Tony Morrison, Desmond O'Grady, James Owen, Peter Parker, Martha Read, Caroline Richmond, Eric Shorter, Don Stacey, David Twiston Davies, Hugo Vickers, Martin van der Weyer, Sebastian Wilberforce, Austin Wormleighton and Sir Peregrine Worsthorne.

We would also like to thank our stalwart desk manager, Teresa Moore, who keeps the files and knows where the bodies are buried; Morven Knowles, the *Daily Telegraph*'s publications manager and Gordon Wise and Catherine Benwell at John Murray, all of whom have helped us with their advice and encouragement; and Beatrice Ramsay for cheerfully spending a work experience day at the computer, cutting and pasting.

Thanks are also due to obits editors past and present, David Jones, Kate Summerscale, Christopher Howse and Andrew McKie, but above all to the incomparable Hugh Massingberd, whose pioneering work as *Telegraph* obits editor has given huge pleasure to so many, and whose Wodehousian sense of humour continues to permeate the *Telegraph* obituaries desk.

GP and KR

CHIN UP, GIRLS!

A Book of Women's Obituaries from
The Daily Telegraph

Edited by

GEORGIA POWELL AND
KATHARINE RAMSAY

JOHN MURRAY

For Isobel, Beatrice, Harry and Hope

© Telegraph Group Limited 2005

First published in Great Britain in 2005 by John Murray (Publishers)
A division of Hodder Headline

Paperback edition 2006

The right of Georgia Powell and Katharine Ramsay to be identified as the Authors of
the Work has been asserted by them in accordance with the Copyright, Designs and
Patents Act 1988.

1

A CIP catalogue record for this title is
available from the British Library

ISBN-13 978-0-7195-6301-0
ISBN-10 0-7195-6301-1

Typeset in Monotype Bembo by Servis Filmsetting Ltd, Manchester

Hodde   e and
recycl   rests.
The log   to the

Introduction

When Australian Red Cross nurse Vivian Bullwinkel and her little band of fellow nurses awaited their execution by Japanese soldiers, her obituary records that their matron sought to encourage her young charges: 'Chin up, girls,' she said, 'I'm proud of you and I love you all.' Few of the stories in this collection are as harrowing as Nurse Bullwinkel's, yet Matron's exhortation seems a suitable title for a book of women's obituaries. 'Chin up, Girls' suggests a doughty quality – courage in the face of adversity – which they all share. There are no shrinking violets here.

Ever since Hugh Massingberd took over the *Daily Telegraph*'s 'obits' page in 1986 and turned it into a glorious celebration of human oddity and idiosyncrasy, women's obituaries, though in a minority for obvious reasons of history, have stood in a class of their own. Where men can be intrepid, resourceful, comic, depraved or slightly dotty, women often push the boundaries a bit further. There is a special quality to women's obituaries which sets them apart. Never formulaic and enlivened by unexpected twists and turns, they tend to be more vividly colourful, more heedless of convention than their male counterparts.

It is impossible to conceive of a masculine equivalent of that confection of tulle and pancake, Dame Barbara Cartland. Her obituary records that she once circulated to newspaper editors a folder tied with pink ribbon labelled: 'The History of Barbara Cartland and How I Want to be Remembered'. It included the fact that 'In 1981, I was chosen as Achiever of the Year by the National Home Furnishing Association of Colorado Springs.' A love of shameless self-publicity is not exclusive to either sex, but Dame Barbara took it to new extremes.

When the writer Simon Sebag-Montefiore set much of his

fictional university memoir *King's Parade* (1991) at the house of his old Cambridge landlady, Sadie Barnett, his publishers are said to have found the character based on Mrs Barnett beyond belief, and she was duly excised.

And not even the most imaginative novelist would conceive of so improbable a character as Bapsy, Marchioness of Winchester, the Indian-born third wife of the nonagenarian 16th Marquess and an early example of the 'bunny boiler'. During their well-publicised marital disputes, she stalked her husband and his friend Eve Fleming, raging in vitriolic letters: 'May a viper's fangs be forever round your throat. And may you stew in a pit of your own juice.'

Most of those whose lives are celebrated in this book reached their prime at a uniquely exciting time – between universal suffrage and the Sex Discrimination Act – between women gaining a right to be heard and women being accepted as having a right to equal opportunities. This was the generation of women who made it possible.

They had a lot to put up with. Dame Sheila Sherlock, liver specialist and first woman professor of medicine, graduated top in her year from Edinburgh University but was prevented from holding a house job in a hospital because she was female. The obituary of Violet Webb, Britain's first woman Olympic medal winner, records that women athletes who entered the 1928 Olympics, were told that 'at the Olympic games [the woman's] primary role should be like in the ancient tournaments – the crowning of the [male] victors with laurel.' In 1955, Baroness Wootton of Abinger was inspired to write *The Social Foundation of Wages Policy* by her discovery that her salary as a female don was the same as the money earned by an elephant giving children rides at Whipsnade Zoo.

That many who achieved something in their own right developed a tough carapace is hardly surprising. The formidable Dame Sheila, her obituary records, had a short way with Fleet

Street hacks, who no doubt formed a substantial percentage of her clientele: 'How much do you drink,' she would demand brusquely. 'We all know that journalists drink a lot, but how many do you have before breakfast?' Hermione, Countess of Ranfurly recalled that she was forced to contend, as a child, with the fact that 'I started life as a disappointment because I wasn't a boy. I continued being a disappointment because I was ugly. Instead of minding, I determined to ride better, run faster, be funnier and give more generous presents than the rest of my family.'

Many who left their mark had private means, and of those some also enjoyed the inestimable advantage (at least as far as their obituaries are concerned) of being born into the aristocracy, certain sections of which have never played by the rules which govern the lives of lesser mortals. The daughters of such characters as the 7th Earl Beauchamp KG 'who after acts unpardonable was obliged to leave the country and settle on the Continent', could hardly be expected to lead a regular life.

Nor is it an accident that many of the women in this book were unmarried. Some decided that marriage would hold them back from what they wanted to do. Marjorie Courtenay-Latimer, the local museum curator who discovered that the coelacanth – a prehistoric fish thought to be extinct – was still alive, broke off an early engagement when she found her fiancé 'didn't like my madness in collecting plants and climbing trees after birds'. For some, tragic circumstances deprived them of a happy married life, but spurred them on in other directions. Baroness Wootton's husband was killed in action five weeks after their marriage. She went on to become an academic, a governor of the BBC, a peeress and the first woman to sit on the Woolsack.

War was liberating in other ways too. Susan Travers, who was to become the first female member of the French Foreign Legion, abandoned a vapid and somewhat superficial youth to

3

drive officers and nurse the wounded in France and Italy: 'I had become', she later wrote, 'the person I always wanted to be.' The author Mary Wesley described the effect of war on many women: 'They'd escaped from home, got jobs, lived absolutely for the moment, slept with their lovers – because the next day they might be dead.'

As they explored new opportunities, some women went a little over the top in their efforts to prove that they could be as good as their male counterparts. The obituary of Beatrice 'Tilly' Shilling, inventor of Miss Shilling's Orifice, a device which enabled Spitfire pilots to dive without stalling their engines, records that 'she could braze a butt joint with the skill of a fitter' and that visitors to her house were 'astonished by the variety of motorcycle parts scattered around'. Elsie Widdowson, the nutritionist who helped develop the wartime diet, injected herself with all manner of unpleasant substances at great risk to her own health, in order to discover their effects on the body.

The sex war is only a small part of the story. With one or two exceptions (notably the splendid battling feminist Bella Abzug) few of these women had much time for 60s-style Women's Lib. The fearsome Rear-Admiral Grace Hopper, who helped develop the computer language Cobol and coined the term 'bug', was delighted to be named the first Computer Sciences Man of the Year in 1969. 'I'm thoroughly in the doghouse with the women's liberation people,' she remarked. 'They once asked me if I had ever met prejudice and I said I've always been too busy to look for it.'

Almost to a woman our subjects would have been horrified by today's 'victim culture' and would have taken a dim view of introspection. Whether they are enduring torture by the Gestapo (Mary Lindell) or getting the 'fuzzy end of the lollipop' in love (too many to list), there is never a tremor of self-pity. 'Don't bring me flowers,' snaps the Labour *grande dame* Olive Gibb as she nears her end, 'I'm not dead yet.' Nor is there any whingeing about male chauvinism, though most of them faced it to a degree that would be almost unimaginable now.

Much more striking is the puppyish sense of excitement of women who found themselves free at last to follow their own star. 'Cheerio, Mummy,' calls Peggy Salaman as she sets off in her single-engine Puss Moth to beat the London to Cape Town light aeroplane record: 'I'm determined to do or die and, believe me, I'm going to do.' And she does. Her obituary records that, not content with breaking the record, she picked up a couple of lion cubs *en route*, bottle fed them in mid air and brought them back to the family home in Bayswater where 'there were disagreeable odours – despite unsparing applications of eau-de-Cologne – and ineradicable scratches on the parquet floor.'

But this collection is not some worthy litany of women's achievements played out to the accompaniment of shattering glass ceilings. In these post-feminist days we can welcome the fact that freedom for women means not only freedom to be good, brave or clever, but freedom to be mad, bad or dangerous to know – sometimes all three.

What are we to make of Eileen Fox, the rotund and talkative 'Queen of Soho', who was given to removing her clothes in public when she felt she was being paid insufficient attention and sued British Airways after being bitten on the bottom by a flea? 'A patriot,' her obituarist notes, 'she could seldom hear *Rule Britannia* without loosening her bra straps.' Or Shoe Taylor, the butcher's daughter from Oldham who was inspired to adopt an alternative lifestyle by *The Sound of Music*. Her obituary records that before becoming the devoted mistress of right-wing toff Jonathan Guinness, she spent ten years as a wandering hippy, doing drugs, sex and alternative therapies, before ending up 'a bulimic recluse living in a stone hut in the foothills of the Pyrenees, reduced to scrounging around restaurants and guzzling leftovers which she would then immediately vomit'.

None of the women whose lives are chronicled here had their careers mapped out for them. They could not follow their fathers into the family regiment – or inherit a title. No rich uncle would take them to his club to introduce them to his contacts in the City. As a consequence their stories often have a freewheeling, anarchic quality, full of surprises and sudden changes of direction. Muriel Walker, alias K'tut Tantri, alias Surabaya Sue, began her career in Hollywood writing about film stars for magazines, ditched her husband, upped sticks and moved to Bali to become a painter, fell in love with a Balinese prince, became a hotelier and then an Indonesian freedom fighter in the war against the Dutch.

Choosing the obituaries to include has not been easy. The 'long list' we assembled after several months of trawling through the archives would have filled many volumes. With one or two exceptions, we have tried to avoid the too obviously famous. The great strength of the *Daily Telegraph*'s obituaries page (and a source of immense pleasure for those who work on it) is its concern with the little-known figures whose stories, untainted by familiarity or made tedious by repetition, can bring an era vividly to light. Some obituaries have appeared in previous collections (although we have attempted to keep the numbers down). We make no apology for this, as it would be odd, in this sort of compendium, to omit the best.

We have sought to include as wide a spectrum as possible but this book does not pretend to be remotely comprehensive or even representative. Our selection is highly subjective, our main demand being that they should be good stories written well and in a way which should provoke a strong response in the reader. If you don't cry at the harrowing story of Nurse Bullwinkel, or laugh out loud when reading the obituary of Fanny Cradock, the 'irascible *grande dame* of the kitchen', then there's no hope for you.

Georgia Powell and Katharine Ramsay

HEROINES

*

VIVIAN BULLWINKEL

*Lone survivor of a massacre of young Australian nurses by the
Japanese on a tropical island in 1942*

✳

Vivian Bullwinkel, who has died in Perth, Western Australia,
aged 84, was the sole survivor of a massacre of young nurses by
Japanese soldiers in 1942, a crime which, when it came to light
after the war, stirred Australians to a new pitch of anti-Japanese
sentiment.

A nursing sister with the notional rank of lieutenant, Vivian
Bullwinkel was one of 124 women of the Australian Army
Nursing Service stationed in Malaya in 1941. Their units were
attached to two brigades of Australia's 8th Division, sent to bol-
ster the British defence. On 12 February 1942, with Singapore
on the point of capitulation, Vivian Bullwinkel and 64 other
nurses were ordered aboard the SS *Vyner Brooke*, a small island
freighter bound, with luck, for Sumatra or Java. They hated to
go; they were needed then more than ever. Some 300 evacuees
were crammed aboard, men and women and children.

For nearly two days, steaming at night, the *Vyner Brooke* gave
Japanese warships and aircraft the slip, but bombers caught her
in daylight halfway down Bangka Strait between Sumatra and
Bangka Island. Vivian Bullwinkel, unable to swim, dog-paddled
in her life jacket to an upturned lifeboat and clung there with 11
other nurses, three civilians and a ship's officer. A Japanese aeroplane made a final strafing run, killing survivors in the water.

Many hours later, Vivian Bullwinkel's group had propelled
their boat to Bangka Island. By daylight some hundred survivors
were clustered on a beach; they included British servicemen
whose ship had also been sunk. There was nothing for it but to
surrender; the Japanese controlled the island. While most of the

survivors headed inland to give themselves up, the nurses remained on the beach with stretcher cases and with the British servicemen to await the Japanese.

A contingent arrived purposefully. The men were marched around a nearby headland; 40 or 50 shots were heard and the Japanese returned, cleaning their bayonets. Next, they ordered the 22 surviving nurses, two of them wounded, together with an aged woman, to march into the sea, line abreast. It was about noon; the sea was tranquil, a light breeze played, palms lined the tropical shore. The nurses wore their grey dresses and Red Cross armbands. They knew what was to happen. Vivian Bullwinkel heard their matron, Irene Drummond, say, as they moved through the water, 'Chin up, girls! I'm proud of you and I love you all.' A nurse said drily: 'There are two things I hate in life, the Japs and the sea, and today I've got both.' Vivian Bullwinkel saw no tears and heard no lament.

They were almost up to their waists when a machine gun raked them from behind, back and forth. Vivian Bullwinkel, hit high on the left hip, was knocked over. For a long time, she allowed herself to float with the tide, to all appearances dead like the rest, until she was washed into the shallows. The beach was deserted.

The bullet had gone through with no great damage. That night she slept in a large fern in the jungle lining the beach. Looking for water next day, she heard a voice ask, 'Where have you been, nurse?' It was a British soldier, Private Kinsley, who had been among stretcher cases bayoneted on the beach after the nurses were shot. He had been run through twice, but had managed to crawl away. Vivian Bullwinkel nursed him and herself as best she could for more than ten days, fed by the women of a local village where the men were afraid to help. By then it was clear that the two would have to give themselves up and take their chances.

This they did. Kinsley, who had a wife called Elsie and who came from East Yorkshire, died a few days later. Vivian

Bullwinkel wore a water bottle on her hip to hide the evidence of the wound. She found herself reunited in prison camp with other nurses who after surviving the *Vyner Brooke* (which 12 did not) had fallen into less brutal hands than she did. She spent the next three-and-a-half years in a series of prison camps on Bangka Island and in Sumatra. The nurses buried eight of their companions, dead from malnutrition, ill treatment and disease.

And yet the story has uplifting elements. The steadfastness of Vivian Bullwinkel and the nurses who died at the beach had an echo in the courage and comradeship that helped sustain those in the camps. Twenty-four of the *Vyner Brooke* nurses survived, and Vivian Bullwinkel gave evidence of war crimes to the Tokyo Tribunal. The Japanese officer thought to have ordered the massacre committed suicide; a camp commandant was sentenced to 15 years' imprisonment.

'Bully', as she was known to friends, was 26 years old when captured; tall, slim, with a gentle face, generous mouth, soft blue eyes and fair hair cut in a sort of Eton crop. Naturally reserved, she could nevertheless find humour sometimes when humour was scarce.

Vivian Bullwinkel was born at Kapunda, South Australia, of distant German descent, on 18 December 1915. She was educated in the mining city of Broken Hill, where she began her nursing career.

After the war, she rose to the top of her profession, retiring as Matron of the Queen's Memorial Infectious Diseases Hospital, Melbourne. As a Lieutenant-Colonel in the Citizen Military Forces she commanded a nurse-training unit. She played a prominent role in various civil nursing and service organisations. When in London she was invited to meet Queen Mary, who delighted her with a 40-minute conversation and a signed photograph. She was appointed MBE in 1973, and an officer of the Order of Australia in 1993. She was also an Associate of the Royal Red

Cross, and in 1947 she was awarded the Florence Nightingale Medal, given every two years by the International Committee of the Red Cross as the highest distinction a nurse can receive.

She married, in 1977, Colonel Frank Statham, of Perth; he died in 1999. In 1993 they had attended the unveiling of a memorial to the nurses who died, erected at her urging on Bangka Island.

17 July 2000

DAPHNE PEARSON GC

WAAF who won the George Cross for dragging a pilot from a blazing aircraft loaded with bombs

*

Daphne Pearson, who has died aged 89, was the first woman to be awarded the George Cross, after rescuing a pilot from his burning aircraft.

In 1940 she was a 29-year-old medical corporal working as an attendant in the sick quarters of the RAF base at Detling in Kent. At around 1 am on 31 May she was sleeping fitfully when she heard the noise of a plane in distress. One engine was cutting out and it seemed to be heading directly towards the base. She quickly dressed, put on gumboots and a tin hat and dashed outside in time to see the plane crash through the trees and slam into the ground. 'A guard told me to stop but I said "No",' she later recalled. 'I ran on, opening the gate for an ambulance to get through.'

There was a dull glow where the plane had come to rest. She scrambled over a fence, tumbled down an incline, was stung by nettles in the ditch and finally reached the field with the wreckage. As she neared the aircraft, others appeared on the scene and started dragging the pilot clear. Running towards them, she yelled: 'Leave him to me – go and get the fence down for the ambulance.'

On her own, she began to drag the pilot further away from the blaze, but he was groaning in pain and she stopped to give first aid. Unclipping his harness, she found that his neck was injured and she feared a broken back. The pilot then mumbled that there was a full load of bombs on board, so she pulled him further away, reaching the other side of a ridge just before the petrol tanks blew up. Daphne Pearson at once threw herself on top of the pilot to protect him from blast and splinters, placing her helmet over his head. As they lay there, a 120lb bomb went off, and she held his head to prevent any further dislocation. A soldier then crawled forward and lent her a handkerchief so that she could clean him up (there was a lot of blood around his mouth and a tooth protruding from his upper jaw) and she was about to examine his ankle when the plane went up in another huge explosion. The air around them seemed to collapse and the breath was sucked out of them. They were showered with splinters and debris, and other helpers were blown flat as before a hurricane-force wind.

Fearing that other bombs would go off, Daphne Pearson ran to the fence to help the medical officer over with the stretcher. Shortly after the pilot had been removed by ambulance, there was yet another, even fiercer explosion. Daphne Pearson was undaunted, however, and went back to the wreckage to look for the fourth member of the crew, the wireless operator; but he was dead. Afterwards, she returned to the base to help the doctor, and was on duty as usual at 8 am that day.

Daphne Pearson was awarded the Empire Gallantry Medal on 19 July 1940, the first woman to receive a gallantry award during the Second World War. This was converted into a George Cross in 1941. Her action earned a mention in the House of Commons by Sir Winston Churchill.

Joan Daphne Mary Pearson was born on 26 May 1911 at Mudeford in Hampshire, the daughter of the Reverend J. H. Pearson. After St Brandon's Clergy Daughters' School in Bristol, she apprenticed herself to a photographer. For eight years she worked as a photographer, with her own studio at St Ives.

Ill health persuaded Daphne Pearson to sell the studio in the mid 1930s, after which she worked variously as a chauffeuse and as the manager of the retail fruit section of a large farm in Kent. Much of her spare time was taken up with flying lessons and she was only a few hours away from gaining her pilot's certificate when war broke out. She enlisted in the WAAF in 1939 and was accepted as a medical orderly. A month after her courageous action at Detling, Daphne Pearson was commissioned, and served throughout the War with Bomber Command. In August 1940 she was transferred to RAF West Drayton as Temporary Equipment and Gas Defence Officer, and her subsequent string of postings were mainly in recruitment, although again she was dogged by ill health.

After demobilisation in 1946, Daphne Pearson began a job as assistant governor of a women's borstal at Aylesbury, Buckinghamshire. In the meantime she began evening classes in horticulture. She later became assistant to the keeper of the herbarium at the Royal Botanical Gardens, Kew. She subsequently owned a shop at Kew selling gardening equipment, fresh produce and flowers. In 1959 she emigrated to Australia, where for many years she helped a friend run a farm outside Melbourne.

She never married.

26 July 2000

PAMELA HILL

A life dominated by a love that withstood war, separation and
madness, only to be tested by a diary in code

*

Pamela Hill, who has died aged 83, lived a life dominated by a single love affair, elevated by her indomitable will into one of the most romantic stories to emerge from the Second World War.

The affair began in March 1939, when she met Donald Hill, a good-looking RAF pilot. It was to involve not only the joys of falling in love, but the pain of war and separation, the bitter-sweetness of reconciliation, and a diary written in a code that took half a century to crack.

Pamela Hill had been born Pamela Seely Kirrage at Tunbridge Wells on 16 February 1917, the eldest of three daughters. Her father, Henry Kirrage, was general manager of an insurance company. Pamela's middle-class background was underpinned by an education largely devoted to learning to dance and to play tennis at Hamilton House, a school 'for the daughters of gentlemen'.

When she met Donald Hill, Pamela Kirrage was a model, and, in her own words, 'interested in nothing but having fun'. Hill was more serious, but their first dance proved a *coup de foudre* for them both. That summer of 1939, they were together for every moment that could be spared from Hill's flying duties. In July they exchanged rings; and they were planning their marriage when Hill was ordered to the Far East.

Almost seven years were to pass before they saw each other again. The war put an end to Pamela Kirrage's plans to fly out to join her fiancé. In December 1941, the Japanese invaded Hong Kong; when the colony surrendered on Christmas Day, Flight Lieutenant Donald Hill was taken prisoner. For 18 months, Pamela Kirrage did not even know whether he was alive. She continued, however, to write to him every week. She found work first in the Red Cross, later for the Political Warfare Executive, responsible for black propaganda. At their head-quarters at Woburn Abbey, there was no shortage of unattached, glamorous men interested in a beautiful and seemingly unat-tached girl. Among the most persistent suitors was the songwriter and SOE officer, Eric Maschwitz, who wooed her by taking her to the Mirabelle and singing to her his hit song *A Nightingale Sang in Berkeley Square*. But she resisted all her admirers. 'I know that today it must seem silly being in love like that,' she said years later, 'but Donald was the one person who made me feel complete.'

It was not until the summer of 1944 that an answer came to her letters. 'My darling,' Donald Hill wrote, 'Last week a mira-cle happened. I received a letter from you, dated 11th July 1942. My first letter, darling, and what a difference it made. I was so excited that I started reading it upside down. To know after all these months you are alive and well. Darling, what more could I ask . . . I just live for the day when I shall see you again, my darling. I shall probably be struck dumb.'

At the outbreak of war he had started to keep a diary. To con-ceal an activity punishable by torture or death, he encrypted the entries and disguised the rows of figures as mathematical tables. After the war, he was decorated for his conduct during the battle and for maintaining morale in camp. However, the effects of malnutrition and maltreatment were severe, and on release he was sent to recuperate in New Zealand. Not until January 1946 were he and Pamela re-united.

Ten days after his return they were married, and over the next decade had three children. But Hill, like so many former pris-oners of the Japanese, had suffered deep psychological scars. Increasingly, Pamela found her husband becoming more with-drawn, and prone to violent swings of mood. He would not talk about what had happened in camp, nor would he decode the diary he had brought back. 'I can think of more enjoyable things to read,' he would reply, brushing the subject aside. They began to quarrel. For Pamela, the diary became a symbol of the locked-away part of his personality that she could no longer reach. Their estrangement grew, and eventually the marriage broke down. In 1978 they were divorced. Donald re-married, but away from Pamela his mental state deteriorated rapidly. In a violent flash-back, he assaulted his second wife, and was remanded to a mental hospital. There Pamela found him again. She began to visit and help to look after him. Gradually their old intimacy returned. On her 65th birthday, he bought her flowers.

'Darling,' he declared, 'you know you're the only woman I've ever loved.' Although still legally married to his second wife, he insisted they have an unofficial wedding ceremony. The ring he slipped on to her finger was the engagement ring she had given him in 1939. When he died in 1985, she was holding his hand.

Among his few possessions was his coded diary. It became Pamela's mission to decipher it. Over the next decade she sent it to institutions like the Imperial War Museum and the RAF Museum, but each time it was returned, the code unbroken. Finally, it arrived on the desk of Dr Philip Aston, a mathematician at Surrey University. With the university's resources, he felt the puzzle might be solved in a weekend or two. But Donald had buried his secret deep in layers of code.

For five months, Dr Aston ran endless permutations through a computer, gradually breaking through each layer, but at the heart of the puzzle Donald had placed a final keyword. It defeated all logical attempts at solution until one night, lying sleepless in bed, Dr Aston suddenly understood that it could only be what was most important to the prisoner. Putting together the two names – Donald Samuel Hill Pamela Seely Kirrage – in a single word, he applied it to the diary, and all at once the chaos resolved itself into coherence.

When the decoded diary was given to her in 1996, Pamela found in it no terrible revelations but only Donald Hill's sense of vulnerability. It was his fear of betraying to his captors his deepest feelings that had driven him to hide them. 'Thank God for you Pammy darling,' he had written, 'your memory is ever with me.' 'It feels as though the man I first loved has been restored to me,' Pamela said after reading his diary. Recently, a book about the Hills – *The Code of Love* by Andro Linklater – has been published. Although gravely ill, Pamela Hills was determined to live until it appeared. She attended the launch in a wheelchair. 'Now I can let myself die,' she said.

She is survived by two daughters and a son.

5 April 2000

MARY LINDELL

Head of the French Resistance at Lyons where she ran an escape route out of occupied France

*

Mary Lindell, the Comtesse de Milleville, who has died in Germany aged 91, was an outstandingly courageous British-born heroine of the French Resistance in the 1939–45 War; codenamed 'Marie-Claire', she headed the Resistance organisation at Lyons where she ran an escape route out of occupied France for Allied airmen, soldiers and refugees.

In 1942 she smuggled the only two survivors of the celebrated 'Cockleshell Heroes', Major 'Blondy' Hasler and Marine Bill Sparks, out of France to Spain following their successful raid on German blockade-running ships at Bordeaux. This Commando mission was described by Mountbatten as 'one of the most courageous and imaginative operations of the Second World War'.

Recalling the event 40 years on, the Comtesse said: 'Because of a mix-up in instructions from London I waited for Major

Hasler at the wrong place and it was an anxious time, with the Germans knowing some Commandos had escaped before I was able to contact him and Sparks. It was vital to get them back to England for British Intelligence and I delegated my son to take them through southern France into Spain using one of our escape routes through the mountains. The whole area was swarming with Gestapo men, informers and troops. But they got through safely.' She herself was frequently imprisoned and interrogated by the Gestapo. Finally, in 1944, she was shot through the head and thrown into the notorious Nazi concentration camp for women at Ravensbruck near Berlin, where, as she later put it, 'conditions were pretty dim for the general public'.

In 1983, after Klaus Barbie, the 'Butcher of Lyons', had been returned to the city following his extradition from Bolivia, the Comtesse revealed that she had paid 45,000 francs to Barbie during the war for the release of her elder son from Fort Montluc prison. She told how she had asked an SS officer how much he wanted for her son Maurice de Milleville's release. He had replied: '30,000 or 40,000 francs.' Then she produced the bank notes, torn in half, and said he could have the rest when her son was brought to her alive at the home of some friends in Lyons. M. de Milleville was duly released, having been badly beaten and looking 'like strawberry jam'.

The Comtesse's younger son, Octavius, was deported by the Germans and died in Mauthausen concentration camp. Her daughter also worked for the Resistance. 'My mother had a very narrow channel of interest,' Maurice de Milleville said. 'Her heart was in getting people out of France. There was no other thing.'

Although married to a French Count, Miss Lindell remained invincibly, and somewhat imperiously, British. 'We were sick to death of the French,' she recalled in the Yorkshire Television programme, *Women of Courage* (1980), 'and knew that someone would have to stay behind and stand up to the Jerries and see things through.' She steadfastly retained her British passport during her encounters with the Gestapo, although, as she said, 'I always made out I hated England as part of my cover.'

The Comtesse was not, by all accounts, easy to work with. Some of her Resistance colleagues complained that she would not obey instructions. She herself admitted to arrogance and attributed this to having been well-to-do all her life. She claimed never to have known fear and because of this refused to take credit for the bravery that brought her a fistful of medals. She won the Croix de Guerre twice, once for her bravery as a Red Cross nurse at the Western Front in the 1914–18 War and again for her services to the Resistance in the 1939–45 War. She was also eventually appointed OBE.

After the war her tiny autocratic figure was a familiar sight at meetings of the RAF Association in Paris where she lived with her dachshund Tommy.

10 January 1987

PATRICIA MORPHEW

Fire service driver in the Blitz who kept driving after her car was holed by a bomb

*

Patricia Morphew, who has died aged 80, was awarded a BEM for conspicuous bravery as a young staff car driver for the National Fire Service during the London Blitz.

She was driving to a fire along Dowgate Hill, near the Monument, in the City of London, on the night of 10 May 1941, when a high-explosive bomb detonated only 15 yards from her car. 'It was a hell of a night,' she later recalled. 'I had to drive my chief, District Officer Craggs, to a fire which had just started. I got soaked from a hose, but before I had time to think, there was a flash.

The car leapt into the air and came down 25 yards away. Somehow I was still holding the wheel. A whole building seemed to be coming in on us. The chief threw himself over me and stopped a lot of bricks and debris. Then I found that the car was on fire.'

There was mayhem and confusion all around. But with 'courage a man can envy', in the words of Craggs, she coolly climbed out of the hole in the car's roof and extinguished the flames. She then drove the car on three flat tyres back to her fire station, where she calmly requested a 'cup of tea, please, and another car'. The air raid lasted another 12 hours, during which she remained on duty, scotching incendiaries with anything she could lay her hands on, sometimes stamping out flames. At the height of the attack, she saved a building from fire by promptly removing two incendiary bombs from an upper floor.

She recorded in her diary how, during a brief lull in the bombardment, she sat down to rest in front of some wooden doors but quickly got up again when she realised that the green paint behind her was bubbling with the heat. On 11 May, her diary entry simply read: 'Leave, full moon, slept.'

She was born Patricia Dorothea Dewing on 6 June 1917 at Southsea. When she was a year old, her father, Lieutenant-Colonel Robert E. Dewing, DSO, was killed in action leading the 10th Battalion of the Royal Berkshire regiment in France. Her mother died shortly afterwards in the great influenza epidemic of 1919. Patricia and her sister were brought up by their grandfather and, when he died, by two uncles. She was educated at Ancaster House, Bexhill and then at a finishing school in Montreux, where she learned skiing and 'a little French'. She began training as a physiotherapist in the French town of Rennes, then returned to England to complete her training at King's College Hospital, qualifying shortly before war broke out.

She volunteered for the Fire Service because, she explained, she had a 'girl's love of fire engines with bright red pumps and clanging bells'. She was immediately posted as a staff car driver to

Cannon Street Fire station. She had to drive officers through an area which included London's docks, Beckton gasworks and the City of London, including St Paul's. During the Blitz, Patricia Dewing's station had to cope with massive destruction. The docks were a constant target; the vast reinforced concrete plant at Beckton was blasted into gargantuan wreckage and in one night six million books blazed in the publishers' warehouses around St Paul's. It made Patricia's driving duties something of a challenge.

'Called to St Paul's about 12pm. Spent unhappy time outside waiting for Craggs,' read a typical entry in her diary, for 16 April 1941. 'No one in sight. Bombs very near all around. Things crashing down. Many fires. Land mine on church, and several dead. Tried to give First Aid to one man covered with dust, but he was dead.'

On another occasion she volunteered to go into the street to give first aid to some injured firemen, regardless of the danger from falling bombs. Afterwards she helped fight a fire in the station itself, and prevented the flames from spreading. During another raid, she recalled, she was working on a bombed site, and tugged at some ropes in the dark, lost her balance and fell into a warehouse basement into a tank full of oil, ruining her uniform. By daylight it turned out that the ropes were attached to an unexploded parachute mine.

When not employed driving her car, she would often be sent off on other errands. She recalled being instructed by one fire officer to 'just nip up to the dome [of St Paul's], girl, and tell us how the fires at Cheapside are going.'

After the war, she returned to her practice as a physiotherapist. She was twice married. Her first marriage, to Martin Burnett, was dissolved. She married, secondly, Christopher Morphew, who died in 1986. She is survived by a daughter by her first marriage.

15 June 1998

SYBIL BANNISTER

*Englishwoman who spent the war in Germany and was nearly
burnt to death during the massed Allied bombing of Wuppertal*

*

Sybil Bannister, who has died aged 86, was an author whose
experiences as an Englishwoman alone in Germany during the
Second World War remained painful to the end of her life.

She was born on 29 May 1910, the daughter of a Sussex
farmer. In the summer of 1933, while she was in Germany learning the language, she met a handsome medical student called
Kurt Falkenberg. Three years later they married and Sybil settled down to life as a housewife in Danzig, where her husband,
by then a doctor, worked.

At 5 am on 1 September 1939 she was woken by the roaring of
guns: German troops had crossed the Polish frontier. Two days
later Britain declared war, and three days after that, Sybil gave birth
to their son, Manny. Soon she was dependent on messages from
the Red Cross for news from her family in Sussex. As war deep-
ened, her marriage began to fail – due in part, she believed, to the
differences of nationality. Nevertheless, when Falkenberg told her
that he wanted a divorce late in 1941, she was wholly unprepared.
Hearing the news, she felt a rush of fear, which left her cold and
shivering, a feeling matched only in the worst of the air raids to
come. She was allowed to keep Manny, but Sybil Bannister was
now effectively adrift in Nazi Germany. An invitation followed
from her ex-husband's parents to bring their grandson to stay for
a holiday in Wuppertal-Barmen, in western Germany.

On the night of 29 May 1943, as she and her sisters-in-law
sipped wine to celebrate her birthday, they heard the sound of the
Wuppertal anti-aircraft guns firing at massed Allied bombers.
Sybil Bannister ran to take her son from his attic bedroom to the

vaulted cellar of the house. As she opened the cellar door a series of huge explosions shattered the house above. Neighbours in their night clothes crammed into the cellar carrying the wounded and burnt, while flames lit the streets outside. The stifling heat from the burning house above made it increasingly clear that those in the cellar must either face the flaming streets, or suffocate. Outside the air was filled with smoke, and the tar of the roads was melting with the heat. The burning phosphorus from incendiary bombs clung to debris as it fell into the streets. Wrapping Manny in a rug so that he would not be scorched, Sybil Bannister stumbled through the streets, at one point running through knee-high flames to escape the burning buildings. Eventually, too weary to go on, she fell to the ground half-conscious, aware only that she and Manny would both burn to death where they lay. As the flames reached the child's feet he screamed and kicked, awakening her to further efforts. Within seconds, a motorcycle and side-car drew up and the two were driven to safety. Not until she reached it did she feel pain and realise her legs were burnt from knee to ankle, with third degree burns down her calves.

It was the first Allied raid of such intensity, and Wuppertal was destroyed. She later said that although many realised she was English, none of her fellow sufferers railed at her for her nationality, either then or during later raids.

After her wounds had healed, in 1944 she was ordered by the Gestapo to hand her son over to the National Socialist Party Welfare Association; otherwise, she was told, he would be taken forcibly and placed in an institution. Though terrified, she went to see the Gestapo Chief, but her pleadings were to no avail. In the event she gave up Manny to his father and his new wife in Bromberg, seeing him only briefly, once a week, until January 1945, when the Russians were at the gates of the city. Sybil, Manny, her husband's new wife Hedi, and their adopted baby Uwe, just managed to board a train out. It was a 30-hour train journey to Berlin: the passengers were squeezed together without heating or sanitation; one woman went mad before their eyes; and through the windows they glimpsed open wagons carrying wounded soldiers who had frozen to death.

In Berlin, Sybil Bannister had to leave Manny again to be taken by Hedi, with Uwe, to Pomerania. Reaching Hamburg, she found the city razed. She pretended to be German and took a health visitor's job, visiting the huts occupied by the bombed-out citizens. She was frequently caught in raids as she worked. When the British took the city in May 1945, she found herself in the unsettling position of being a 'peeping Tom', as she put it, a Briton viewing the British occupiers through a German subject's eyes.

Her child, a refugee again, survived a long journey, walking and begging for lifts and food from Pomerania to Hamburg, but his adopted baby brother Uwe died on the road. When she and her son finally managed to return to England, Sybil Bannister found it hard to talk about what she had experienced, and harder still to find listeners who wanted to hear. In the immediate post-war years few English people wanted to believe that there were any good Germans, such as the friends who had sheltered her and helped her survive. When neighbours spoke with awe of the effects of the Blitz on London, Sybil Bannister learnt that it was best not to point out that the scale of destruction in Germany was so much greater.

She later worked as a secretary in Sussex and, a keen amateur musician, sold programmes at Glyndebourne each year. A book she wrote to exorcise her experiences, *I Lived Under Hitler*, found only a few readers when it was published in 1957. She was pleased when a new generation discovered it on its re-publication by Penguin in 1995, though re-living her experiences distressed her deeply.

Sybil Bannister did not re-marry, and is survived by her son.

24 May 1997

TRAILBLAZERS

*

DAME SHEILA SHERLOCK

The world's foremost authority on the liver and the first woman
in Britain to become a Professor of Medicine

*

Dame Sheila Sherlock, who has died aged 83, was the world's leading liver specialist. Aggressive, ambitious and audacious, Sheila Sherlock was a small bundle of energy, and her output – written, clinical, research, and teaching – was phenomenal. She was the first woman in Britain to be appointed a Professor of Medicine and the first to become vice-president of the Royal College of Physicians. She wrote the first serious modern text-book on her subject, *Diseases of the Liver and Biliary System*, in 1954; it ran to 11 editions and was translated into at least six languages.

In the 1950s, no one knew much about liver disease, but her clinical research and teaching soon improved diagnosis and treatment. Previously, the only way to take a sample of a person's liver was by using open surgery, often impossible as many patients with liver disease are unfit to receive a general anaesthetic. She popularised needle biopsies, making an exact diagnosis possible.

Jaundice was common in Allied troops during the Second World War, and the biopsy material revealed its causes, which included blood transfusion. In 1966 she helped to create what is now a standard test in diagnosing primary cirrhosis of the liver, later showing (with Deborah Doniach at the Middlesex Hospital) that it was caused by an auto-immune reaction. In 1971 she showed that it could be treated with steroids. Later she showed that hepatitis often leads to cirrhosis and thence to cancer, and that hepatitis could be prevented by vaccination.

Sheila Patricia Violet Sherlock was born on 31 March 1918. From Folkestone Grammar School she was rejected by several medical schools, which had few places for women, and went to

Edinburgh University, graduating top in Medicine in 1941. Prevented from holding a house job because she was female, she became clinical assistant to James Learmonth, Professor of Surgery. She called him 'Poppa'; he taught her how to do research and how to write it up. The following year she moved to the Hammersmith Hospital, west London, as house physician to Professor John McMichael. Three years later she received an Edinburgh MD and Gold Medal for a thesis on acute hepatitis. After a Rockefeller Fellowship at Yale University and a further year at the Hammersmith, she was appointed Lecturer and Honorary Consultant Physician. She was still only 30. By the time she was 35, she and her liver unit were internationally known. She had become a Fellow of the Royal College of Physicians in 1951, aged 33, by far the youngest woman to be elected. In 1982 she was narrowly defeated for the College Presidency. In 1959 she moved to the Royal Free Hospital and medical school. When she retired in 1983 she moved to the Department of Surgery, where she worked, wrote and saw private patients until shortly before she died.

Her liver unit gained an increasingly wide reputation. At one time all the world's leading liver specialists had been through it. She did a weekly ward round for them, treating them like small children; they took it like lambs. A mother hen to those working under her, she did all she could to teach them and advance their careers, pushing them out of the nest when she felt they were ready. On occasion she reduced male junior doctors to tears, and she could tear up a third and fourth draft of a research paper while detailing her criticisms. She could harrumph with indignation if she received similar criticism. But her staff respected and loved her.

If she was maternal to her staff, she was paternalistic to her patients. She knew what was best for them and would tell them what she thought and what she was going to do. There was little place for patients' feelings: 'How much do you drink?' she asked a sick newspaper journalist. 'We all know that journalists drink a lot, but how many drinks do you have before breakfast?'

In the 1950s and 1960s, consent to carry out research on patients was rarely questioned or discussed. Most patients adored Sheila Sherlock and would submit to almost anything. But in 1969, in his book *Human Guinea Pigs*, Dr Maurice Papworth questioned the ethics of experimenting on patients, and cited Sheila Sherlock's work as a prime example. A controversy ensued, and she never forgave Papworth.

Sheila Sherlock let her hair down at parties, played tennis competitively, could name the Kent county cricket team, understood rugby football and supported Arsenal. She received many awards and honours, and was appointed DBE in 1978. In 2001, she was made a Fellow of the Royal Society.

She married, in 1951, Dr Geraint James, who survives her together with their two daughters.

20 February 2002

PEGGY SALAMAN

*Aviatrix who beat the London to Cape Town flying record with
a couple of lion cubs*

*

Peggy Salaman, the aviatrix who has died in Arizona aged 82, became an international celebrity while still a Bright Young Thing when she beat the London to Cape Town light aeroplane record, picking up a couple of lion cubs on the way.

On 30 October 1931 – with a 'Cheerio, Mummy, I'm determined to do or die and, believe me, I'm going to do' – Miss Salaman waved her mother good-bye and flew off into the night from the Channel coast airfield at Lympne in Kent. Peggy

Salaman's flight captured the imagination of the press; here was 'The Girl With Everything Money Could Buy Who Had Got Bored With It All'. Such details as the fact that she had packed an evening gown for Cape Town – and that she had brought along packets of chewing gum to seal any petrol tank leaks – were lovingly chronicled.

Five days, six hours and forty minutes after she left Lympne she landed in Cape Town – accompanied by Gordon Store, her South African navigator and fellow-pilot. Her time knocked more than a day off the previous record of Lieutenant Commander Glen Kidston, who that spring had completed the journey in six days and ten hours. But, taking into account the fragility of her little single-engined De Havilland Puss Moth, it was an even greater achievement than the figures indicate. Kidston had flown a heavier and more powerful Lockheed Vega – in effect, a Mini compared with a Rolls. Indeed the Moth was hardly more than a standard flying club machine, maximum speed 125 mph. There was, however, an additional fuel tank and a metal propeller to add about 5mph to the speed. Navigation lights were fitted but there was no radio. The Moth, which she called the Good Hope, was a present from her mother. It was dressed in a livery of navy blue with a pale blue stripe – 'Like the perambulator I had for her as a baby,' said her mother.

The daughter of a businessman and property developer, Peggy Louise Salaman was born in London in 1907 and educated at Queen's College, Harley Street, and Bentley Priory (which, in 1940, was to become Dowding's HQ during the Battle of Britain). Finished in Paris, she did a London Season before, in pursuit of her passionate determination to fly, taking lessons at Hanworth with Capt. Finley, a former RFC pilot. She obtained an 'A' licence, and in July 1931 she entered the Moth in the King's Cup air race, where – accompanied by Lieutenant Geoffrey Rodd as her pilot – she won the prize for the fastest machine.

That October, as she headed for Le Bourget in Paris on the first leg of her epic flight, Miss Salaman's only sartorial concession to aviation was a helmet. The rest of her attire in the cockpit comprised grey flannel trousers and a white sweater. A pith helmet and shorts were packed with the ball gown for the tropics. With Store navigating, she flew the old 'Red Route' of the British Empire. After Rome and Athens came Juba, where she was much taken by a pair of lion cubs. She duly bought the cuddly young creatures for £25 and named them Juba and Joker; they were bottle-fed on board as the Good Hope progressed towards Entebbe.

Then it was on to Bulawayo, but the combination of nightfall and a hilly area urged caution, and she landed in wild bush country between Abercorn and Broken Hill, Northern Rhodesia. Came the dawn and take-off was found to be impossible until a strip had been prepared. Fortunately Store had armed himself with a machete and Peggy had a revolver with which she felled some young trees. An elephant trench was filled with earth to clear a runway. Airborne again, Store, as she recalled, 'threaded his way through Africa as easily as a taxi-man in London'.

In the last stages of the adventure Miss Salaman left the 18-day-old cubs at Kimberley to be sent on by train. They had become too much of a handful. On arriving at Cape Town and hearing that she had broken the record, she trilled: 'How perfectly lovely!' She added: 'We could have got here much earlier, but we slowed to 90mph over gorgeous mountains and admired the magnificent scenery.'

Afterwards she was told the Moth was now unfit to fly. Store stayed on in South Africa, but she sailed home with the lion cubs in the liner *Warwick Castle*. At sea she heard that the celebrated aviator Jim Mollison, already chasing her record, had crashed in Egypt. She cabled to him: 'Hard lines. You missed our luck.'

Back in London she returned to the family in Cambridge Square, Bayswater. The cubs resided in the cloakroom, but as they grew the maids complained. Not only were they considered potentially dangerous but there were disagreeable odours – despite unsparing applications of Eau de Cologne – and ineradicable scratches on the parquet floor. Bertram Mills came to the rescue but he was unable to tame them for his circus; eventually the lions, by now renamed Romeo and Juliet, were housed in a private zoo.

Subsequently Peggy Salaman gained a commercial licence in America, where she entered a Los Angeles Air Derby and finished 42nd out of 80. During the 1939–45 War she served in the WAAF, as a plotter, and then in the WRNS. Afterwards she helped to look after displaced children at a camp in Brittany.

Miss Salaman was married briefly to Denis Flanders, the architectural and landscape artist. During a visit to America in the 1950s she met her second husband, Walter Bell, an electrical engineer and airman with two private aircraft. Flying around America together, they landed one day at Phoenix, Arizona, and were so enchanted that they bought a house in the adobe style and settled there.

12 September 1990

CATHERINE GRIFFITHS

Oldest survivor of the Welsh suffragettes who was jailed for breaking into the House of Lords

*

Catherine Griffiths, who has died aged 102, was a remarkable Welsh nurse of fiery temperament and said to be the oldest survivor of that determined band, the Suffragettes, celebrated for their militant 'Votes for Women' campaign.

Between 1911 and 1914 in particular, they made some highly

imaginative and inventive demonstrations: Mrs Griffiths's contribution was to gain access to the chamber of the House of Commons and strew tin tacks upon the seat of Lloyd George ('To make him sit up' she later explained). Subsequently she was jailed for breaking into the House of Lords.

After female suffrage was won, she went on to make a solid contribution to local government politics, eventually becoming Mayor of Finsbury. She joined the Labour Party as soon as membership became open to individuals (1918), was a founder-member of its Women's Section in North London, and gave distinguished service to the Co-operative Women's Guild. Mrs Griffiths cherished vivid memories of Keir Hardie, Clem Attlee, Aneurin Bevan and other stalwart socialists. In 1987 she received an award and a standing ovation at the Labour Conference, responding with a happily-phrased speech. At 100 years old she still climbed three flights of stairs to her flat, but at 102 would consent to a short rest en route.

Born Catherine James in 1885 at Nanyffyllon, near Maesteg, she was the daughter of a miner and granddaughter of the village blacksmith. Her father was literate and spoke both Welsh and English. Her mother was unlettered and knew only Welsh. Catherine was proud of her Welsh ancestry and always retained the attractive lilt of her mother-tongue. She was one of five children brought up in the old respectable tradition of clean pinafore for school, Bible always on the parlour table, Sunday chapel and weekly Band of Hope meetings. She graduated from 'board school' to higher school, then trained for three years as a nurse at Merthyr Tydfil. Since probationers were unpaid, the family provided her with money for clothes – the mark of a modest social standing but still a struggle – and when her pay rose from 10 shillings and then to 15, she was quick to 'run home to Mam' with it.

Working as a Queen's Jubilee Nurse (district nurse) in Merthyr and Cardiff she often had to deal with mining and docklands injuries. What she saw in poor homes made her a radical and a suffragette. 'A woman was just a slave – there to attend to the needs of men,' she would recall. Illiteracy was widespread and she was often asked to write letters (sometimes in very stilted phrases) for the families she visited. But so great was the opposition to radicalism and the suffrage movement that some householders ordered her away rather than have their families attended by her.

She settled in London in the 1914–18 War when her husband's work in education brought them to Finsbury. After his death in 1948 she concealed her age to get back into nursing work and even when forced to retire in 1965, undertook regular weekly voluntary work at the Great Ormond Street Children's Hospital until she reached 100. Even after this she remained a governor of Dulwich College, and Prior Weston School, and worked for the Amwell Society, a local conservation group.

Some of today's radical causes failed to win Mrs Griffiths's support, sometimes to the surprise of younger people. 'You can't put words in her mouth, can you?' remarked one young BBC interviewer after Mrs Griffiths had declared of NHS abortion: 'It's against nature.' And she would often refer nostalgically to the firmer discipline of bygone days.

Mrs Griffiths is survived by a son and a daughter.

23 March 1988

MARGARET MEE

Botanical artist and traveller who braved snakes, spiders and cannibals in her pursuit of rare species

*

Margaret Mee, the intrepid and brilliant botanical artist who has died aged 79, devoted her life to recording the threatened flora of the Amazonian rainforests. Besides being one of the foremost experts of the art of flower portraiture, Margaret Mee was a redoubtable traveller in the great female tradition of Mary Kingsley and Freya Stark. Wearing a straw hat and packing a pistol along with her sketch pad, brushes and water-colours, this deceptively frail and intensely feminine woman braved snakes, poisonous spiders, cannibals and blood-sucking buffalo gnats to penetrate the deepest Brazilian jungle in pursuit of rare species.

She would make her way in a small boat, with a local boat-man as her only companion, and suffered several bouts of malaria and hepatitis. One night a band of drunken gold prospectors burst into her hut in an Indian village, but she sent them on their way, reminding the ruffians that it was not proper to enter a lady's hut when she was alone. When the leader of the gang unwisely made another incursion into the hut some hours – and bottles – later, he found himself looking down the barrel of Mrs Mee's .32 Rossi revolver.

'I haven't had a lot of shooting practice,' she recalled, 'but really I think I'm quite good. After all, a steady hand and a good eye are absolutely essential qualities for a painter, wouldn't you say?'

Her last Amazon expedition took place this May when she fulfilled her long-held ambition to record the *Selenicereus wittii* (the Amazon Moonflower). On previous journeys in the Igapo flooded forest she had seen the celebrated cactus (which flowers just once, on one night a year) but never succeeded in capturing it with her brush. Once, in the late 1970s, she caught a glimpse of it in bud, but its surrounding creek proved impenetrable in the dark and when she returned in the light of day the flower had closed. But on her final journey Mrs Mee succeeded in painting the opening flower and, for the first time in the wild, noted many points of its unusual natural history. In her diary she recorded how she waited for the buds to open: 'As I stood there with the dim outline of the forest all around, I was spellbound.

Then the first petal began to move and then another as the flower burst into life.' She then had merely a few hours of darkness left to commit the flower to paper for posterity.

Margaret Hendersen Brown, of Swedish seafaring descent, was born at Chesham, Bucks, in 1909 and, although she studied art as a girl, made her initial mark in the political sphere. In 1937 she was delegate of the Union of Sign, Glass and Ticket Writers to the TUC in Norwich, where she made a stirring speech.

During the 1939–45 War she served as a draughtsman in an aircraft factory and afterwards resumed her art studies at the Camberwell School of Art under Victor Pasmore and then at St Martin's, where she met her second husband, Greville Mee, a commercial artist. In 1952 the Mees moved to Brazil, where her sister lived, and Margaret began her travels to capture the beauty of flowers. In the course of her early journeys, she concentrated her efforts in the coastal rainforest around São Paulo, finding a host of subjects which she illustrated with unerring accuracy and a sensitive technical style. These early paintings are all the more important because this coastal rainforest has since virtually disappeared. They were exhibited in Brazil in 1958 and in London in 1960 when she was awarded the Grenfell Medal of the Royal Horticultural Society.

In the early 1960s, her journeys were into the arid north-east of Brazil where she sketched and painted for Dr Lyman B. Smith, the authority on the family *Bromeliaceae*. These studies were made under the patronage of the Insititute de Botanica, São Paulo, and the Smithsonian Institution, Washington.

Margaret Mee's great Amazonian odyssey began in 1956 with a visit to the Gurupi river which forms a border between the states of Pará and Maranhão. In 1962 she visited the Mato Grosso, and in 1964 the Upper Rio Negro along the borders of Colombia and Venezuela. In 1967, sponsored by the National Geographic Society, she became the first woman traveller to climb on the south side of the Pico de Nebline, Brazil's highest mountain. From this journey her interest in and concern for the future of the forest Indians began and then grew in intensity over the years.

A high point in Mrs Mee's career came in 1967 when she exhibited at London's Tryon Gallery, a show timed to coincide with the publication of a folio edition of *Flowers of the Brazilian Forests*, containing 32 plates. The edition was created under the patronage of Prince Philip and the paintings were widely acclaimed. Wilfrid Blunt, the art critic and historian wrote of them: 'They could stand without shame in the high company of such masters as Georg Dionysius Ehret and Redouté.'

More Amazon journeys followed, with two in 1971–2 funded by a Guggenheim Fellowship. These were immensely successful as Mrs Mee discovered an area south of the main Amazon stream which was rich in new species – notably *Aechmea polyantha* and *Aechmea Meeana*, bromeliads which have never been found since and which are known only from Margaret Mee's Amazon Collection of 60 paintings.

The next 18 years of her life were devoted to further Amazon journeys from which the major part of the Collection was derived. Margaret Mee's paintings were seen at exhibitions held in 1980 at the National History Museum and in 1986 at the Missouri Botanical Garden. She was appointed MBE in 1975 and elected a Fellow of the Linnean Society in 1986. For ten years she was an honorary associate of the Botanical Museum of Harvard University.

At the time of her death, in a motor accident in the English Midlands, she was campaigning passionately for the conservation and future of the Brazilian jungle and promoting her remarkable new book, *In Search of Flowers of the Amazon Forests*. Mrs Mee, who saw the beginning of the destruction of the Amazon forests in the late 1960s, realised the scientific value of her work and determined never to sell an original first painting of any species. Thus she created a unique record of Amazon plants in permanent gouache, a medium which, if well conserved, should last forever. It was her hope that this collection should be deposited in its entirety at the Royal Botanic Gardens, Kew, and this is one of the aims of the Margaret Mee Amazon Trust, of which she was an active vice-president.

She is survived by her husband.

3 December 1988

BARONESS WOOTTON OF ABINGER

Socialist grande dame who overcame wartime bereavement to become an academic criminologist, writer and the first woman to sit on the Woolsack

*

Baroness Wootton of Abinger, who has died aged 91, was one of the most eminent women of her generation, as an academic, a writer on social and economic questions, a JP for more than 40 years, a governor of the BBC and one of the first life peeresses in the House of Lords, where she was the first woman to sit on the Woolsack.

A lifelong socialist, Lady Wootton once described the Lords as 'a very nice club' with a 'lot of interesting people in it', adding that it was 'extraordinarily futile' and that she looked forward to its abolition. She nevertheless played an active part in its proceedings – introducing the Bill to abolish the death penalty, for example – and spoke often and lucidly on such questions as legal reform. In 1968 her report on soft drugs caused a considerable furore by its recommendation of more lenient sentences for offences involving cannabis, and was dismissed patronisingly by James Callaghan, the Labour Home Secretary, as 'over-influenced by a lobby in favour of legalising pot'. In 1970, however, Callaghan introduced legislation broadly in line with the Wootton proposals.

Though she was a staunch liberal on social questions, Lady Wootton had no time for the pseudoscientific cant that often accompanies such a position, especially in her specialist area of criminology. Of the excessively psychological approach to crime, for example, she observed that: 'Two hundred years ago we used to make a practice of treating lunatics as criminals; nowadays we are much more inclined to treat criminals as lunatics.'

The daughter of two Cambridge dons, Barbara Frances Adams was born in 1897. She learned to read at the age of three, but was educated at home until she was 13, when she went to the Perse School for Girls, Cambridge. She later said: 'I never learned anything at school except possibly some command of the English language.' She nevertheless won a classical scholarship to Girton College. In 1917, while still an undergraduate, she married Captain John Wootton. The next day he joined his regiment in France, and five weeks later he was killed. As she recalled bitterly in her autobiography, *In a World I Never Made* (1967): 'His blood-stained kit was punctiliously returned to me.'

After this traumatic experience Barbara Wootton pressed on with her studies, switching in her final year to the economics tripos, in which she won a starred first. This resulted in the award of a research scholarship at the London School of Economics and an invitation to lecture in social science at Westfield College. In 1920 Barbara Wootton was back at Girton as director of studies and lecturer in economics. She also joined the University Labour Club and, brimming with socialist fervour, gave up the easy and pleasant life of a don to join the research department of the Trades Union Congress and the Labour Party. At election time she wrote speeches for Labour candidates, and sometimes went to meetings to hear how her efforts turned out: 'It put me off for ever from wanting to stand myself – so phoney!'

In 1924 she was the only woman invited to join a departmental committee under Lord Colwyn to report on taxation and the national debt – an appointment which, she complained, resulted in 'persecution' by journalists, who pestered her with questions about her qualifications, recreations and love life. The committee sat for three years, but failed to reach agreement – though Barbara Wootton was one of the four Labour members who produced a minority report.

At the age of 28 she was made a magistrate, which delighted her but at the same time struck her as absurd, since women at that time were not allowed to vote until they were 30.

Lack of prospects in her Labour party job drove Barbara Wootton in 1926 to take the post of principal of the Morley College for Working Men and Women; but the next year she was offered the new post of director of studies for the extra-mural undergraduates of London University. During her 17 years in that job she travelled widely – to Russia, Norway, America and Mexico – and began her series of books and pamphlets. She wrote 14 books in all, the most scholarly of which was *Social Science and Social Pathology* (1959). Others ranged from the overtly political – *End Social Inequality* (1941), for example – to studies of crime (*Crime and the Criminal Law*, 1964) and wages policy. She was inspired to write *The Social Foundations of Wages Policy* (1955) by her discovery that her salary as a don was the same as the money earned by an elephant giving rides to children at Whipsnade Zoo.

For four years from 1948 she was Professor of Social Studies at London University, then concluded her academic career as Nuffield Research Fellow at Bedford College from 1952 to 1957. Barbara Wootton was a governor of the BBC from 1950 to 1956, and a magistrate in the Metropolitan Courts – taking a particular interest in juvenile offenders, whom she thought should never have appeared before her in the first place – until 1970. Aside from her work in the House of Lords – to which she was nominated by Hugh Gaitskill in 1958, and where she served as Deputy Speaker – most of her public work was on Royal Commissions (on the press, the Civil Service and the penal system) and on a number of departmental committees. She was also a member of the BBC's Brains Trust. She held innumerable honorary degrees, and was appointed CH in 1977.

Though she kept the name of her first husband, Barbara Wootton remarried in 1935, to George Wright, a taxi driver, who died in 1964.

13 July 1988

MARGARET LOUDEN

Surgeon whose pioneering treatment saved people crushed by buildings in the Blitz

✳

Margaret Louden, who has died aged 88, was a skilful general surgeon, involved during the Second World War in developing treatment for Crush Syndrome, a condition which afflicted patients dug out from bombed buildings.

When the Blitz of London began in earnest in September 1940, it was noted that some of those who had been extricated from the ruins without any apparent external injury, unaccountably collapsed and died after a few days. It seemed that they were suffering from uraemia, the accumulation in the blood of constituents normally eliminated in the urine. Margaret Louden saw several such cases at the South London Hospital for Women and Children, and played an important part in piecing together the process of degeneration. Victims trapped under heavy weights had the blood cut off from the compressed muscles, which suffered irreversible damage. After they had been rescued, the blood returned to the dead muscle, which released both myoglobin and potassium. Myoglobin caused blockages within the kidney, which would swell up and cease to function; potassium produced irregularities in cardiac rhythm. Another symptom was swelling in the leg. In fact, Crush Syndrome had been identified in a German publication during the First World War, but the British medical profession, not being well read in enemy literature, had to start from scratch.

A medical team was sent to Newcastle in 1941 to investigate civilian industrial accidents; it included the philosopher Ludwig Wittgenstein, who had resigned his Cambridge professorship to become a mortuary porter at Guy's Hospital. He showed a particular talent for cutting sections of frozen lung. The team emphasised the importance of blood and fluid replacement. In 1943 a Ministry of Health memorandum advised that the patient should drink copious amounts of a fluid containing sodium bicarbonate to neutralise the effect of the myoglobin. All too often this treatment was administered too late. But in 1944 Margaret Louden was responsible for a conspicuous success. A woman trapped in her house by a bomb on 5 July 1944 was given one and a half pints of fluid before being dug out. When she was admitted to the South London Hospital for Women and Children, her right leg was swollen and blistered with pressure marks. The leg continued to swell, reaching its maximum size between the 11th and 12th days. At the same time, though, the intake of fluids ensured that the myoglobin was gradually expelled in the woman's urine. Within a year she had recovered completely, save for some numbness and loss of power due to the dead muscles.

Had Margaret Louden chosen to publish an account of her work on Crush Syndrome she might have won considerable renown. But it was not until December 1990 that the above case appeared in the *British Medical Journal*, in an article by E.G.L. Bywaters.

After the war it became recognised that renal failure which had previously been attributed to the toxic effects of alcohol or drugs, might similarly be due to the manner in which the weight of the unconscious body had acted upon muscles.

Margaret Mary Crawford Louden was born on 6 April 1910 in Palmers Green, north London, and educated at the Princess Helena School in Dulwich and at St Paul's Girls' School, where she was senior foundation scholar. Talented at both music and art, she also captained the cricket and swimming teams. In 1928, she entered the London School of Medicine for Women (now the Royal Free Hospital School of Medicine). Six years later she had not only qualified as a surgeon, but also won prizes for obstetrics; and in 1938 she became a fellow of the Royal College of Surgeons.

As a registrar at Guy's Hospital, Margaret Louden worked under Sir Heneage Ogilvie. Later she was consultant general surgeon at the South London Hospital for Women and Children. During the war she dealt not only with victims of Crush Syndrome, but also with wounded soldiers and pilots. After air raids, victims would be lying on stretchers and improvised beds in the corridors, and on at least one occasion Margaret Louden worked three nights and two days without a break. One of those she treated was Sir James Martin, the inventor of the ejector seat, who had been injured in an encounter with gypsies. They became fast friends, and after the war Margaret Louden advised Martin on the effects of ejection on the human skeleton.

For 30 years from the end of the Second World War she continued to devote herself to the South London Hospital for Women and Children (which was staffed only by women doctors). From 1975 to 1977 she worked part-time at the Elizabeth Garrett Anderson Hospital. In retirement, Margaret Louden continued to take an active interest in medicine, and from 1983 to 1985 took a forceful role in the attempt (which proved unsuccessful) to save the South London Hospital for Women and Children from closure.

As a surgeon, Margaret Louden combined technical skill with psychological insight, and took infinite pains in everything she did. Unfazed by crises, she was always prepared to take on cases that others had abandoned as hopeless; at the same time, though, she only operated when she deemed it absolutely essential.

Margaret Louden married first, in 1937, Derek Martin, Museum Curator to the Hospital for Sick Children, Great Ormond Street; they had two daughters. She married secondly, in 1962, Bernard Simpson, a consultant engineer.

19 February 1999

THELMA CAZALET-KEIR

Tory MP who championed women's rights and initiated Churchill's only defeat in the Commons

*

Thelma Cazalet-Keir, who has died aged 89, was a doughty fighter for women's rights and a pioneering Conservative MP who earned a place in history for initiating Churchill's wartime defeat in the House of Commons.

There was a moment of rare drama for MPs – then sitting in the House of Lords because of the bomb damage to the Commons – when she moved her amendment to R.A. Butler's Education Bill of 1944. Seconded by Peter Thorneycroft, it required that the Minister, in approving teachers' salaries, should not discriminate between men and women 'solely on the grounds of sex'. This was the first real opportunity that Parliament had had to write into legislation equality between the sexes. The amendment was carried by a single vote (117 to 116). With D-Day only a fortnight away and much else on his mind, Churchill's reaction was one of blind fury. He turned the issue into a matter of personal confidence in his premiership and successfully persuaded the Commons to delete the amendment, with Mrs Cazalet-Keir, MP for East Islington, voting against her own amendment. But Churchill's anger was more apparent than real, and before the debate he announced the appointment of a Royal Commission to consider the question of equal pay for men and women for equal work. He swiftly forgave Mrs Cazalet-Keir and when he formed his brief 'caretaker government' in 1945, he appointed her Parliamentary Secretary to the Education Minister.

Mrs Cazalet-Keir lost her Parliamentary seat in the General Election of that year but persevered with the principle of parity between the sexes in her role as chairman of the Equal Pay Campaign. By 1956 she felt enough progress had been made to disband the committee.

Earlier, she had distinguished herself as the youngest member of the London County Council in the 1920s and as the first woman Conservative MP to be appointed a parliamentary private secretary – to Kenneth Lindsay, the Parliamentary Secretary to the Board of Education, in 1938. After the War, Mrs Cazalet-Keir ceased to be active in party politics, though she continued to be a prominent public figure as president of the feminist Fawcett Society, a governor of the BBC and a member of the Arts Council.

Thelma Cazalet was born in 1899 into a well-known sporting dynasty of Huguenot descent. Her father was a racehorse owner with stables at the family seat of Fairlawne in Kent, where her brother Peter later trained Queen Elizabeth the Queen Mother's steeplechasers. Another brother, Victor, who sat in the Commons at the same time as his sister, was killed in the same aircraft as General Sikorski at Gibraltar in 1943.

Although diminutive in stature ('I remember two maids spending long periods pulling on my legs in a desperate attempt to make me taller'), Thelma Cazalet more than kept her end up in the family's games-playing traditions. She played tennis for Kent and was a formidable competitor in the Parliamentary golf handicap. Even as a girl, however, she had leanings towards more serious matters: she spoke on political platforms while still at school. With her direct, straight-forward manner – tending to dispose of conversation rather than indulge in it – she made an immediate impression on being elected to the LCC for East Islington in 1925. She soon acquired a sound knowledge of London's educational and housing problems, as well as taking an active part in child welfare schemes. In 1931 she carried Baldwin's standard in the East Islington by-election when he was visiting Lord Beaverbrook's 'Empire Crusade' – but lost.

Later that year, however, she was elected as a National Conservative. In the Commons she took a special interest in education and was among the early advocates of comprehensive schools. During the 1939–45 War she was a member of a committee of inquiry into conditions in the women's Services and of the committee on equal compensation (civil injuries). From 1943 to 1946 she was a driving force in the Tory Reform Committee, which did so much to change the image and policies of the Conservative party after the war.

Mrs Cazalet-Keir was a member of the executive committee of the Contemporary Art Society and in her lifetime had a remarkably wide circle of friends, ranging from Lloyd George, Kipling and Barrie to Augustus John and the film star Elizabeth Taylor. To 'LG' she was an 'honorary daughter' (having been at school with the Liberal politician's daughter, Megan). He once told her that she was 'one of the only two women who never bore me'.

Mrs Cazalet-Keir was also a redoubtable champion of P.G. Wodehouse (the stepfather of her sister-in-law Leonora, first wife of Peter Cazalet, the trainer). She advised him to stay in France at the end of the war when the great humorist was being subjected to hysterical recriminations over some innocent broadcasts he had made to America after his internment in a German camp. In 1973 she edited *Homage to P.G. Wodehouse*, a delightful collection of tributes by Lord David Cecil, Malcolm Muggeridge, Auberon Waugh, William Douglas Home and others.

At one stage she ran a market garden in Kent as well as a London shop to sell her produce. Mrs Cazalet-Keir was a Christian Scientist. She was appointed CBE in 1952.

In 1939 she married the author and journalist David Keir, who died in 1969.

17 January 1989

JOAN LITTLEWOOD

Visionary director whose Theatre Workshop for the working-class was hijacked by West End audiences

*

Joan Littlewood, the theatrical director who has died aged 87, led an extraordinary revolution in British theatre in the 1950s; a Left-wing visionary, she had founded in 1945 a company called Theatre Workshop, a collective that toured shows aimed at working-class audiences in the North of England.

It was using Bertolt Brecht's principles before Brecht had been heard of in Britain. When it moved to London in 1953 it became, after winning much honour abroad, fashionable. But as it lacked subsidy it grew to depend for income on the profit of transfers to the West End, which Joan Littlewood despised. The transfers grew so numerous that they depleted the company and its resources, and eventually she gave up and went away to try her hand at children's theatre and associated matters – anything to be free from the blandishments of the commercial theatre.

But it was an exciting decade while it lasted, because from the East End it blew great gusts of fresh air into the more conventional West End. While other gusts were felt from further west in Sloane Square, these came from new writers at the Royal Court, whereas Theatre Workshop was a long-established, self-contained company with its own writers, director, designers and philosophy; it had a style of staging all its own and a style of acting of equal distinction.

Out of all this energy and struggle came some famous shows, many of which were popular enough not only to move into the West End but also to be made into films. The most successful productions included Ewan MacColl's version of Hasek's *The Good Soldier Schweik* and Brendan Behan's *The Quare Fellow* (both 1957); Shelagh Delaney's *A Taste of Honey* and Behan's *The Hostage* (1958); Frank Norman and Lionel Bart's *Fings Ain't Wot They Used T'Be* and Wolf Mankowitz's *Make Me An Offer* (1959); Stephen Lewis's *Sparrers Can't Sing* (1960); then, after the theatre had been closed for two years, *Oh! What A Lovely War* (1963) and *Mrs Wilson's Diary* (1967).

All these shows typified the extemporising Littlewood tradition drawn from the music hall: rapid rewrites at rehearsal, a peppering of songs, and jokey asides. Small wonder that productions took so long to polish – though in fact Joan Littlewood did not believe in polish. What they never lacked, however, was atmosphere: a sense of spontaneity and freshness induced by Joan Littlewood, the chain-smoking, toothy woman in a woolly hat with an eagerness to disconcert the middle-classes, particularly those who liked straight, respectable plays with beginnings, middles and ends.

But Joan Littlewood's dream of addressing the working-class in the theatre was never to be fulfilled. Theatre Workshop stood in the middle of the East End with its cheap, refurbished and charming little late-Victorian playhouse, staging song-and-dance plays for the local people; but the local people never came, though they lived within yards of the Theatre Royal with its convivial bar and barrels of draught beer, and someone at the piano to lead the sing-song before the show.

People from further west on the other hand went in hordes, in their furs and smart cars. The trek eastwards was a tribute to the vitality, vulgarity and originality of Joan Littlewood's Theatre Workshop. But when she left in 1975, while other people strove to retain the theatre's Cockney spirit, the Littlewood gusto had gone and so had the key to the company's creativity. Writers who had thrived under Joan Littlewood's tutelage seemed to lose their inspiration. Actors whom she had drawn into the company, and who had made their names by working for it, lost direction without the director.

Joan Maud Littlewood was born to an unmarried girl of 16 at Stockwell, south London, on 6 October 1914, and mostly brought up by her grandparents. She was five when her mother married, and she was the bridesmaid. There were no books in the house and if her mother saw her with a book she would throw it on the fire. But Joan would slip off to the library, and read with a candle under the bedclothes. Educated at a local convent school, she showed a talent for writing and painting and at the age of 11 staged *Hamlet*, playing all the roles herself. She later claimed that as a schoolgirl she detested nearly all the classical productions at the Old Vic except for Gielgud's *Hamlet* in 1930, which she pronounced intelligent but 'too decorative'.

At 16, Joan won a scholarship to the Royal Academy of Dramatic Art but, finding it 'full of debs learning elocution', she left before completing her studies. Intending to hike to Liverpool, then stow away on a boat to America, she packed a bundle and walked 130 miles to Burton-on-Trent, where she collapsed, exhausted. Taken in by a working family, she moved to Manchester. There, moved by the miseries of the Depression, she founded an amateur company called Theatre of Action, which played in the streets. When she met and married Ewan

MacColl, the musician and author, in 1935, they set up a group called Theatre Union. This disbanded on the outbreak of the Second World War, during which she worked for the BBC on wireless documentaries.

In 1945, at Kendal, her third and last company, Theatre Workshop, was established to create original, frequently political, plays, and to put fresh, again frequently political, slants on the classics. Gerry Raffles was its administrator, and profits were split equally. Joan Littlewood and Raffles fell in love, and her marriage to MacColl was dissolved.

For eight years Theatre Workshop played to predominantly working-class audiences in Britain, Scandinavia, Germany and Czechoslovakia. Meanwhile, in 1947, Joan Littlewood staged her first London production at the Rudolph Steiner Hall, called *Operation Olive Branch*, Ewan MacColl's version of the *Lysistrata* of Aristophanes. In 1952 MacColl's play *Uranium 235* did so well at Swiss Cottage that it moved to the West End, with such actors as Howard Goorney, George Cooper, Avis Bunnage, and Harry Corbett, who were to set up Theatre Workshop at the derelict Theatre Royal, Stratford East.

This proved to be the home of many triumphs, although for its first two seasons nobody took much notice of what it was doing. The critics went to Devon to see its production at Barnstaple of the English premiere of Brecht's *Mother Courage*, because by 1955 Kenneth Tynan had alerted everyone to Brecht, and Joan Littlewood was supposedly a Brechtian director. There had also been a commendable revival of *Richard II*, in which Harry Corbett gave a good performance. But Stratford East remained off the beaten track for theatre-goers until 1955–56, when Theatre Workshop won golden opinions at the Paris International Theatre Festival with *Arden of Faversham*, *Volpone* and *The Good Soldier Schweik*. Honour abroad suddenly drew home audiences to the forgotten little playhouse. In spite of Joan Littlewood's dread of 'going commercial', nine shows transferred successfully to the West End. And she herself successfully directed the film of *Sparrers Can't Sing*. In 1964, for the Edinburgh Festival, she conflated both parts of Shakespeare's *Henry IV*, but without great success; and she staged other shows at Stratford, following the huge success of *Oh! What A Lovely War* in 1963. But the need to profit from the transfers of so many productions drove Joan Littlewood's theatrical inclinations in other directions, particularly into working with children. This spelt the end of an era.

Gerry Raffles had, meanwhile, taken care of all things domestic in Joan Littlewood's life: cooking, chauffeuring, even buying her clothes and giving her pocket money. When he died in 1975, she walked out of the Theatre Royal, never to return.

In her autobiography, *Joan's Book* (1994), she said nothing of her life after that, during which time she lived quietly in France, where Raffles had died. There she enjoyed a close, though not romantic, friendship with Baron Philippe de Rothschild, until his death in 1988. She called him 'Guv' and his château a 'stable'. When *Playboy* came to interview him, she came down to dinner wearing two bedraggled rabbit ears and a pompom for a tail.

23 September 2002

AIR COMMODORE BRIDGET GRUNDY

WAAF pioneer who began her wartime service by inspecting drains and ended up 30 years later outranking rival men officers

*

Air Commodore Bridget Grundy, who has died aged 77, was one of the earliest members of the Women's Auxiliary Air Force in the Second World War, and afterwards became the first member of the Women's Royal Air Force (apart from the director) to reach Air Rank.

The Women's Royal Air Force was originally founded in 1918, but disbanded two years later. It was not re-formed – as the Women's Auxiliary Air Force (WAAF) – until June 1939, so that the arrival of Biddy Martin (as Bridget Grundy then was) at RAF Wittering a few days after the declaration of war occasioned some surprise. "Ere you buggers,' an RAF sergeant told his men, 'stop yer swearing.'

Biddy Martin joined a motor transport section, though her previous experience in this field had been confined to the diocesan bishop's car, which she had driven while serving in the 41st Leicester Company of the Women's Legion. Now, paid 1s 4d a day, and kitted out in buff overalls and blue beret (no uniform was available before Christmas 1939), she became the commanding officer's driver. Very soon she was known as 'the Whizzbang' – rather unfairly since she only smashed the staff car twice. Biddy Martin also drove an enormous fire tender. With her dirty and greasy overalls she felt infinitely superior to those whom she derided as 'the rather snooty clean girls who worked in the ops room'.

During the Battle of Britain she served at Wittering, a No. 12 Group fighter station. Commissioned in October 1940, she found that her first task was to inspect the WAAF blocks' drains, and her second to persuade an airwoman that it would be wiser not to swallow a tin of Harpic cleaner. Early in 1941, Biddy Martin was posted to the WAAF depot at Harrogate. By this time recruits were arriving in their hundreds; as a junior officer she was responsible for removing their head lice. After two months she was posted to St Athan in South Wales, from which 200 WAAF non-commissioned officers passed out every fortnight. Overall, WAAF numbers climbed from 2,000 in 1939 to 182,000 in 1943.

One of Biddy Martin's duties was to arrange lectures.

Impressed on one occasion by a large turn-out, she congratulated the lecturer, who, it turned out, was a Piccadilly prostitute who was regaling her audience with a history of her experiences 'on the game'.

In September 1941, Biddy was posted to Canada as the youngest and most junior of three WAAF officers who had been selected to help the Royal Canadian Air Force to introduce women. Paid Canadian rates, she felt like a millionaire. Returning home in the New Year of 1942 as a Flight Officer, she helped to retrain as mechanics WAAFs who had previously been working on barrage balloons. 'They were a really tough lot,' she recalled, 'and I wasn't sorry when I was posted to the Air Ministry in January 1943.' As the WAAF became better integrated with the RAF proper, Biddy Martin was assigned to lecture on RAF courses. She recalled an RAF chaplain who politely declared that he was very interested in his women, and a senior NCO who initiated a stream of complaints with the declaration that he was old enough to be her father.

On 6 June 1944, D-Day, Biddy Martin arrived at RAF Chivenor, north Devon, to command 350 WAAFs at a station which was heavily involved in backing up the invasion. 'By that time,' she recalled, 'the WAAF worked in almost every part of the station. My job was to administer them and make certain their conditions of work were as good as possible.' Despite the breakdown of segregation in work, the WAAF quarters were surrounded by barbed wire. 'Almost every morning the station warrant officer presented small scraps of airmen's blue serge,' Biddy Martin recalled. Faced with this evidence, she invariably counselled 'no further action'.

Her next move saw her in command of the WAAF section at the flying boat base at Castle Archdale, Northern Ireland. Delapidations at headquarters were so far advanced that when it rained an umbrella was used on the stairs to protect visitors. Biddy Martin ended her war preparing WAAFs for their return to civilian life, whither she herself followed them after a spell as a squadron officer with a signals unit. But it was no means the end of her service in the forces.

She was born in London on 28 September 1920, although her home was in Leicestershire where her father, Lieutenant-Colonel Charles Martin, was High Sheriff. She was educated at Ancaster House, Bexhill-on-Sea. After her wartime responsibilities, it did not take her long to become disillusioned with her civilian employment as a buyer in a department store. So in 1946 she returned to the WAAF. Soon afterwards permanent service for women was introduced, and in 1949 the WAAF was absorbed in the recreated Women's Royal Air Force. 'We achieved the doubtful honour of becoming eligible for men's punishment, including detention,' Biddy Martin observed.

In 1950, she received command of the women's officer cadet training unit at Hawkinge in Kent. Four years later she was one of the first two members of the WRAF to pass staff college. 'The only concession to our sex,' she remembered, 'was an eight-foot wall dividing us from the men in our hut. But the partition served as a challenge. Male students tried to vault it and I stood on the other side with a glass of beer for those who succeeded.'

Next Biddy Martin was posted to the intelligence staff at the Air Ministry. 'It was at times very difficult to keep my mouth shut about the fascinating things that came through the office,' she recalled, 'but I was so scared of being charged under the Official Secrets Act that I managed to remain dumb.'

After spells at Fighter Command Headquarters and in Cyprus, she returned in 1961 to the Air Ministry, at first in the WRAF Director's department, and then with the director-general of manning. Subsequently she took over the mammoth task of helping to re-organise the trades' structure of the Service, and then in 1964 took over from her deputy director in the rank of group captain.

In 1968 Biddy Martin escaped from Whitehall to join No. 22

Group headquarters as Staff Officer Administration. As a training group, 22 Group embraced the university air squadrons whose dinners she enjoyed. 'The students were always intrigued with a female group captain,' she recollected. Finally, in 1971, Biddy Martin, having gained promotion in competition with male group captains, was posted in the rank of air commodore as director of personnel management at RAF Innsworth.

Shortly afterwards, she married Edmund Leigh Grundy, a stockbroker whom she had met on a fishing trip in Scotland. Believing that she could not be at the same time a good RAF officer and a good wife, Air Commodore Grundy took early retirement in 1972. The Grundys went to live in Hertfordshire, where Biddy contributed enthusiastically to county life. She was president of the Hertfordshire Red Cross from 1978 to 1988, and a deputy lieutenant for the county.

26 May 1998

JENNIFER D'ABO

*Entrepreneur driven by the thrill of the deal who showed a talent
for turning round moribund companies*

*

Jennifer d'Abo, who has died aged 57, was one of Britain's best-known women entrepreneurs. Statuesque and strong-voiced, she was a striking presence in any gathering, not least for her trademark heart-shaped spectacles. She made a dynamic impression on everyone she met, and had a knack of charming financiers into backing her projects. But she sometimes felt herself patronised and discriminated against in the male-dominated world of big business.

'The City is still terribly cautious about women,' she told one interviewer. 'If I put up a feasibility study for a business project, it's read by ten analysts as opposed to two because I'm a woman.'

Jennifer d'Abo's motivation was the thrill of the deal and the satisfaction of turning round moribund companies, rather than personal enrichment. She acted intuitively, brought a sense of fun into her business dealings, and was never afraid to defy convention. Though she invested in many different ventures – by no means all of them successful – she was best known for her achievement in reviving Ryman, the office stationery chain.

Shopping in a Ryman branch one day in 1981, she was horrified to find how shabby it had become. Ryman's owner, the Burton group, was willing to sell, and d'Abo and her management team moved in to revamp the Ryman image, giving it a complete facelift and a lively new product range. Filing cabinets, for example, now came in bright pinks and greens, rather than gunmetal grey. Perhaps d'Abo's cleverest innovation, however, was the introduction of the self-adhesive Post-It note. She returned from a Frankfurt trade fair with a sample of the gummed notepads, then available only in white. But she sensed that they needed to be more eye-catching, and ordered them for Ryman in yellow, pink and blue. They became an essential item on every British office desk. Ryman survived financial peril and struggles with its unions to become one of the sharpest retail brands of the 1980s. It was floated on the stock market in 1986, and taken over by Pentos – for £20 million, double the flotation price – a year later.

Meanwhile, another City play produced a less satisfactory outcome. Through a shell company called Stormgard, Jennifer d'Abo launched a hostile bid in 1986 for Selincourt, a small, traditional textiles group. The battle was hard fought, and just as it was won some of her bankers withdrew support, leaving her to find £25 million of new financing in three days. Having leapt that hurdle, she found herself locked in a two-year management struggle, eventually having no choice but to resign. She described this episode as 'the nastiest time of my life', but it did not deter her from other entrepreneurial gambits over the following decade.

Jennifer Mary Victoria Hammond-Maude was born in London on 14 August 1945. Her father, a diplomat, was often away, and her mother's health was poor; so Jennifer spent much of her childhood with her grandmother. She attended nine schools, the last of which was Hatherop Castle in Gloucestershire, where she passed five O levels. She went on to a finishing school in Paris, but hopes of going to art school were abandoned after her mother's death when Jennifer was 17. A year later she married David Morgan-Jones, an officer in the Life Guards, with whom she had a daughter, Sophie.

One of Jennifer's first jobs, as a teenager, had been as an office junior at Keith Prowse, the theatrical ticket agency owned by Peter Cadbury, a scion of the chocolate dynasty whom she met when he bought her grandmother's house. In 1970, having divorced Morgan-Jones, she married Cadbury, who was her senior by 27 years; they had a son, Joel. She became a strong support to Peter Cadbury in his sometimes colourful business dealings. In particular, Cadbury credited Jennifer with helping him to weather a crisis at Westward Television, where he was ousted as chairman in a blaze of media attention, only to be reinstated eight days later.

She also took over the running of his investment portfolio – a skill she had learned from her grandmother, a keen investor – and was irritated to find that women were still barred from taking the stock exchange exams. In 1973, to Peter Cadbury's initial fury, she decided to sell all his shares; the market crashed a few weeks later, and her husband's rage turned to grateful admiration.

Life with Cadbury was a glamorous whirl of hunting, holidays in Nassau, Rolls-Royces and private planes – both husband and wife held a pilot's licence. But the marriage lasted only six years; according to Cadbury at the time, it broke up because 'she's a better entrepreneur than I am'. They remained good friends – as indeed she did with both her other ex-husbands, sometimes in later years entertaining all three to dinner at the same time.

Her third marriage, which lasted until 1987, was to the stockbroker Robin d'Abo. Initially they were relatively poor, and Jennifer set out to earn a living by taking on a Wavy Line grocery shop franchise at Alton, in Hampshire. The work was backbreaking, but it gave her a taste for the retail trade. In 1977 she acquired Burlington Furnishing, a department store in Basingstoke which she revamped in the style of Peter Jones and sold for a healthy profit. Her next investment, in 1980, was Jean Sorelle, a Peterborough-based maker of toiletries and fragrances.

In 1988 Jennifer d'Abo and her former Ryman team acquired Roffey Brothers, a compost-making company, to which in due course they added T. Parker & Sons, a supplier of 'turf dressings' to golf courses. When the golf course boom went into reverse in the recession, these businesses also suffered and were eventually sold. But Jennifer d'Abo had better luck with her last major investment, the florist Moyses Stevens, where she developed a successful import-export business. She was also at various times a director of Channel Four Television and the London Docklands Development Corporation; a member of the Industrial Development Board for Northern Ireland; and a council member of Cancer Research UK.

In the late 1990s Jennifer d'Abo was herself diagnosed with cancer and advised to give up all her business interests. But she continued to live life to the full, remaining a generous hostess to a wide and eclectic circle of friends who were, in turn, devoted to her. She was a brilliantly creative cook. She published, in 1999, *Jennifer d'Abo at Home*, subtitled 'recipes for stylish people in a hurry', which offered tips from a range of celebrity contributors. In the last year of her life Jennifer d'Abo moved to southwest France, where she renovated a beautiful house.

2 May 2003

OLIVE GIBBS

*Formidable Labour grande dame and passionate campaigner for
unilateral disarmament*

*

Olive Gibbs, who has died aged 77, was a formidable figure
in Labour politics in Oxford, where she served twice as lord
mayor; she was also chairman of the Campaign for Nuclear
Disarmament (CND) from 1964 to 1967.

The passion with which Olive Gibbs espoused causes made
her a tough campaigner, and she did not indulge the vanity of
male opponents. Her opinions, though, never came in packages;
if she was fierce in combat she was equally warm in friendship.
Her commitment to nuclear disarmament preceded her dedication to the Labour Party. In August 1945 she was at a dance –
she always convivial – when the news broke that Americans had
dropped an atom bomb on Hiroshima. Most of the revellers
cheered, but Olive Gibbs remained pale and trembling in her
seat. 'In a world which held the atom bomb,' she decided, 'there
could never be any path for me but pacifism.'

When CND was founded in 1958, she took charge of the
Oxford group and led it on several Aldermaston marches. She
remembered breaking off from the head of one march to visit a
public lavatory in a subway only to discover that hundreds of
marchers had followed her underground. Her own reaction was
thermo-nuclear when, in 1959, the Women's Voluntary Services
published a pamphlet which described radiation sickness as 'a
kind of nasty tummy ache'.

The next year she organised a march to the American airforce
base at Brize Norton, where she conducted a four-hour vigil
that was an anticipation of later and considerably longer demonstrations at Greenham Common. But Gibbs was outraged by

CND supporters who daubed slogans on the walls of All Souls. Not only did she offer to help to remove them; to mark the strength of her feelings she refused to join undergraduate members of CND on a march.

When she took over from Canon Collins as chairman of CND in 1964 – initially 'for just six months' – the organisation was in disarray, and with no formal membership to pay the subscriptions there were grave financial problems. Gibbs's energy, spirit and conviction soon reactivated the campaign and restored the finances. Faced in 1966 with a debt of £3,000, she declared that CND should close down if it could not meet its obligations, and within weeks had raised more than the sum required. By the end of her term new subscription-paying members were joining at the rate of 1,200 a month.

She revived the Aldermaston March (which had lapsed in 1964) and strove to give the movement a broader platform. CND espoused the cause of underdeveloped nations, criticised racial divisions and demanded an independent foreign policy. Olive Gibbs herself animadverted upon 'the ghastly situation' which the Americans had brought about in Vietnam. British membership of a nuclear alliance, she warned, was 'no less dangerous because it is negotiated by a Labour Prime Minister.' These opinions brought her into close alliance with Michael Foot: 'We shared just about everything,' she remembered, 'except a sleeping bag.'

A printer's daughter, she was born Olive Frances Cox on 17 February 1918 in a shabby area to the west of Oxford which she tellingly evoked in her autobiography *Our Olive* (1989). It was not so much the appalling poverty as the community spirit which she remembered – a spirit that seemed to disappear when the slums were demolished. Olive was educated at Milham Ford School, where she set a record of 37 successive detentions. At home she was regularly beaten by her father.

In 1940 she married Edmund Gibbs, an accountant who

would precede her as leader of the Labour group on the Oxford Council. She herself had yet to find her political vocation, and to the end of her days mocked those who claimed to have been party members since birth. No intelligent person, she thought, could be expected to swallow everything in a party's programme.

It was not until the county borough closed five nursery classes in south and west Oxford in 1952 that Olive Gibbs became active in the Labour cause. Riled by a Tory councillor's remark that 'young children are much better off being looked after by their mothers than being at school', she stood successfully for West ward. She fought hard to preserve the community at Jericho, and to stop a road being built through Christ Church Meadow. This latter cause she adopted with such passion that she was temporarily expelled from the Labour group on the council. But Christ Church Meadow remains.

In 1967 Olive Gibbs was arrested, together with a fellow of All Souls, a former sheriff of Oxford and two clergymen, for displaying insulting signs likely to cause a breach of a peace outside a hairdresser's shop which operated a colour bar. Her view of civil rights was never partial. When a fascist wanted to hire Oxford Town Hall in 1958 she insisted that the building belonged to all the people of the city – whether Labour, Conservative, Communist or Fascist – and that it should be available to them accordingly.

Olive Gibbs served her first term as mayor from 1974 to 1975, flying the peace flag from Oxford town hall. Another term followed in 1983 (after the incumbent had died in office) and two years later she was elected as lady mayoress to complement a widower lord mayor. She also sat on Oxfordshire county council from 1973 to 1985. It was a sign of the respect in which she was held that, although there was a Conservative majority, she was elected as the council's first woman chairman in her last year.

Latterly she fought a long and courageous battle against cancer. 'Don't bring me flowers,' she would say, 'I'm not dead yet.'

Olive Gibbs is survived by her husband and two sons.

30 September 1995

BATTLEAXES

*

DAME BARBARA CARTLAND

*Author of more than 700 romantic novels who championed
vitamins, honey, gypsies and the colour pink*

*

Dame Barbara Cartland, who has died aged 98, was a confection entirely of her own making: a romantic novelist of unrivalled output, a doughty champion of unlikely causes, the most reliable sound-bite artiste of her times, and step-grandmother of Diana, Princess of Wales. In her later years, she cut an unmistakeable figure in a froth of pink ball gown with extravagant, almost clown-like, make-up – her cheeks pulled back with sadly visible bits of sticking plaster. This façade of pancake and tulle, however, concealed an iron constitution, a steely determination, and a mind which, though often contrary and in an eccentric orbit of its own, was seldom less than razor sharp. She was a formidable fairy queen.

She boasted, in a *Who's Who* entry which took more than a page merely to list her 700 books, that she was the best-selling author in the world, with sales of 750 million. Some doubted. Although there was once public embarrassment when it was discovered that an inaccurate birth-date appeared in *Who's Who* (secretarial error, claimed the Dame) she was actually born Barbara Hamilton Cartland on 9 July 1901, at her grandparents' house at Edgbaston. Her parents, she later claimed, would have preferred a boy.

Although Dame Barbara was always at pains to stress her aristocratic ancestry the truth of the matter is that her antecedents were solidly middle class. Her financier grandfather, James, lost a fortune in an unwise speculation on the Fishguard railway and shot himself one Sunday morning. As a result, her childhood was spent in relatively reduced circumstances. Her father, Bertie

Cartland, tried without much luck to retrieve the situation through gambling. He enjoyed a modest income as Provincial Secretary of the Primrose League, but maintaining the standards to which he aspired was always a struggle. He was killed in the Great War leaving his widow, Polly, in financial straits with Barbara and her two younger brothers to bring up. Luckily Dame Barbara's mother, who also lived on into her nineties, was indomitable too, and somehow ends were met. 'Poor I may be,' Polly once remarked, 'but common I am not.' The phrase became a sort of unofficial family motto.

In some respects, her daughter Barbara was a crashing snob. One interviewer asked her whether she thought class barriers had disappeared and was told that of course they had – otherwise, why on earth did he suppose someone like her would be talking to someone like him. Yet she always appealed to every class of society and, in her inimitably eccentric way, was a great champion of those to whom she would refer as 'ordinary people'.

Barbara herself was educated at Worcester High School and Malvern, which she hated. She boarded with families in and around Bath before going to a finishing school on the Solent called Netley Abbey.

For most of her life she was fascinated, professionally and personally, by the relationship between the sexes. In private she would discuss sexual matters with an explicitness verging on the bawdy (she was fascinating on the subject of the Duke and Duchess of Windsor's private parts); but in public she proclaimed a virginal romanticism verging on the prudish. Her first brush with men came in the Bath period, when a libidinous major invited her to his bedroom in order to show her 'how his revolver worked'. But in 1919, on holiday, she first discovered the thrill of male company. She claimed to have received three proposals of marriage that fortnight alone. In time this rose to around 50.

In order that Barbara could come out and enjoy the London season, her mother took a rented house in South Kensington.

There was still not much money though Barbara had an annual allowance of £50. Gay, vivacious, fascinated by 'society', she danced all night and did her best to fulfil her ambition (as she confessed to her much loved brother Ronald) to 'get to know everybody in London'. There was even an engagement to one of the many young men who proposed. He was an officer in the Life Guards. However, when her mother warned her about the 'facts of life' Barbara was so disgusted that she broke it all off. Her jilted fiancé, in the fashion of the time, threatened to shoot himself with his service revolver outside the coffee stall in Hyde Park where debs and their delights repaired after a night of partying. He did not carry out the threat, but it may have helped mould the romantic novelist in her.

Barbara Cartland had been practising her gift for story-telling by teaching at Sunday school, but one evening at a cocktail party she bumped into a man from the *Daily Express* who suggested she might supply paragraphs for his gossip column at five shillings a time. Before long, she had graduated to writing feature articles. Soon she attracted the attention of the *Express*'s proprietor, Lord Beaverbrook, and became a regular luncheon guest at his house in Hurlingham. Beaverbrook seems almost certainly to have made some sort of pass at his young protegée, but she resisted. However, she always said that it was Beaverbrook who taught her most about writing. Certainly the short sentences, short paragraphs and short words that characterised her work are very much the style of *Express* editorials of the day. Beaverbrook also inculcated the notion that name-dropping was a useful device, especially when the names had titles attached to them.

She had begun her first novel before meeting Beaverbrook and in 1923, *Jigsaw*, a thinly disguised autobiography of a young society girl, was published by Duckworth. It had been sent in on spec, and appeared, priced 7s 6d, on the same day as a novel by another future Dame, Edith Sitwell. The reviews were mixed, but the young author was a mere 23 years old.

Despite these precocious literary endeavours, she remained hard up. For a while her mother ran a woollens shop called Knitwear, and she herself had a hat shop which foundered, not least because the boss was so often away, tripping the light fantastic, probably wearing one of her own hats. Millinery was clearly not going to be the answer to her financial predicament. As with others of her sex and generation, the obvious solution was marriage. In 1927 she became engaged to Alexander 'Sachie' McCorquodale, son of the chairman of the country's largest printing company. It did not last. For someone whose whole career was founded on the notion of romantic love, she always wrote of the marriage in surprisingly prosaic terms. She bore him a daughter, Raine; he gave her a house in Mayfair and a Rolls-Royce, but he had a serious drink problem and before long was conducting an affair with a major's wife, details of which Barbara discovered in the drawers of his desk. The resulting divorce case was spectacular. Thanks to connections of Ronald's she retained the services of Sir Patrick Hastings, while her husband had Sir Norman Birkett. These were the two leading Silks of the day. The headlines read: 'Divorce suit by novelist. Husband's cruise in liner. Cousin cited in cross petition.'

It was alleged that she had been conducting an affair with her husband's cousin Hugh. He had a key to her house and used to go to her bedroom, kiss her on both cheeks and she would mix him cocktails and address him as 'Darling'. Cutting a demure figure in the witness box, Barbara protested that all her friends – of both sexes – were treated in similar fashion. She was believed. Nevertheless, in 1936 she married Hugh and the couple lived happily ever after. Or at least until Hugh's death many years later.

Satisfactory though this second marriage was, it was her brother Ronald who loomed largest in her life. Very early in married life, Hugh was going off on Scottish fishing holidays while his wife and Ronald went on reading and walking holidays to Switzerland. She once said that she and her brother had everything together with the single exception of sex.

In 1933 Ronald Cartland had been adopted as Conservative candidate for King's Norton, and Barbara acted in effect as his campaign manager, writing ferociously in order to augment his meagre funds, speaking and canvassing on his behalf and becoming completely absorbed in his political career. Barbara Cartland was always fascinated by politics, and later made some forays into political life on her own account. But her most absorbing political moments were lived vicariously through Ronald.

She was always flamboyant, and a past mistress at publicity stunts. She was largely responsible for revamping the fashionable Embassy Club; she was the force behind the first glider-towed mail delivery – the aircraft was named after her; and she drove an MG around the track at Brooklands. Apart from her journalism, she continued to write novels, though before the war they were not on the whole the sort of books that came to be associated with her when she blossomed as the world's most prolific romantic novelist. She tended to write about contemporary life, though a reviewer observed sharply that another novel was 'a safe distance from everyday life'. Nevertheless, she aspired to be taken seriously as a popular middlebrow novelist, and she often succeeded. Nor did she then write at such a breakneck speed – in 1937, when her son Ian was born, she had completed 17 novels in the 14 years since her debut. Quick work, certainly, but nothing compared with the hundreds of romances that she produced in her seventies and eighties.

The greatest tragedy of her life occurred in 1940: both her brothers were killed at Dunkirk. For the next 50 years and more she used to say that Ronald frequently appeared in her dreams and even – she being susceptible to the preternatural – in visions.

She herself took the children to Canada early in the war, but then, characteristically, felt under-employed and cowardly, so managed against all odds to return to England. Here she became a welfare officer with the Women's Voluntary Services. Her most impressive coup was to organise a wardrobe of white wedding dresses so that girls serving with the forces did not have to get married in uniform. By the end of the war she had accumulated more than 1,000 dresses. Many of these wartime brides were to write to her on their golden wedding anniversaries to thank her for giving them the chance to wed in white.

By the end of the war, smarting at not having been awarded even a 'measly MBE', she was 44 and, despite her happy home life, felt that her whole world was 'smashed in ruins'. Two Conservative Associations apparently asked her to stand in the 1945 election campaign but she thought she was too old, and that Raine, now 17, Ian 8, and Glen 5, needed a mother's love. Some of her energies were channelled into launching Raine on the world, and it was due to Barbara as much as her daughter that Raine became 'Deb of the Year' in 1947. A year later, Raine married Gerald Legge, heir to the Earldom of Dartmouth.

A woman's magazine, spurred by this romantic event, asked Barbara to write a historical romance. This was *Hazard of Hearts*, the first of her novels which belongs decisively in the genre which the world has now come to recognise as Barbara Cartland's own. From then on she wrote historical Cinderella stories with heroic heroes and heroines, villainous bad guys of both sexes who always got their come-uppance, and happy endings with definite, though understated, sexual connotations. At her most productive, dictating from the depths of her chaise-longue she 'wrote' them at the rate of about one every fortnight.

After Raine's marriage, she, Hugh and the boys moved to a house near Potter's Bar in Hertfordshire, a Victorian pile where Beatrix Potter had originally conceived *The Tale of Peter Rabbit*. This was home for the rest of her life.

In the gaps between writing fiction she found time to serve on the local council, beavered away on behalf of the St John Ambulance and championed the cause of honey and vitamins.

(She once sent Patrick Campbell a bottle of vitamins to 'cure' his stutter.) She fought for the rights of local gypsies, entertained visiting journalists to lavish cream teas, conducted a quasi-romantic liaison with Lord Mountbatten, and generally worked at creating an image for herself which one of her several biographers identified as 'The Crusader in Pink'.

One of her sons became head of Cartland Promotions and the two worked assiduously on promoting her books, which sold prodigiously not just in Britain and America but also in Third World countries, where she was much pirated. Colonel Gaddafi of Libya was reputed to be a fan. In 1991, thanks (she liked to intimate) to the personal intervention of the Queen Mother, she was appointed Dame of the British Empire – a belated compensation for the wartime failure to gain even that 'measly MBE'.

Outliving her few rivals as the 'Queen of Romantic Fiction', she became almost a self-parody, and yet was saved by herself from becoming as absurd as her detractors might have liked. She had a wry self awareness, never more so than when she declined to appear on stage with Danny la Rue, on the grounds that no one in the audience would know who was who. Consumately professional to the last, she was a journalist's dream, always ready with a pithy aphorism for every occasion, answering the telephone herself and producing a quotable sentence at a moment's notice.

Of generous habits, she always said that 'one could never say thank you enough' – though she was also a good harbourer of grudges, far more formidable than her marshmallow appearance suggested. She was one of the few people on Anthony Clare's wireless programme *In the Psychiatrist's Chair* to emerge not only unscathed but victorious.

Despite failing eyesight, she continued to produce novels until almost the very end and became an aged pin-up, widely loved. In 1991 she circulated to newspaper editors a folder tied with pink ribbon, labelled in blue felt-tip: *The History of Barbara*

Cartland and 'How I Want to be Remembered'. It was wholly positive in approach. 'In 1981, I was chosen,' she told the world, 'as Achiever of the Year by the National Home Furnishing Association of Colorado Springs.' It lists every one of her hundreds of novels as well as 'Her Other Wonderful Books' including biography (*Metternich – the Passionate Diplomat*) and five cook books (the recipes were devised by her long-serving chef, Nigel). Her final addition was 'being published in Poland and the Arab world because I am moral'.

Her husband Hugh died in 1963. She is survived by her daughter and two sons.

22 May 2000

ELISABETH MANN BORGESE

Intellectual who taught a dog to play the piano

*

Elisabeth Mann Borgese, who has died aged 83, was the last surviving child of the German novelist Thomas Mann and successful herself in several different fields: as an anthropologist; as a political scientist; as an environmentalist with a special interest in oceans; and as a writer of short stories. One of her more outlandish achievements, at the end of her life, was to train an English setter to play piano duets with her. To this end she had a special piano made – with no legs and no black notes, and with keys twice as wide as normal.

A visitor wrote the following account of the performance: 'Mrs Mann Borgese sat down on the floor at the left of the keyboard, and the dog took his place to the right of middle C. They performed two short duets, one by Schumann and the other by Mozart. Encouraged by praise, pats on the head and pieces of meat fed to him during unscored pauses, the dog mostly hit the right note at the right moment. Certainly he had a good sense of rhythm. He made a few mistakes, but she explained this by saying he'd gone for three weeks without practising while she was away.'

Elisabeth Mann was born in Munich on 24 April 1918, the fifth of Thomas Mann's six children. In 1933, when Thomas Mann's opposition to the Nazis forced him to leave Germany, Elisabeth accompanied him to Switzerland, where she attended the Freies Gymnasium at Zurich. A talented pianist, she then studied for a diploma at the Conservatoire at Zurich, where she fell in love with her professor, Giuseppe Borgese. They married in 1939.

Thomas Mann had settled in America in 1936. Elisabeth joined him there, working as a research associate at the University of Chicago from 1945 to 1955. In 1950, as chairman of the World Federal Government Movement Executive, she came to Britain to give a talk to MPs. Subsequently she edited *Perspective USA*, and served on the editorial board of *Encyclopaedia Britannica*.

In 1963, as author of *The Ascent of Women*, Elisabeth Mann Borgese advanced a curious anthropological theory that women, in wearing wigs, might be preparing themselves for future development as a race of bald Amazons. She had inherited from her father a love of the sea, and was determined that the oceans should be preserved as a common heritage. In 1970 she organised a conference entitled Peace in the Oceans, which would prove the first of 30 such meetings held in different parts of the world. She was also chairman of the International Centre for Ocean Development from 1986 to 1992. Meanwhile, in 1979 she had been appointed to the chair of Political Science at Dalhousie University, New Brunswick, Canada. From this base she continued to campaign for world leaders to revise their attitude to marine resources.

Elisabeth's most notable work of fiction was a book of short stories, *To Whom It May Concern* (1960). Although she warned that the collection had 'nothing to offer conservative tastes,' and announced that her fiction was akin to the painting of Mondrian or the music of Alban Berg, she proved adept at concocting tales suggestive of the ambivalence of scientific progress. Thus a scientist kept alive by refrigeration for 100 years proves to be a tremendous bore when thawed out.

Elisabeth Mann Borgese was appointed a member of the Order of Canada in 1988, and in the same year was awarded the Gold Medal of the Foundation for International Studies, Malta. She had two daughters.

18 February 2002

JENNIFER PATERSON

Eccentric but much-loved cook who latterly achieved recognition as one of television's Two Fat Ladies

*

Jennifer Paterson, who has died aged 71, was a fat, loud, outspoken, laughing cook much loved in society despite her eccentricities, but known to the nation only in her last years as one of the Two Fat Ladies in the television series. Under the direction of Patricia Llewellyn, the show was immensely successful, as the Fat Ladies jumped through ever more unlikely hoops – legging a canal boat though a tunnel, performing aerobatics in a light aircraft – and presented stewed brains or puddings like volcanoes of cream to surprised communities of nuns in Irish castles or boy scouts at midge-infested lakesides.

While the other Fat Lady, Clarissa Dickson Wright, would reminisce in a collected manner about her drunk relations and men's legs, on screen Jennifer Paterson was always an actor. Scripts were abandoned because neither Lady could keep a straight face, but Jennifer Paterson could always produce a good line. In a memorable sequence in which both extracted meat from a lobster with the help of violently wielded choppers, Jennifer Paterson demonstrated the best way of killing the crustacean in the first place, reserving for the faint-hearted the remark: 'If you don't want to know the score, look away now.'

She was familiar with the upper classes but refused to observe the ordinary conventions, and these characteristics combined to interesting effect when, for a decade from 1978, she was the cook at the *Spectator*'s weekly lunches. The Russian ambassador was not surprisingly puzzled when the woman who had just brought in the mackerel mousse joined in the conversation by saying: 'My brother knows all about Ulan Bator.'

The Prince of Wales asked her advice on organic products for his farm at Highgrove after visiting her in the poky *Spectator* third-floor kitchen. One day, in a rage, she threw from its window a pile of dirty coffee mugs left there by the accounts staff; they landed in the next door garden of the National Association of Funeral Directors. Her subsequent sacking by Charles Moore, the magazine's editor, was rescinded within a fortnight.

If a visitor suspected that this check-trousered figure with bright lipstick and a bejewelled crash helmet was merely a frustrated spinster he would have underestimated her. She was clever, even if the punctuation for her 'receipts' (as she insisted on calling her recipes for the *Spectator*) was provided by Lady Clare Asquith. Her formal education had ended when she was 16, apart from a course at Kingston School of Art which underlay her wide knowledge of painting. She was perfectly sure of her own taste, rather liking the Etty nude that hung in her drawing room, but preferring the Lowry still life.

Her knowledge of the Roman Catholic faith was accurate. She loved the Latin liturgy and disliked even a small admixture of English prayers with Latin choral pieces at High Mass at Westminster Cathedral; thus, although she lived on the doorstep of the Cathedral, she rode across London each Sunday morning to the Brompton Oratory. The Catholic religion informed her whole outlook. During her night prayers she would say: 'Dear God please stop all this in Yugoslavia, it's too terrible.' She was generous and trusting; 'Oh, I'll lend it you,' she said at lunch to a friend who was £5,000 short of a deposit to buy a house; and she did. In Lent she ate onion soup and gave up drink; but otherwise she must have drunk the maximum compatible with survival and sanity.

Jennifer Mary Paterson was born on 3 April 1928 at Redcliffe Gardens, Kensington, though she was proud to point out that she had been conceived in China. Her father, a 6ft 3in officer of the Seaforth Highlanders, had been posted by his civilian employers, the Asiatic Petroleum Company, to China, and it was there she spent most of her first five years, with an amah to look after her and unclean water to drink, which, she liked to think, made her immune from food-poisoning for the rest of her life.

She was naughty at school – the Convent of the Assumption at Ramsgate – where she developed her talent for showing off. Some of the nuns were French and worked culinary wonders with home-grown vegetables despite the War. As punishment for her disruptive behaviour, she was made to eat her meals in isolation behind a screen in the school hall. She subverted this discipline by peeking over the top at the assembled schoolgirls. She had to leave, so that, in the Reverend Mother's hopeful phrase, the school might 'calm down'.

For the rest of her life she lived a peripatetic existence. Her first job was as an assistant stage manager at the Windsor Rep. Then in 1946 she went to live in Berlin, where her father had been posted. Always fond of music, he had requisitioned a grand piano; with the help of cheap spirits and cigarettes, it was easy to create a party atmosphere. Though she loved parties and flirting with men, Jennifer Paterson followed the morality of the Catholic Church (permissive on drink, strict on sex). She was never to marry, and she had little money. But she was determined to make the most of things. She next took a job looking after some children in Portugal. She regarded herself as rather good with children, and certainly toddlers enjoyed having raspberries blown on their tummies or being thrown in the air. In Portugal she discovered the Mediterranean preference for food that tastes. Bacalao, garlic, anchovies, olives, shellfish and robust red wine were unfamiliar to most British people of the time.

Her next stop was Sicily, where (because of her love of swim-ming) she became known to the diet guru Gayelord Hauser as the 'Mermaid of Taormina'. He once turned down lunch with Greta Garbo because he preferred to keep an engagement with Jennifer Paterson. She swam strongly on the rocky coast, made friends with Truman Capote and consolidated her value at parties with a good memory for song lyrics and no inhibition in performing them. Only later did a habit of two packets of Woodbines a day roughen her fine baritone in Bessie Smith's 'Gimme a pig's foot and a bottle of beer . . .' Next came Benghazi, where she contrived to cook large meals on a Baby Belling stove, with saucepans balanced on one another. She learnt too that freshly slaughtered meat is too tough to eat, but that, treated cor-rectly, almost every part of a beast may be devoured.

Back in London in the year of the Coronation she found a job working on magazines from an office in Trafalgar Square. She made more friends: Tony and Peter Shaffer; Fiore Henriques, the fiercely individualistic sculptor at whose studio she lodged for a while; Olga Deterding, the unhappy millionairess who choked to death one night; Jonathan Routh, with whom she worked from 1960 on his series *Candid Camera*, helping to set up the hoaxes. After a few months as an unlikely matron at Padworth School, where she dosed the girls with gin, she found a billet as cook-housekeeper at the Ugandan legation in London.

This ended when she berated diplomats for bringing back tarts at night. Cooking at the *Spectator* was more congenial, though drunken lunches that ended at five tried her patience. It was Charles Moore's idea to get her to write as well as cook for the *Spectator*. Her prose style was chiefly exclamatory, but in addition to recondite details of saints' lives, she provided recipes that were usually cookable.

She had never been reluctant to make friends with the aristocracy, but she also took to some of the livelier members of the republic of letters, such as Peter Ackroyd, Richard Ingrams, Beryl Bainbridge, A.N. Wilson, Anna Haycraft and Andrew Barrow. She relished the Colony Room Club when Muriel Belcher was its proprietrix. As a young woman Jennifer Paterson had something of the looks of Doris Day, whom she could not abide; later she was fat but solid with fine dyed-black hair. A good emerald ring, once the property of the late Violet, Duchess of Westminster, became familiar to viewers who saw it as she mixed dough, her strong fingernails bright with red varnish. She sometimes washed her hands, but hygiene was not her first anxiety. Once she was found tossing the salad for a *Private Eye* lunch in the washbasin of the gents at the Coach and Horses, Soho. One December day a friend going to the lavatory at her flat was surprised to find the bath seemingly occupied by a dismembered body. 'Oh, it's the turkeys and stuffing for the Fathers of the Oratory,' she said.

Her daily routine at her flat behind Westminster Cathedral when she was 70 would be to get up at 6.45 (awoken by her uncle on his way to daily Mass), drink tea and read the paper, ride her motorcycle to the swimming pool and swim 32 lengths, shop in the open market at Tachbrook Street, write an article for the *Spectator* or *Oldie* on a manual typewriter, drink vodka, lunch late on pasta and red wine, take a two-hour siesta, go to a party or watch rather loud television, sitting on an upright chair with a whisky until 11 pm.

She always rode home from boozy lunches fantastically over the limit; her only precaution was to suck a creosote cough lozenge, lest she meet a policeman. Once, puzzled by the big roundabout at Shepherd's Bush, she rode up on to the grass for a better view. Luckily she never killed anyone.

11 August 1999

BELLA ABZUG

Feminist activist proud of her big hats, big mouth and big ideas

*

Bella Abzug, who has died aged 77, was a fiery figure in the American women's movement and the first Jewish woman to be elected to Congress. Flamboyant and pugnacious, with a distinctive Bronx accent, Bella Abzug gloried in liberal causes and large hats; the latter were usually of the floppy-brimmed variety, which she adopted as a lawyer because, she said, it distinguished her from the secretaries.

Woe betide those who underestimated her. When a campaign opponent called her a radical knee-jerk pacifist, she whacked him on the jaw. During her years in Congress, from 1971 to 1977, newspapers fell over themselves to think up new sobriquets for her, ranging from 'Battling Bella' to 'Mother Courage'. 'Some guys would like to dismiss me with silly comments about my hats or my four-letter words or my figure,' she wrote in her autobiography, *Bella!* (1972). 'All I can say is that anybody who thinks he can take me lightly because I'm fresh and colourful had better watch out.'

She was as good as her word. She worked for welfare reform, demanded Nixon's impeachment so early that she was accused of headline-grabbing, and promoted public transport over oil and car interests. In 1976, when she discovered the CIA had been keeping tabs on her civil rights and anti-war protests for 20 years, she insisted on a public apology from the agency's head, William Colby. Bella Abzug's full-throttle style was used by critics to paint her as a caricature feminist. But it also won her admirers. 'I like her,' Nelson Rockefeller once said. 'She's got balls.'

She was born Bella Savitzky in the Bronx, New York, in 1920, to Russian emigré parents. Her father ran a not very successful butcher's shop called the Live and Let Live Meat Market. She had her first thoughts on feminism during visits to the synagogue, when the women were relegated to the back of the balcony. She was educated locally and at Hunter College in Manhattan. After graduating in 1942, she enrolled at Columbia Law School, but dropped out to work in a shipbuilding factory. She returned after the Second World War, by now married to Martin Abzug, a successful businessman, and took a law degree in 1947. During the 1950s she defended civil rights cases in the South, earning threatening references in the editorials of Southern newspapers to the 'white lady lawyer'. She also defended writers and actors accused of un-American activities in the McCarthy witch-hunts. She helped to draft legislation that was incorporated into the Civil Rights Act of 1954.

In the 1960s Bella Abzug became a 'peacenik' when the United States and Russia resumed nuclear testing, and helped to found Women Strike for Peace, a feminist anti-nuclear group. She won her seat in Congress in 1971, representing the 19th Precinct, one of the most ethnically mixed constituencies in New York. 'Believe me, the last thing I needed at this point in my life was to knock my brains out to get myself elected to Congress,' she said. 'There are plenty of people, including my husband, who think I'm nuts.'

She began in typical style. After the official swearing-in ceremony in the House, she held her own ceremony outside on the steps, armed with an enormous megaphone and flanked by 600 followers and a Harlem youth group shouting, 'Give 'em hella, Bella!' The next day she was back on Capitol Hill with 1,000 Vietnam veterans, denouncing the war as 'dirty, immoral and illegal'. Congress, she decided, was a bastion of privilege. She was appalled that there were only 12 women in Congress; and although there were 22 million blacks, Congress had only a dozen. 'No wonder Congress is a smug, incestuous, stagnant institution,' she remarked. 'It reeks of sameness.'

Her voting record was consistent: for such issues as government aid for abortion and co-ed physical education, and against the B-1 bomber and nerve gas. In 1976 she gave up her seat in the House to fight for a seat in the Senate, but lost the Democratic nomination to Daniel Patrick Moynihan. The next year she lost to Ed Koch for the post of Mayor of New York, and also failed to re-enter the House. In 1978 President Carter appointed her co-chairman of an advisory committee on women's rights. Under her, the committee took a militant line, criticising the administration for not doing enough. In a disastrous meeting between the committee and the President, Bella Abzug tore into Carter, lecturing him on his failings. He took exception to her 'confrontational' style, and gave her the choice of resigning or being dismissed.

In recent years Bella Abzug campaigned for women's health care and breast cancer research. She also headed the Women's Environment and Development Organisation, a global network of activists she founded in 1990.

Martin Abzug died in 1986; they had two daughters.

2 April 1998

BARBARA ROBERTSON

*Stalwart of the Bath Music Festival who organised a Roman
orgy at which guests consumed fried dormice*

*

Barbara Robertson, who has died aged 86, was chairman of the
Bath Music Festival from 1970 to 1976; before that she had
gained a reputation as a colourful and inventive hostess,
described on one occasion as being responsible for more jolly
social occasions in the city than anyone since Beau Nash. Under
her aegis a series of outdoor picnics, colourful pageants and
glittering balls added glamour and spectacle to the annual
programme of music. In 1960 she launched the first in a series
of grand social events, during Yehudi Menuhin's era at the helm
of the Bath Festival, that were designed to prick the stuffy exterior of his concerts.

Her most infamous effort came in the form of a Roman orgy
held at the city's Roman baths in 1961. Guests, many of them
from high society, were forced to wear togas as they joined in the
celebrations. They later described a menu that was a tribute to
the Roman diet: fried dormice, nightingales' tongues and sows'
udders. Across the waters floated a boat with slave girls bearing
guests' meals. When the last revellers refused to leave at 4 am, the
city authorities drained the Roman baths.

As riotous pictures of the orgy began to circulate, Menuhin's
patience began to wear thin. In an interview in 1998 he continued to express dismay that Barbara Robertson and her team
had not taken a more serious approach to their merriment. 'I
love frivolity, I love gaiety, I love abandonment,' he said. 'But
to see a lot of rich people get together and find some excuse
for getting drunk – that attitude was at odds with my own feeling about it.' Barbara Robertson, though, was unrepentant:

'Bath tends to be a bit stodgy,' she said, 'so we felt we should liven it up.' Although later events caused less of a ripple, Barbara Robertson continued to organise festival balls, including, in 1962, La Serenissima, a Venetian carnival on the river Avon attended by Princess Margaret. In the same year there was the so-called Cave Rave, a jazz evening held in the caverns at Cheddar Gorge at which guests were invited to dress in animal skins. In 1964 she hosted a party with a Greek mythological theme in the grounds of her home, Combe Hay Manor, three miles south of Bath, which she shared with her husband.

After Yehudi Menuhin parted company with the festival in 1968, Barbara Robertson was appointed chairman in succession to Lord Strathcona, overseeing Sir Michael Tippett's reign as artistic director (1970–74) and his handover to Sir William Glock in 1975. Among many innovations, she allowed Tippett to go ahead with an open air rock concert in the city centre. Although it caused consternation among local people, it was attended by the farmer Michael Eavis, who used the experience as the inspiration for the Glastonbury Festival, today one of Britain's best-known summer events.

Born Barbara Fry at Bristol on 9 May 1915, she was a member of the Fry chocolate and cocoa family. Her brother, Jeremy Fry, was a one-time escort to Princess Margaret. She was educated at Clifton Girls' School, but her mother refused to let her go to university.

In her teens she met Charles Robertson while on a train journey. He was heir to James Robertson and Sons, the jam makers which was founded by his grandfather and famous for its gollywog motif. They married when she was 20. During the war they welcomed evacuees into Combe Hay Manor, and afterwards Barbara Robertson worked as a marriage guidance counsellor. Her husband was managing director of the family firm until 1969, and chairman for a further two years. In retirement he became a noted philanthropist and philatelist, with a rare and valuable collection of Austrian stamps. The couple had a keen interest in architecture, and in the mid-1950s established the Courtauld Institute Summer School at Bath. Barbara Robertson was also a member of the Bath Preservation Trust, serving as chairman from 1969 to 1971.

She was a great enthusiast for the decorative arts. When her son's father-in-law, Canon Fenton Morley, became a chaplain to the Queen, she created a cope for him. It was handmade from more than four yards of gold-embossed brocade, and lined with satin. As one way of diminishing the Bath Festival's mounting overdraft, she collected pebbles from beaches, painted them, and then sold them off as table decorations.

She was appointed MBE in 1976, the year in which she relinquished her chairmanship of the festival, and received an honorary degree from the University of Bath in 1989.

Charles Robertson died in 1983. Barbara Robertson is survived by their two sons and a daughter.

20 April 2002

JULIA SMITH

Creator of EastEnders, the soap that gripped the nation

*

Julia Smith, who has died aged 70, was 'the Godmother' of *EastEnders,* a new kind of soap opera – rough, raw and realistic – first broadcast on 19 February 1985. From the 1960s the BBC had attempted to produce a series to rival *Coronation Street,* but *Compact, United!* and *The Newcomers* all failed to make the grade. By the 1980s, with independent television taking the lion's share of the early evening audience, and the Tory Government making threatening noises, the BBC decided a radical new departure was required.

Two ideas for a soap were suggested to Julia Smith, one set in a shopping arcade and another in a mobile-home park. Neither found favour, but in further discussions the words 'East End' and 'Victorian Square' began to crop up. In February 1984 the rough format which Julia Smith and her collaborator Tony Holland had sketched out was immediately accepted.

Since the East End was too crowded to accommodate film crews, the BBC bought a back lot at Elstree studios, and constructed Albert Square there, with houses made of glass fibre and plywood, and with authentic weeds in the gardens. Julia Smith and Tony Holland retired to Lanzarote, where Angie and Den, and more than 20 other characters sprang out of their imaginations; some of the names, though, were taken from East End cemeteries. Such was the advance publicity that even the first episode had an audience of 17 million, while viewing figures for the two episodes shown on Christmas Day 1986 reached 29.5 and 31.1 million.

EastEnders provided a problem for everyone to identify with. Arthur showed what it was like to be unemployed and disgraced. Den was trapped in a childless marriage with an alcoholic wife. Lofty discovered that being soft and sensitive does not inspire love. Ali worried about his virility. Julia Smith and Tony Holland were determined to confront the grittier issues. Loneliness, cot death, mental illness, prostitution, schoolgirl pregnancy, suicide, Aids and homosexuality all found their place in the story. Characters never minced their words.

'It is at our peril that we allow this series,' warned Mary Whitehouse. 'I'm just as moral as Mrs Whitehouse,' retorted Julia Smith, 'and I care possibly more deeply. The difference is that she believes in sweeping things under the carpet and pretending they don't exist. I believe in showing what does exist and preparing people for the world they live in. My prime aim is to entertain, my second is to inform. I do not preach.' Determined that her concept should not be distorted, Julia ruled the cast with a rod of iron, as though they were the children which she never had. 'A producer has to have a strong hand,' she explained. 'You have to be mercurial and make quick decisions.'

Not only were actors forbidden to tamper with a syllable of the script; they were not allowed to travel more than 50 miles outside London on a weekday, and were compelled to eat in the canteen. 'Perhaps my marriage would have succeeded,' Julia Smith reflected, 'if I hadn't become so involved.' She especially identified with Michelle, the teenager made pregnant by Dirty Den. 'I had a relative who had these problems,' she said, 'and they were mishandled. I wanted to show it needn't wreck her life.'

Julia Smith regarded soap opera as a valuable catharsis for the lonely, providing them with at least some people with whom they might identify. And she saw the genre as possessing roots that stretched far back into the past. 'Soap has been going since Homer and the Iliad,' she explained. 'The Bible was a soap in its way. The world has always needed story-tellers for those who are not highly educated. The Church was formed through story-telling.' Above all she looked back to Charles Dickens. 'He wrote serials for weekly magazines and had the gift of combining reality with fairy stories,' she said.

Julia Smith was born in London in 1927 and, as she put it, 'dragged up on the fringes of the theatre'. The family was based in Bedford Park; her father was principal professor of singing at the Royal College of Music; and her uncle, Herbert Menges, arranged music for the theatre. During the Second World War, she was evacuated to the West Country, where she was educated at a boarding school. Later she went to RADA, where she won prizes but decided against an acting career: 'I would never be a juvenile with my face.' Instead she went into stage management. Her break came in her mid-20s, when the BBC asked her to transfer a stage production of Menotti's *The Consul* to the small screen. She remained with the BBC for several years before leaving to become senior stage manager with the Shakespeare Memorial Theatre.

But in the early 1960s the Corporation reclaimed her for *An Age of Kings*, a television adaptation of Shakespeare's history plays. The success of the series was such that Julia Smith found herself kept waiting in a shop while the assistants argued about the Wars of the Roses. In 1968 Julia Smith directed *The Railway Children*. She was also a script editor on *Z Cars*, collaborating for the first time with Tony Holland, who was directing. The pair worked together on *Angels* in the later 1970s, and on *District Nurse* (1984), before *EastEnders*. On her own account Julia Smith directed 17 episodes of *Dr Finlay's Casebook*.

In 1992 she and Tony Holland launched a new soap opera, *Eldorado*, a concoction of 'sun, sand, sangria and sex' based on the lives of a community of expatriates living in the fictitious village of Los Barcos in southern Spain. But negative press comment and sliding ratings forced the BBC to abandon the project in 1993.

Away from the studio Julia Smith lived in a remote and tiny Dorset cottage, with her poodle Roly, which once had a part in *EastEnders*. She died of cancer.

20 June 1997

DAME VIOLET DICKSON

Grande dame of Kuwait who spent 60 years in Araby and held court over classic English teas

*

Dame Violet Dickson, who has died aged 94, was a celebrated, indeed an awesome, figure in Kuwait, where she lived for more than 60 years, and where she remained for several weeks after the Iraqi invasion. Not until the end of September 1990 was this venerable *grande dame* flown back to England, to spend her last days in seclusion at Goring-on-Thames.

During her 60 years in Araby – half of them as a widow – Violet Dickson knew many of the chief actors in its history, among them King Abdul Aziz ibn Saud of Saudi Arabia, King Faisal of Iraq, four Kuwaiti rulers, and many tribal sheikhs. She moved with equal ease among western diplomats and travellers such as Bertram Thomas, Gertrude Bell, Freya Stark, Wilfrid Thesiger and Ian Fleming. Her knowledge of Kuwait, and in particular her unparalleled grasp of the feuds and rivalries festering among the kingdom's 600-strong royal family, made her an indispensable resource for incoming British ambassadors and visiting notables.

Her 80th birthday party, held in a tent in the embassy compound in the summer of 1976, was a major event in the life of the British community; and the heavens laid on an almighty thunderstorm for the occasion.

Yet, for all her prestige, Dame Violet continued to occupy the modest seafront house that had been her home since her arrival in 1929, when she had been carried ashore in a sedan chair with her husband, Colonel Harold Dickson, the political agent and later the local representative of the Kuwait Oil Company. In the 1950s she looked on regretfully as neighbouring properties were demolished to make space for the concrete commercial temples of modern Kuwait. Her own house was eventually dwarfed by these monstrosities; a cool and dark oasis amidst that blazing heat, it was built of sun-dried mud strengthened with coral rock, with ceilings supported by mangrove poles, and a spacious verandah overlooking the Arabian Gulf. Here, even in extreme old age, Dame Violet would hold court over a classic English tea. Attempts made after her husband's death in 1959 to persuade her to move into a more comfortable and modern abode were doomed to failure, even though it was rumoured that the current ruler Sheikh Jaber Al Ahmad Al Sabah – now in exile – had offered the hospitality of his palace.

But Dame Violet was not content to stay in the town of Kuwait; she made frequent ventures into the desert, both to visit her Bedouin friends – she was an habituée of tribal weddings – and in pursuit of new botanical and entomological specimens. As long ago as 1933 she was sending dried flowers back to Kew; and in the same year the Natural History Museum supplied nets, killing bottles and other equipment to assist her quest for desert insects, especially grasshoppers. A plant – *Horwoodia dicksoniae* – and a beetle – *Julodius speculifer dicksoni* – were named after her. In 1955 she published *The Wild Flowers of Kuwait and Bahrain*, which carried her own illustrations.

Dame Violet was a mountainously large, sturdy-legged woman, who talked in a surprisingly small, sharp voice. She spoke Arabic in a Bedouin dialect, though she never learnt to read or write the language. She was an intensely practical person of simple tastes, never bored, and wholly without intellectual pretensions. The same artlessness was evident in her appearance; the hair was scraped back into a bun, the feet were thrust into ankle socks and flat shoes, the torso enveloped in a huge shapeless dress, and the whole surmounted by a little cotton sun-hat. During the Second World War she donned a shabby coat and skirt made by a Kuwaiti tailor out of a piece of man's suiting.

Dame Violet was dismissive of women and made no secret of her preference for male company. This distaste for her own sex, she happily admitted, was often reciprocated, notably by certain Arab princesses, who hid in the cupboard during her visits to their palace. Though Dame Violet was a good listener, and rarely offered gratuitous advice, her conversation could be robust. She nicknamed one of her favourite desert flowers 'the donkey's penis', and shocked an earnest scholar at an embassy dinner party by explaining that the Arabic word for a sea urchin meant 'the female vulva'.

Her patrician manner made her a revered figure among the middle-class expatriates who came to the Gulf. To the end she did her best to ignore the oil-rich city which had grown up around her, continuing to shop in the souk and to patronise the Central Post Office, in spite of the proliferation of local shops and post offices across the city. She returned to England every summer and – courtesy of Swiss Air – paid annual visits to Switzerland, where she had spent part of her youth. Kuwait, though, had become her spiritual home; she faced life with a wry and deadpan humour and seemed to have gained an almost Islamic acceptance of whatsoever the fates afforded.

Violet Penelope Lucas-Calcraft was born on 3 September 1896 at Gautby in Lincolnshire, where her father was a land agent in charge of the local estates belonging to the Vyners of Newby Hall in Yorkshire. As a child her special delights were collecting butterflies and birds eggs, pastimes interspersed with the trapping and skinning of moles. Young Violet was educated at Miss Lunn's High School, Woodhall Spa, and at Les Charmettes at Vevey in Switzerland, from which she returned with some difficulty on the outbreak of the First World War.

In 1915 she showed her independent spirit by going to work at Smith's bank in Lincoln. Three years later she was posted to Cox's bank in Marseilles, and it was here that she met her future husband when he came in to enquire if he had any mail. A week later the decisive Captain Dickson – then serving in the Indian Army – sent Miss Lucas-Calcraft a telegram proposing marriage. Violet accepted without hesitation, and in the autumn of 1919 the couple were married by special licence in St Thomas's Cathedral, Bombay. After a brief honeymoon at the Taj Mahal Hotel, Violet Dickson found herself swept into the inhospitable conditions of Arabia. Her married life began in Mesopotamia and Captain Dickson – son of the consul-general in Jerusalem, grandson of the physician to the British Embassy in Istanbul and great-grandson of the physician to the Ottoman Pashalic of Tripoli – soon instilled in his wife his enthusiasm for the Near East, and especially for the Arabs of the desert. Their two children, who were given Arab names – Saud for the son, Zahra Freeth for the daughter – were brought up to think of boiled locusts as a special treat.

After Mesopotamia, the Dicksons lived and worked from 1923 to 1924 at Quetta in Baluchistan, from 1924 to 1928 at Bikaner in Rajputana and from 1928 to 1929 at Bushire in Iran, before in 1929 Captain Dickson was appointed political agent in Kuwait. When the Dicksons arrived in Kuwait – then a small, dusty town with unsurfaced roads – the entire European community numbered only 11 souls. Moving into the dilapidated mud house on the harbour, they were obliged to repair its walls with their own hands. Rats were exterminated by scattering barley on a white sheet and shooting the rodents by moonlight with a .410 shotgun.

Violet Dickson's social sway owed much to her husband's long and intimate friendship with Sheikh Ahmad, Emir of Kuwait, who died in 1950. Such was the trust which this ruler placed in the Dicksons' judgment that one evening over dinner he sought Violet's help in finding a suitable wife. Somewhat hesitatingly, she mentioned a beautiful girl whom she had met on one of her forays into the desert. The recollection proved fortunate, for the marriage which the Sheikh subsequently contracted proved extremely happy.

Dame Violet liked to recall how, in 1937, her husband had found Kuwait's most productive oilfield after dreaming about a beautiful girl rising alive from a tomb. Rather more credit, however, might seem due to the native woman who interpreted this masculine reverie to mean that oil would be discovered in an area far removed from contemporary wells, near a solitary side tree.

The Dicksons enjoyed a close friendship with the celebrated

adventurer H. St John Philby, and during a visit to London in the summer of 1957 they entertained Philby and his son Kim – cleared 18 months earlier by the Foreign Secretary, Harold Macmillan, of being the Third Man – to dinner at the Hyde Park Hotel in Knightsbridge.

Dame Violet's somewhat disappointing autobiography, *Forty Years in Kuwait*, was published in 1971. Her services to Anglo-Kuwaiti relations were recognised by her appointment as MBE in 1942, as CBE in 1964 and as DBE in 1976.

She is survived by her two children. Saud has been High Commissioner in Anguilla, and Zahra Freeth, an author of considerable distinction, runs a stall in Colchester antiques market.

5 January 1991

'SADIE' BARNETT

Last of the great Dickensian landladies

*

'Sadie' Barnett, a Cambridge legend, who has died aged 80, was one of the last of the great Dickensian landladies – and certainly the sole surviving private landlady in King's Parade. She presided over the most splendid digs in the University at No. 9 King's Parade, overlooking King's College Chapel and the Gibbs Building.

Mrs Barnett's social expectations of her lodgers were as traditional as the ambience of her rooms – and in this respect she was perhaps more of a Trollopian than a Dickensian figure. She would frequently ask Gonville and Caius College, from which she held the leasehold, to supply her with 'proper young gentlemen'. When Caius undergraduates became too bourgeois for her liking, she turned to Magdalene and Pembroke.

She greeted the representative of one noble family with the words: 'The last time we had a lord here, he hanged himself in room four.' To another, upon receipt of his Coutts cheque at the end of his first term, she declared: 'You're very modest, aren't you? You didn't say you was no Hon.' In later years Mrs Barnett took in undergraduates from less exalted backgrounds, but she took a dim view of their career prospects when compared with their landed co-evals. 'Nah, he's labour,' she would say dismissively – though it was unclear whether by this she meant that he was destined for manual labour or was merely perceived as a supporter of the Labour party. Mrs Barnett never entertained doubts about the rectitude of her grander residents. 'He was such a gent,' she once said. 'When he was sick he was always sick out of the window.'

One recent resident, Simon Sebag-Montefiore, set much of his fictional university memoir *King's Parade* (1991) at her house; but the publishers are said to have found the character based on Mrs Barnett beyond belief, and she was duly excised. Mrs Barnett was always very proud of the achievements of her 'boys', who latterly had included the historians Andrew Roberts and Michael Bloch. She regularly corresponded with her alumni all over the world, and would sometimes stay with them on her travels.

She was born Sarah Wolfschaut on 3 January 1911 at Stepney, east London, the daughter of a Jewish fruit and vegetable trader in Aldgate. Young Sadie was the seventh of ten children and began life in the rag trade, as a dressmaker. At the age of 15 she met a waiter, Michael Barnett, whom she married in 1932. They moved to Cambridge where Mrs Barnett began her career as a landlady. They separated during the Second World War but their childless union was never dissolved.

From the late 1940s Mrs Barnett enjoyed the leasehold at King's Parade. Although kosher herself, she cooked breakfast of eggs and bacon for her lodgers, and had strict rules about women and hours of residence. She regretted the passing of the more deferential undergraduates and after the upheavals of the

1960s felt sorely tried by her more high-spirited lodgers, who preferred an unsupervised existence. Some claimed that Mrs Barnett was an unconscious exemplar of enlightened despotism, but in reality she was a maternal neo-feudalist who exercised great care over her wards. She could display an almost Plantagenet 'ira et malevolentia', which concealed a fundamentally good heart. This fierce protectiveness manifested itself when the constabulary arrived to arrest one tenant after some undergraduate excess: 'You leave him alone, he's not a burglar. He's not a murderer. He's one of my nice young men.' On another occasion, when some anti-field sports campaigners, enraged by the sight of a brace of pheasants hung out of her window by one of her lodgers, sought to gain entry to the house, she gave them short shrift. 'He can kill what he likes,' she told them. 'He's a sportsman, you know.'

Attired in a quilted dressing-gown, Mrs Barnett would sit in her room for much of the day watching the trade test transmission card on BBC. 'I am waiting for the Royals to come on . . . I know they will be on soon – Ascot and all that,' she would say, whatever the season. When some undergraduates tried to disseminate the 'free Mandela' message to her lodgers, she showed them the door with the parting shot: 'Who is this Nelson Piquet anyway?' Mrs Barnett could always detect the tread of women's feet on the stairs and would display remarkable swiftness in bounding after them in order, prematurely, to enforce the official curfew. She was intolerant of the ways of the Modern Girl and when introduced to two of the species at a tea party declared: '"Pickle" and "Pooh"? What sort of names are those? Get out of here, you brazen hussies. You're here for one thing – and for one thing only.' On one occasion she was found on her hands and knees outside the door, eavesdropping. Within, a lodger had a 'punk' girl friend with dyed green hair, whom he hid under a blanket when Mrs Barnett suddenly demanded entry. She poked the bedding with a broom-handle, thereby revealing the naked punk. She threw out the tenant, observing: 'I wouldn't have minded if it was only the hair on her head that was green.'

Sadie Barnett was an efficient landlady who was capable of great kindnesses to those in need – particularly foreign students, who for years afterwards would write her grateful letters. But not for nothing did the university newspaper describe her as 'King's Parade's Boadicean landlady'.

15 August 1991

BARBARA WOODHOUSE

Dog trainer who could teach basic obedience in less than six minutes

✳

Barbara Woodhouse, who has died aged 78, became famous in the 1970s with the BBC TV series, *Training Dogs the Woodhouse Way*, sweeping the nation with her ringing catchphrase: 'Walkies!'

A real life Dr Doolittle in a tweed skirt, Woodhouse enjoyed a magical ability to communicate with animals, using love, enthusiasm, willpower and 'the telepathic communication without which I could never talk to animals at all'. Her personality had a seemingly miraculous effect, as she demonstrated when one nervous dog, terrified of entering Tube trains, jumped straight aboard at her stentorian command. She could train any dog in basic obedience in less than six minutes; one of her own dogs was taught to answer the telephone. Barbara Woodhouse had such rapport with animals that when she kept a boarding school for dogs her charges kept running away from their owners and coming back to her. Altogether she trained more than 17,000 dogs – a world record.

The daughter of a clerical headmaster, Barbara Blackburn was born near Dublin in 1910. Her father died when she was nine, and she was brought up in Brighton and Oxford by her mother and assorted nannies. She once overheard her mother say: 'Why can't Barbara be beautiful, like the other children?' From that moment she decided that she preferred animals, because they did not care what she looked like.

After school at Headington and in Switzerland, she boldly went to Harper Adams Agricultural College in Newport, Shropshire, where she was the only woman among 60 men. She studied veterinary science, building construction and engineering, and gained the second highest marks in the college: she became an expert motor mechanic, and could lay bricks as fast as a professional. After a time running a riding school, the redoubtable Miss Blackburn set off, aged 24, on a cargo boat to seek adventure in Argentina. During her time there she contracted both foot and mouth disease and diabetes. She spent four years on great estates on the pampas, and earned a wide reputation for her skill in breaking wild horses, which was considered an exclusively masculine occupation.

Back in England in 1940, she married Dr Michael Woodhouse, and during the 1939–45 War kept cows, discovering that milk production improved if the animals wore rugs in winter. In 1954 she published her enduring bestseller, *Talking to Animals*, which she had dashed off in only five days. She later wrote more than 20 books, including an autobiography, *Just Barbara* (published in 1981). Her television career began in the early 1950s, when she demonstrated her animal-training skills on Scottish television. After appearances on *Pebble Mill at One*, she was finally given the series which made her a celebrity. Among her most successful pupils were her two Great Danes, which made more than 100 screen appearances, and the famous Old English Sheepdog trained to carry a can of paint for Dulux advertisements.

After suffering a stroke in 1984, she was scarcely able to walk and could only speak very slowly. She nonetheless took 30 to

40 telephone enquiries a day from dog owners and wrote a book advising stroke sufferers how to come to terms with their condition.

In 1987 she used her teaching skills as part of a personal battle against unemployment, training backward jobless youths to read and write. Before her recent second stroke she had been due to appear in a television documentary, *Where There's Life*, in which she defended the right of stroke patients to refuse, as she had done, the painful process of rehabilitation through physiotherapy.

She is survived by her husband, a son and two daughters.

11 July 1988

MAJOR BETTY HUNTER COWAN

Army major and member of a long-standing female partnership known as 'the Cavewomen'

*

Major Betty Hunter Cowan, who has died aged 79, served with distinction in the Women's Royal Army Corps and then settled, with her old friend Major Phyllis Heymann, in Cyprus, where they were affectionately known as 'the Cavewomen'.

The sobriquet derived from their residence, Cave House, situated at Tjiklos, a circular plateau 1,000ft up the Kyrenia Pass, which commanded a spectacular view of the north coast. The Majors themselves favoured the nicknames 'Wracks' and 'Cranks', from the initials of their respective Army corps: Major Betty's WRAC, Major Phyllis's Queen Alexandra's Royal Army Nursing Corps.

Both Majors remained on duty throughout the worst EOKA troubles in Cyprus, and resolutely refused to budge from the place, even when the United Nations urged them to evacuate during the Turkish invasion of July 1974. Because of its strategic location, on the edge of the key three-mile pass to Nicosia – for which there was some of the fiercest fighting of the Turkish campaign – Cave House became a focal point for both sides. In the mountains to the rear was the Greek-Cypriot National Guard, and ahead were the advancing Turkish hordes.

Major Betty, a proud Scot, and Major Phyllis, a feisty Yorkshirewoman, were in their element, and set about marshalling the multitude of refugees who were making their way up the hill, lured by a contingent of Finnish UN troops clustered in the vicinity of Cave House. During the thick of the invasion the Majors billeted the throng around a sheltered old water point, which was used for supplying the UN posts. They rationed what little water remained, and rallied the refugees to help fight the fires, which were devastating vast tracts of spruce and pine forest. At one point some Turkish troops tried to take a short cut through the Cave House estate and were engulfed in the flames. One Turk, wounded in the leg by a bullet and badly burned, crawled within feet of the Majors' rosemary and lavender hedgerow and then shot himself. 'We felt fearfully sorry for him,' said Major Phyllis, 'but I think he did the right thing.'

An Army officer's daughter, Elizabeth Hunter Cowan was born at Tunbridge Wells on 12 August 1912 and educated at St Felix's, Southwold. Young Betty had a peripatetic childhood, staying with a variety of family friends in Britain. She was a gifted musician, and had embarked on training to be an opera singer when the Second World War broke out. She began as a FANY – 'an ancient animal,' as she used to say, 'now practically extinct' – and from 1942 did 'a man's job' as deputy assistant director of supplies and transport in the War Office. In 1947, by now a member of the WRAC, Major Betty went out to serve in the Egyptian Canal Zone. It was there, at British GHQ, that she met Major Phyllis Heymann.

That same year they went to Cyprus, where they fell in love with the estate at Tjiklos. Major Betty's task was to organise motor transport on the island, while Major Phyllis instructed the local military hospital in the latest vaccination techniques. The estate was owned by a friend of Major Betty's, who invited them to return on their retirement in 1960, and fixed a nominal rent of £15 a month for their life tenancy. They remained, stalwart and inseparable, ever after.

After the end of the troubles the Finnish UN contingent stayed on at Tjiklos, and installed a sauna there. The Majors frequented the steamy bath-house at every opportunity, and were justly proud when the 'Fin Con' presented them each with diplomas testifying to their having withstood temperatures of 112°F.

The Majors were dispirited by the sudden transformation, after the immigration of Turks from the south in 1975, of Greek Kyrenia into Turkish Girne. But things looked up again when Sabri Tahir, an old friend of British residents in the area, was appointed Mayor of Kyrenia. In that capacity, the wheeler-dealing Turk – 'the terrestrial rogue of business with many houses', as he was described by Lawrence Durrell in *Bitter Lemons* – began to hold court with his daughter every afternoon at his house, where he was able to explain the newly-named streets and shops to the Majors. The two women also became friendly with Durrell, whom Major Betty described as a typical Kyrenian character: 'Little men are often very aggressive, aren't they?' By the mid-1970s more than half of the 800-strong British community had left, but, in spite of a lamentable shortage of gin, the Majors still enjoyed a stimulating social life. Each week they travelled to the British Council in the Greek south to watch a special matinée film, organised at their request to enable them to return home through the barricades before the 5 pm Turkish curfew.

Besides birdwatching, they worked indefatigably to restore their estate to its former tranquil beauty, doing much to revive the many fields of cyclamen which had been destroyed in the fire.

31 December 1991

MARY WINCH

Veteran litigant who took on the English legal system and lost

*

Mary Winch, who has died aged 76, defied the British legal system in the belief that she was the victim of injustice, but succeeded only in multiplying her troubles. Her struggle, which originated in her determination to stay in her mother's house, persisted for a quarter of a century. Rather than relinquish her claims, she endured both prison and incarceration in a mental hospital.

Her story echoes that of Miss Flyte, the old woman who haunted the Chancery court in Charles Dickens's *Bleak House*, 'always expecting some incomprehensible judgment to be given in her favour'. Miss Flyte kept birds in a cage, naming them Hope, Joy, Youth, Peace, Rest, Life, Dust, Ashes, Waste, Want, Ruin, Despair, Madness, Death, Cunning, Folly, Words, Wigs, Rags, Sheepskin, Plunder, Precedent, Jargon, Gammon and Spinach. Miss Flyte found occasion to release her birds at the conclusion of Jarndyce v. Jarndyce – though by that time the case had swallowed up the entire Jarndyce estate in costs. Mary Winch, by contrast, did gain some compensation, but never rid herself of her obsession.

Yet her first 50 years gave no hint of the ordeal to come. Born Mary Agnes Winch on 14 June 1920 at Birmingham, she spent her early years in the Cotswolds. Her father died when she was ten, after which her mother settled in Wales. Mary was educated at the grammar school in Colwyn Bay. After school, Mary Winch became a secretary in an architect's office at Caernarvon, and in the science department of Bangor University. Later she worked part-time in the office of the Lord Lieutenant.

In 1972 she was living with her mother and her younger sister,

Ruby, at Ganaway, a detached Victorian house in Caernarvon. That year her mother died, and two months later Ruby Winch left the house in order to marry. In no time the sisters were at loggerheads. Mary wanted to stay at Ganaway, but their mother had died intestate and they could not agree a value at which the house should be assessed for the purpose of dividing the estate. They also argued about how to pursue a legal claim for £30,000 which their mother had made against a former business partner. The wrangle simmered on until 1975, when the High Court appointed the Public Trustee to administer the estate; he ordered that the house should be sold, and the proceeds shared. Mary Winch, claiming her doctor's sanction for her determination to remain in the house, countered by issuing a writ claiming on the estate as a dependent. The Public Trustee sought direction from the Court of Chancery, and it was ruled that the house must be sold, and the debt owing to the estate settled. Subsequently Mary Winch, who had been prevented by illness from attending the hearing, was informed that the debt had indeed been settled, at £2,000. But she refused to hand over the deeds of the house, which was now barricaded against her. Summoned before Chancery, she pleaded that she had been denied a fair hearing, and even when threatened with imprisonment continued to withhold the deeds. After nine months in hiding, in 1978 she was discovered by the police in a house in Colwyn Bay and taken to Risley Remand Centre.

'I never thought of giving up except once,' she said later, 'when they put me in a punishment cell at Risley and I was exercising with child murderers.' Meanwhile her possessions were removed from the house. When Mary Winch asked the Official Solicitor to investigate her case, she was moved from Risley to a mental hospital at Denbigh, where she remained for a year. 'I was terrified,' she recalled. 'I thought, if they threaten to give me electric shock treatment I'm going to go missing, whatever it takes.' That horror never materialised, but her experiences were ghastly enough. 'The food was all soft stuff,' she remembered, 'because they had to take everyone's dentures out in case they choked. There was one woman who kept throwing herself under my bed in the middle of the night. I would just see a flash of light, and there she would be.' Meanwhile the Public Trustee, having taken out insurance against the absence of the deeds, sold Ganaway for £11,500 – well below market value, in Mary Winch's opinion.

Released from hospital at the end of 1979, and still full of fight, she moved to Eastbourne. At first she found no one to take up her cause, but eventually, with help from the pressure group Justice, she set about wringing compensation from the doctors who had declared her mad. In the Court of Appeal in 1985 Sir John Donaldson, the Master of the Rolls, granted her leave to bring such proceedings. If everyone who fell foul of solicitors was pronounced insane, he observed, 'our mental institutions would be over-full'. Four years later Mary Winch's case came before the High Court, and the Home Office and Area Health Authority, as employers of the doctors, agreed to pay her £27,000 in compensation. Subsequently, she pursued her case against the Public Trustee, and in 1995 she settled out of court for a payment of £15,000.

The complications of the case had been labyrinthine, and Mary Winch instructed solicitors in droves. At one point her current firm was suing its immediate predecessors for failing to pursue, within the legal timescale, actions against two other firms which had been employed still further back in the case.

In her will Mary Winch expressed a desire to assist a number of charities, including Guide Dogs for the Blind, the Royal Society for the Blind, and various organisations which help the poor, the lonely and the aged.

15 October 1996

FANNY CRADOCK

Grande dame of the kitchen who appeared on television in
Norman Hartnell ballgowns

*

Fanny Cradock, the irascible *grande dame* of the kitchen who has
died aged 85, rejoiced in her singular combination of haute couture and haute cuisine. In her various television series in the
1950s and 1960s Mrs Cradock eschewed aprons and appeared in
Hartnell ballgowns while roaring gravel-throated orders – 'More
wine, Johnnie! More butter! Don't stint!'- at her forbearing
companion, a kindly-looking cove sporting a monocle.

She also wrote children's fiction and romantic novels, and was
a prolific journalist – principally for the *Daily Telegraph*. With the
late Johnnie Cradock (her third husband) she wrote articles about
restaurants, food and wine under the pseudonym 'Bon Viveur'.

It was easy to make fun of Fanny Cradock and the much-put-
upon Johnnie – she was, for instance, guyed as 'Fanny Haddock',
the husky-voiced harridan in the wireless comedy shows *Beyond
Our Ken* and *Round the Horne* – but she did much to awaken
British regard for cooking after the War, and to improve the
standards of commercial catering. Her aim was to make good
cookery easy and fun for the post-war generation of housewives,
who had grown up during the years of food shortages. But she
was dedicated to classical cookery, and refused to cut corners.
She was particularly proud of the fact that in 1956, before an
audience of 6,500 *Daily Telegraph* readers in the Royal Albert
Hall, Queen Elizabeth the Queen Mother said that she believed
the Cradocks had been largely responsible for the improvement
in British catering. *The Cook's Book* and *The Sociable Cook's Book*,
which the Cradocks wrote for the *Daily Telegraph* at the request
of readers, were both extremely popular.

Yet latterly Mrs Cradock became as celebrated for her bad temper as for her cooking. 'I have always been extremely rude,' she boasted, 'and I have always got exactly what I wanted.' Her broadcasting career finally came to an end in 1987 when she was sacked by the BBC for attacking the mild-mannered presenter Pamela Armstrong in front of a studio audience. 'Nobody, but nobody, goes on my set!' she shouted at the bemused Miss Armstrong. 'I've never seen such a bloody shambles in all my life!' The BBC discontinued her spot on the show. 'It's obvious she's not feeling too well,' a spokesman said, 'we think it better if she doesn't appear.'

She was born Phyllis Pechey in the Channel Islands on 26 February 1909. Her father, Archibald Pechey (alias Valentine or Mark Cross), was a butterfly collector and a writer of novels, pantomimes and plays; his greatest success in the theatre was the Aldwych farce *Tons of Money* (1922). Fanny's mother, Bijou, was an actress and a singer. At the age of one, the infant Fanny was given to her grandmother ('the Belle of Leicester') as 'a birthday present', and remained with her until she was 10. She later claimed to have learnt almost everything about food and wine from her grandmother. 'All the food was pink,' she recalled of one of their elegant soirées, 'pink mousse on pink glass plates chilled in pink ice into which pink moss rosebuds had been frozen.'

Away from the table, young Fanny spent her early childhood dress-making and communing with the dead: 'I was on intimate terms with the court of Louis XIV,' she recalled.

She was sent to board at the Downs, which she described as 'the hell pit', 'prison' and 'that awful hole'. At 15 she was expelled for encouraging other girls to contact 'the spirit world'. Although her parents wanted to send her to a finishing school Fanny was determined to stay with her grandmother. She earned her keep by cooking dinner each evening: 'They insisted I was in evening dress and in my place by the time the fish was served.

To save time I wore my Schiaparelli beaded frock and slave bangles in the kitchen – that's how I learned to cook in ballgowns.'

At 17 she eloped with her first husband to Brighton, but he died a few months later in an accident, leaving Fanny a pregnant widow. After her father went bankrupt in 1928 she was reduced to earning a living by washing up at a Roman Catholic canteen. She pawned some clothes in order to place an advertisement for a dress-making service in a local newsagent's window. Another source of income was demonstrating Swiss roll mix, and selling vacuum cleaners door-to-door. She made a second marriage, though it is not mentioned in her memoirs, *Something's Burning.*

In 1939 she met Johnnie Cradock, an amiable Old Harrovian, and began an association which lasted until his death in 1987; they did not marry until 1977. Initially they lived in a house which was celebrated for both its ghosts and its hospitality. 'Our cooking used to amaze our friends,' Fanny Cradock recalled. 'They thought we had black market supplies from Fortnum's.' Locally available food would be ingeniously disguised: 'Bracken shoots were asparagus and I used liquid paraffin for my pastry. We caught and cooked sparrows from the garden and often ate baked hedgehogs (rather like frog's legs).'

While Johnnie Cradock served in the Army during the Second World War, Fanny spent her time writing novels. She had some success with such bodice-rippers as *The Lormes of Castle Rising* and *Storm Over Castle Rising*, under the name Frances Dale. After the war she turned to cookery writing, publishing *The Practical Cook* (1949) and *The Ambitious Cook* (1950). Fanny Cradock also wrote a 'Hair and Beauty' column for the *Daily Telegraph* (as Elsa Frances); a cookery column for the *Daily Mail* (as Frances Dale); a series of articles on the lost city of Atlantis (as Philip Essex); and two more columns for the *Daily Telegraph* (as Nan Sortain and Bon Viveur).

Mrs Cradock liked to savour the memory of numerous 'run-ins' with hoteliers, restaurateurs and members of the public. She recalled one contretemps with some youths outside a hotel who refused to move their car: 'I went in kicking low. I can still remember how exhilarating was the slosh of handbag on fleshy nose.' The youths fled.

In 1954 the Cradocks toured Britain lecturing on cookery for the Brains Trust. Two years later they gave the first live televised cookery demonstration. Before the show Mrs Cradock was so nervous that she had to leave the set, run to the nearest church and pray for 20 minutes before she could face the cameras. Johnnie Cradock's encouragement was more prosaic. He froze and was pushed on to the set by a technician who whispered: 'Get a move on, you silly sod, you're on.'

Fanny Cradock went to enormous lengths in the service of television. She dieted rigorously and even had plastic surgery on her nose when technicians told her it was 'too big' and was 'casting shadows over the food'. As the years advanced she became increasingly eccentric and temperamental. In 1964 she was charged with careless driving, and fined £5; the arresting officer described her as 'abusive and excited'. When he asked her to move her Rolls-Royce (parked across the stream of traffic) she called him a 'uniformed delinquent' and told him to wait while she finished her conversation. When he insisted she move her car, she reversed into the car behind. 'You told me to back up,' she said in court, 'I was just doing as I was told.'

In 1968 the Cradocks published a plan to produce a 'second Fanny and Johnnie'. The couple searched for two teenagers: 'We want to groom them so that in the future they can continue to educate people towards decent standards of cuisine,' announced Mrs Cradock. Later that year a film crew visited *chez* Cradock, where they found that one cupboard contained 60 wholesale-sized packets of cornflakes, and another was packed with cases of sardines. Mrs Cradock claimed that the cornflakes were eaten entirely by her 'houseboy' – 'sometimes as many as three packets at a time'. She ate the sardines herself. Her speciality was a dish called 'Dog's Dinner': mashed sardines and boiled egg, squashed on to brown bread.

By the 1970s her memory for detail – always somewhat unreliable – seemed to be failing. When, in 1977, she finally married Johnnie Cradock at a registry office there was confusion over both her age and her name. Mrs Cradock claimed she was 55, even though her elder son was then 50 and her second son 48. She thought her family name was de Peche rather than Pechey, and, when pressed, claimed it was Valentine.

In 1983 Mrs Cradock was prosecuted for dangerous driving. She had swerved across her lane (perhaps following her grandmother's advice to chauffeurs to 'stick to the middle of the road') and caused a collision. When the other driver tried to talk to her she shouted, 'How dare you hit my car!' and drove off. The other driver followed her for 15 miles, 'honking and signalling'. He finally overtook her and stood in front of the car, waving her down. Mrs Cradock proceeded to run him over. In court she told the judge that the other driver's 'threatening behaviour' had made her afraid to stop. Country neighbours of the Cradocks used to complain of Mrs Cradock's erratic behaviour, especially of her distressing tendency 'to lash out with her walking stick at those who got in her way'. In 1987 Mrs Cradock went missing for seven days during a court case involving jewellery stolen from her home. She eventually appeared, claiming that the police search had not been very thorough: 'I was at home all the time.'

The Cradocks received numerous gastronomic awards, including the *Grand Mousquetaire d'Armagnac*, and were appointed *Chevalier et Grande Dame de la Tripiere d'Or*.

29 December 1994

SPORTSWOMEN

RIXI MARKUS

First woman bridge grandmaster and member of a partnership
known as 'Frisky and Bitchy'

*

Rixi Markus, who has died aged 81, was the first woman in the
world to become a bridge grandmaster, and with the late Fritzi
Gordon made up the most formidable women's bridge partnership in the world.

A native of Austria, Rixi Markus emigrated to London
before the Second World War, and in 1950 became naturalised,
eligible to represent her adopted country. The next year she was
selected with Doris Rhodes for the European women's team
championships, held in Venice. At half-time in the final match,
when Britain was trailing Denmark in the lead, Sidney Lee, the
non-playing captain, decided to pair Rixi and another member
of the team, Fritzi Gordon. Britain won the title, and within a
couple of years Fritzi and Rixi had become an internationally
celebrated bridge double-act. In all, they captured seven
European and four world titles for Britain: the women's pairs in
1962 and 1974, the mixed teams in 1962 and the women's teams
in 1964.

Their success at the game did not make for an easy relationship, though. They were an excitable, argumentative pair, and
their habit of venting their frustrations in public earned them
the sobriquet 'Frisky and Bitchy'. Rixi certainly had a volumi-
nous ego, and thought nothing of confiding that a team mate
was 'a selfish bitch'. At the same time, away from the competitive baize, she was a loyal and warm-hearted personality. She
always regretted the aggressive image she gained in the game. 'At
the bridge table I had to be a killer,' she would recall with a sigh.
'Well, no, a tiger.'

She was born Erika Scharfstein on 27 June 1910, into a prosperous Jewish family in Gura Humora, a part of the Austro-Hungarian Empire that is now Romania. The family was forced to flee ahead of the Russian advance in 1916, and eventually settled in Vienna, where Erika learned her first card game, Preference, common in central Europe at the time. By the age of ten she was playing whist, and two years later, while holidaying with an uncle in the Netherlands, she picked up bridge. On her return to Austria, she was careful to keep her new hobby a secret from her parents, who 'would not have considered it at all a proper pastime for a young girl'. She remained a vehemently protected child, and after private education was sent to a finishing school at Dresden, Miss Wallerstein's Pensionat for Jewish Daughters of Good Families.

In 1928 Erika met and married Salomon Markus, a shoemaker twice her age, who also played bridge. It proved a disastrous union – 'Salo', the inferior player, became brutally jealous of his wife's game, and accused her of flirting with whomever she happened to be playing. Mrs Markus increasingly took refuge from her unhappy domestic life at the Vienna Bridge Club. After the third European Bridge Championships were held there in 1934 she turned professional. Paul Stern, the vice-president of the Vienna Bridge Club, soon invited her to join the Austrian Ladies' Team, which was preparing for the first European Women's Teams Championship to be held in Brussels in 1935. Rixi, as she was now known, proved an invaluable asset: Austria won the Europeans that year and the next, then gained a stunning victory at the first Women's World Championship in Budapest in 1937.

On 11 March 1938, when Hitler's troops entered Austria, Rixi Markus was at the bridge table as usual. Within a few days she had resolved to flee the country – her husband would not leave his business – and to join her parents, who had settled in London in 1936. Clutching her young daughter (born in 1929), her bridge trophies and 200 schillings, she boarded a train in Vienna and fooled the authorities by going via Germany and then Belgium to Britain. Her husband joined her some months later, but the marriage was by then irrevocably damaged, and they separated soon after the outbreak of war. In London Rixi worked as a translator for the Red Cross, supplementing her income with her winnings at rubber bridge. It was then the custom for women's teams to be captained by a man, which caused a degree of tension. 'The captain was only a human being,' she recalled, 'and it was inevitable that he would choose one woman rather than another.' Nonetheless Mrs Markus quickly learned the value of discretion. 'I preferred to choose my romantic affairs outside bridge,' she declared. 'I don't have too much respect for the bridge male.'

Meanwhile she suffered her fair share of tragedy. Her elder sister perished in a concentration camp; her father was killed in a motor-car crash; and a love affair with Walter Carr, a member of the newspaper family, ended with his death from a brain hae-morrhage. In her memoirs, *A Vulnerable Game* (1989) – which contained no hands – Markus also told of her 13-year romance with Harold Lever (now Lord Lever), a minister in the Wilson Government. It was during that affair that she persuaded politicians to start an annual bridge match between the two Houses of Parliament. She was organising the next bout, to take place soon after the election, shortly before she died.

Rixi Markus was the author of a dozen books, and was bridge correspondent of the *Guardian* for more than three decades. In 1975 she was appointed MBE.

Her daughter predeceased her.

6 April 1992

DIANA, DUCHESS OF NEWCASTLE

Fearless promoter of women's racing who held a jockey's licence in
four countries and once competed in the Monte Carlo Rally

*

Diana, Duchess of Newcastle, who has died aged 77, made a significant contribution to horse racing, both as a competitor and as a campaigner for the rights of women jockeys. Beautiful, courageous and unconventional, with a fondness for 'getting going', Diana Newcastle's interest in speed was not confined to riding. During the Second World War, she served as a motor-cycle dispatch rider for the Motorised Transport Corps, and in 1954 she entered her Sunbeam Talbot for the Monte Carlo Rally, finishing the event with a respectable place in the forties.

From childhood days she was keen on horses, but it was not until 1955 that she rode in her first point-to-point, when she was master of the Wylye Valley Foxhounds in Wiltshire. It was then too, that she acquired King Henry's Road, whom she was to ride to numerous victories. She chanced upon him in Surrey, while looking for horses for the hunt. Then an eight-year-old gelding who had been put out to grass, he was said to 'lack bone' and to have a bad temperament. Nonetheless, Diana Newcastle struck up a remarkable rapport with the horse; together they enjoyed a decade of success. In her first season, she entered five races, including the Larkhill, Bradbury Rings and South Devon. She won three and was placed in the other two. In 1956 she suffered a severe fall, but was back the next year and won the Queen's Cup 1½ mile women's flat race in Jersey. By 1958 she had progressed to class B races, in which amateurs and women could compete.

Fiercely competitive, and ever keen to take on the best, she was soon promoting the cause of women jockeys, who were then forbidden to race on the flat in mainland Britain. From

1960 she began expressing her views in lively articles for *Horse and Hound*, sparking a vigorous debate with more conservative-minded readers. There were calls for 'Rossetti-ish dream maidens to stay at home with their knitting'. One correspondent demanded that women be banned from riding point-to-point altogether because of the number of accidents to 'the fair sex'. Diana replied with demands for more women's races, not fewer, arguing that the fault lay with inexperienced riders, unschooled horses, bad tack and worse stewarding. It was to be another 11 years before the rules were changed.

Meanwhile, she rode against men in flat races at Longue, Aix-les-Bains, La Roche-Posay, Vichy, Dieppe and Chantilly. The French were not alone in their admiration for the flying Duchess and she eventually held a jockey's licence in four countries, even qualifying as a 'Gentleman Rider of the Fegentri Club'.

She was never put off by her injuries. In 1960 she persuaded Vincent O'Brien to procure her a ride in the amateur Grand National at Merano, Italy. Halfway round, she came off at the timber jump and ended up in hospital. The committee, distressed that a visiting 'Amazone' had come to grief, had the obstacle removed. Three months later, Diana Newcastle was back in the saddle at Larkhill, the first point-to-point of the season. 'I had a collar bone which dislocated from time to time,' she recalled, 'but a horse jumped on me that day and I never had any trouble again.'

Mary Diana Montagu-Stuart-Wortley-Mackenzie was born on 2 June 1920, the second daughter of Viscount Carlton, who succeeded his father as the 3rd Earl of Wharncliffe in 1935. Her mother, the former Lady Elfreda Wentworth-Fitzwilliam, was the eldest daughter of the 7th Earl Fitzwilliam and a redoubtable figure who ran her own munitions factory in the Second World War and was Master of the Ecclesfield Beagles. Young Diana was brought up at the family seat at Wortley Hall, near Sheffield, where she was educated by governesses. Besides riding, her mother laid great emphasis on speaking French, but this was never Diana's strongest subject. She was more interested in gipsy customs, and told a childhood friend that they must make an oath of life-long fidelity by cutting themselves and mixing their blood in a phial. It was a fact that her loyalty to her friends never waned.

Dark-haired, with piercing blue eyes, a quick smile and an uninhibited laugh, Diana grew up as free a spirit as her huntress namesake. She liked people with dash and style, and was a friend of such air aces as Hugh Dundas and Johnnie Johnson. She wore her father's scarlet Guards jacket to hunt balls and would startle the assistants in Harrods by flinging a leg on the counter to demonstrate the brand of stockings she was after.

In 1939 she joined the MTC. Three years later she was posted to Cambridge as a dispatch rider, making the 120-mile round trip to London several times each week. Mud-spattered, with her crash helmet under her arm, she would break her journey by joining her father for lunch at the Ritz. The speed at which these trips were accomplished earned her the nickname 'Hurtle Wortle'. By the end of the war, she was working for ENSA, driving companies of actors across France in a troop-carrying half-track, weaving rapidly between shell craters. Among her passengers were Yvonne Arnaud and Basil Radford. The accommodation was variable and included a billet above a former brothel. One summer day, when the war seemed all but won, she was wandering through the woods outside Brussels, when the sound of close, unfriendly sniper fire alerted her to the fact that not every German had surrendered.

In 1946, she returned to England and married, as his second wife, the 9th Duke of Newcastle. They went to live at Boyton Manor, Wiltshire, and had two daughters. Though the couple had wholly different temperaments, the marriage was happy until Pelham Newcastle decided to move home to Rhodesia in 1948. Diana did not like Africa. By 1950 she was back in England. Her marriage withered into estrangement and was dissolved in 1959.

In Wiltshire, where she was to remain the rest of her life, Diana Newcastle found accommodation for herself and her two daughters in a house beside the kennels of the Wylye hunt. Later she moved to Cortington Manor, where she hosted meets for the South and West Wilts; she was also a guest of the Beaufort and the Belvoir.

In 1972 the rules were at last changed to permit women to race on the flat. Diana Newcastle was by then 52. She refused to be cheated of an opportunity she had so long fought for. In six weeks of rigorous dieting, she lowered her weight to nine stone and entered races at Folkestone, Doncaster and Salisbury.

To the last she remained a stimulating, funny and occasionally intimidating companion. On one occasion, during her usual thorough security check before going out, she accidentally locked a male guest in the downstairs lavatory. Her only response to his complaint was: 'I hope you flushed it.'

She bore her final illness with typical courage. Even when her health began to deteriorate from cancer, she could be seen doing her shopping at Warminster market, or driving her battered car, at speed, through the Wiltshire countryside.

She is survived by her two daughters.

22 September 1997

BEATRICE 'TILLY' SHILLING

Engineer and racing motor-cyclist described as 'a flaming pathfinder of women's lib'

❋

Beatrice 'Tilly' Shilliing, who has died aged 81, was not only a notable aero engineer, responsible for remedying a defect in the Rolls-Royce Merlin engine during the Second World War, but also a renowned racing motor-cyclist; in the 1930s she stormed round the Brooklands circuit and was awarded a coveted Gold Star for lapping the track at more than 100mph on her Norton 500. 'Tilly' Shilling was once described by a fellow scientist as 'a flaming pathfinder of women's lib'; she always rejected any suggestion that as a woman she might be inferior to a man in technical and scientific fields.

In 1940, when Hurricane and Spitfire pilots encountered a life-or-death carburettor problem, she was already a highly regarded scientist at the Royal Aircraft Establishment at Farnborough. The problem which landed on her desk in the carburation department was this: pilots were obliged to turn on their backs in combat to dive because the 'negative-G' of simply putting the nose down resulted in starving the engine, causing it to splutter or cut out. This was a critical defect since the fuel-injected Daimler-Benz engine powering enemy Me109s permitted Luftwaffe pilots to perform the manoeuvre unhindered. Miss Shilling came up with a simple stop-gap device – which cost less, as it happened, than a shilling. Nicknamed 'Miss Shilling's Orifice', it was a metal disc about the size of an old threepenny bit, with a small hole in the middle. It was brazed into the fighter's fuel pipe, and when the pilot accelerated in a dive the disc stopped even momentary starvation of the Merlin engine. By March 1941 Miss Shilling's Orifice had been installed throughout Fighter Command, sufficing until replaced by an improved carburettor.

A butcher's daughter, Beatrice Shilling was born at Waterlooville, Hampshire, on 8 March 1909, and after working as an electrician and electrical linesman she took an engineering degree at Manchester University. In the 1930s she was recruited as a scientific officer by the RAE and began on a small salary doing fairly menial work. Even as a senior member of that establishment she was renowned for rolling up her sleeves and getting her hands dirty – shop floor workers respected the fact that she could braze a butt joint between two pieces of copper with the skill of a fitter. When she married George Naylor, whom she had met at aerodynamics night-school classes, colleagues presented her with a set of stocks and dies. It was said that she turned her own wedding ring on a lathe in stainless steel.

After the War she shone in charge of investigations at Farnborough – such as a probe into aquaplaning by aircraft taking off or landing on wet runways. These occurrences raised particular public alarm when an Elizabethan airliner crashed on take-off in slush at Munich, killing most of the Manchester United football team. Her investigation of the related problems included conducting a series of trials for the Engineering Physics Department to assess braking performance on an experimental high-friction runway surface in conditions of heavy rain. She summoned a convoy of bowsers to spray water on the concrete, while a wingless naval Scimitar ran up engines as if for take-off.

Miss Shilling shared her passion for speed on wheels with her husband, and visitors to their home were astonished by the variety of motor-cycle parts scattered around. In the 1950s she successfully raced her 1935 Lagonda Rapier at Silverstone, her skilful engine-tuning producing a speed of more than 100mph. She also participated in sports-car racing at Goodwood, and another of her pastimes was pistol shooting.

Miss Shilling was appointed OBE in 1948 and retired in 1969, after 36 years at Farnborough. She is survived by her husband.

18 November 1990

MERVYN SUTHERLAND PILCH

*Elder of the golfing Barton girls who vied with her sister for
domination of the English game in the 1930s*

*

Mervyn Sutherland Pilch, who has died aged 85, possessed one of the most beautiful swings in women's golf; and if she never quite matched the achievements of her younger sister Pam Barton, who held both the British and American women's championships at the same time, she did not fall far behind in natural talent. She hit the ball vast distances with leisurely power, and had a brilliant short game; on her day she could seem unbeatable. But she lacked the killer instinct, and, though she was capable of fighting her way out of difficulties, her elegant action could become rather too easy and loose under pressure.

'The trouble with Mervyn,' it was affectionately remarked, 'is that she is far too nice.' One admirer resorted to verse to explain her failure to live up to her potential:

> *This is a song for Mervyn*
> *The girl with the beautiful swing.*
> *Lousy at concentration*
> *Lacking this one vital thing –*
> *Hitting the ball so far – so far.*
> *Everything going your way,*
> *Then you forget just where you are*
> *And throw all the holes away.*

Mervyn Sutherland Pilch was born Patricia Barton on 11 January 1915, the eldest of three children. Her father worked in London as a director of Lyons, and she went to school in Holland Park. When she was 14 she and her sister Pam (who was two years younger) were taken for a golf lesson with the great J.H.

Taylor, five times Open champion between 1894 and 1913. Pat Barton was unimpressed: 'He hadn't a clue how to teach.' Fortunately, Sir Dunbar Plunket Barton saw the girls in action at the Mid-Surrey course, and constituting himself an honorary uncle, arranged for them to have lessons with Archie Compston. 'He had us hitting balls until we were flat on our faces,' Pat remembered.

Compston turned both sisters into champions. In 1933 Pam beat Pat in the final of the Girls' championship – and then wept at her own victory when she realised Pat would be ineligible for the event in future years. It was at this stage that Pat Barton changed her first name to Mervyn, to avoid confusion with her sister at tournaments.

Playing together, the Barton sisters won the autumn four-somes at Ranelagh, Barnes, in 1934. In singles, however, the auburn-haired and outward-going Pam proved the tougher competitor; in that same season of 1934, still only 17, she reached the final of the British Women's championship at Porthcawl and won the French championship at Le Touquet. She also played for Britain against the USA in the Curtis Cup; this was the second match of the series, and the first played in America. In 1935, the Barton sisters met in the semi-final of the British Women's championship at the Royal County Down Links at Newcastle. Pam was five holes up with six to play, but Mervyn, playing superlatively, then won four holes in a row before bury-ing her hopes in a bunker at the 17th. 'Well played Pam,' she vol-unteered. 'Hard luck Mervyn,' came the reply.

In 1936, Pam, still only 19, won the British Women's Amateur championship at Southport and Ainsdale. She then crossed the Atlantic and carried off the American title at Canoe Brook Country Club, New Jersey. Such was her dominance in America that she only had to play the 18th hole once – in the 36-hole final. Pam Barton's celebrity only seemed to strengthen the bond between the sisters, and if one of them was beaten early in a tournament, she would stay behind to watch and support the other's progress.

Mervyn Barton also had her triumphs, reaching the semi-final of the Women's championship at Burnham in 1938. Later that year Mervyn Barton married Reginald Sutherland Pilch. In order to attend the wedding, Pam Barton gave up her place in the Curtis Cup side going to America. But Mervyn's marriage separated the sisters, since Reggie ran a business based in Calcutta, which sold cars over a vast area between Aden and Shanghai.

In 1939, Mervyn Sutherland Pilch was favourite to win the All-India Ladies' Golf championship, but after playing superbly in the early rounds she lost in the semi-final. She stayed in India during the War, giving birth to two sons. In November 1943 she had a dream that her sister Pam had died; and soon afterwards the premonition was confirmed. Pam, who was serving in the Women's Auxiliary Air Force, had been to a dance with a pilot. Afterwards, taking off from Manston airfield in Kent, her escort forgot to switch on the fuel supply, and crashed on take-off. The pilot was thrown clear and survived; Pam, strapped in, did not. She was 26 and the reigning British amateur champion, having won the title on the last occasion it had been contested, in 1939.

After the war Mervyn Sutherland Pilch and her husband lived mainly in London until 1960; then at Rudgwick and West Chiltington in Sussex. Mervyn continued her golf career with undiminished skill, performing many stalwart deeds for the Royal Mid-Surrey Club and as a member of the Surrey side which won the women's title four times between 1946 and 1956. In 1949 she was robbed of a place in the semi-finals of the English Women's championship when she had an 18-inch putt to win but was unintentionally stymied by her opponent Lady Katherine Cairns.

Though Mervyn Sutherland Pilch never played in the Curtis Cup, she represented England against Canada in 1953 and, though four down after the 14th, halved her singles match. In

1958, she was non-playing captain of England for the home internationals at Hunstanton. In 1961, despite conceding eight strokes in the final, she won the Family Foursomes at Burhill with her younger son Jeremy. She crowned her career in 1968 when she finally won the Surrey Women's championship (a title her sister had won in 1936), having been runner-up in 1955, 1956 and 1958. She still holds the course record of 68 at West Sussex Golf Club. She was quondam President of the Surrey Ladies, and also of the Veteran Ladies Golf Society.

Reggie Sutherland Pilch died in 1983. They had two sons.

10 June 2000

LADY CUSACK-SMITH

*Fearless and colourful Master of Foxhounds in County Galway
who stood no nonsense and loved to Tango*

*

Lady Cusack-Smith, who has died aged 85, was one of the most colourful and senior figures in the world of Irish foxhunting; she was Master of the Bermingham and North Galway from 1946 to 1984, a term as MFH only exceeded in the British Isles by the late 'Master', the 10th Duke of Beaufort. She co-founded the hunt with her husband, Sir Dermot Cusack-Smith, Bt, in 1946. During the war, from 1939 to 1943, she had been sole Master – the three male Masters having gone off to fight – of the celebrated County Galway Hunt, 'The Blazers'. She was a great-great-great niece of the founder of the Blazers, John Dennis, whose great hunting portrait hung in her dining room at Bermingham House.

North Galway country stretches from the north of Galway city, along Lough Corrib in the west and north, and extends northwards into Co. Mayo and eastwards into parts of Co. Roscommon. Stone walls, four or five feet high, are a common feature of the landscape, and Mollie Cusack-Smith was celebrated for her fearless jumping – though if her hunter Hippo did not like the look of a wall, he would turn his back on it and kick it down. Her accomplished blowing of the horn was much admired, and she stood no nonsense out hunting; many people have had their vocabularies broadened by 'Lady Mollie'. The annual ball she held at Bermingham on the second Friday after Christmas was for decades an eagerly awaited date on the calendar. Dinner would be announced with a stirring blast of the hunting horn, and the party would end in the small hours, after wild dancing, with Irish folk music – and with the hostess warbling *The West Awake* in her rich contralto. Perhaps not surprisingly, Mollie Cusack-Smith was someone to whom stories frequently became attached. A local farmer, observing her heading home after a hard day's hunting, is said to have remarked to her: 'The old horse is sweating up a bit, Lady Mollie.' She replied: 'So would you be if you'd been between my legs for six hours.' She did not exactly admit to the truth of the story, but was, she said, indignant when she heard it attributed to someone else.

She was born Adela Mary O'Rorke in Dublin in 1912, the daughter of Charles Trench O'Rorke, a scion of the O'Rorkes of Breffni. Young Mollie grew up at Bermingham House and aged ten was hunting her father's hounds. 'He used to go into Tuam,' she recalled, 'to do some steady drinking – good for his asthma – and people would tell him that they had seen "Miss Mollie cursing horrid".'

After an unsuccessful spell at Sherborne School for Girls – 'They gave me two out of 100 for "trying" in mathematics, but I told them I wasn't trying' – she was sent to be finished in Paris, where she learned to sing. At home she had had a governess who taught her sewing and dressmaking, and so after Paris – and after a row with her father over a horse – she moved to London and set up a dressmaking business in Mayfair. Her customers included Princess Marina, Duchess of Kent.

The sound of Mollie O'Rorke's hunting horn was occasionally heard in Berkeley Square, and away from the shop her boyfriend ('married, thank God!') taught her to ride with greater skill. When she had patched things up with her father he lent her two horses and she joined the Pytchley, where some of the stuffier elements looked askance at her not riding side-saddle, and at her untidiness. She much enjoyed hunt balls – 'I used to turn backward somersaults for miles down the passages – revealing nothing, I may say' – and in London she went dancing, which she liked even better than hunting, most nights. She was a regular at the Four Hundred, and a friend of the Savoy bandleader Caryl Gibbons. The Tango and Latin American dances were her favourites.

When her father fell ill in 1937, Mollie returned to Bermingham to look after him. After an uncle had said of her 'Mollie will never be any good, she is a jack of all trades and master of none', she decided to become a Master of Foxhounds. 'My operatic contralto,' she said, 'which I knew how to project, came in very useful when controlling the field.'

After numerous spills and fractures cheerfully borne, Mollie Cusack-Smith gave up hunting at 71; she had hoped to do 40 seasons, 'but my old horse, Willy, could do no more'. She was pleased, though, that her beloved hounds continued to be kenneled at Bermingham; 'I'd go anywhere and do anything for them,' she confessed. 'I've had a gorgeous, wonderful life,' she said in 1994, 'but I have no money. I've got nothing left. And the roof occasionally blows off, which is very awkward.'

She married Sir Dermot Cusack-Smith, 6th Bt, as his second wife, in 1946; they had a daughter. Sir Dermot died in 1970.

20 February 1998

VIOLET WEBB

*Winner at the Los Angeles Games in 1932 of Britain's first
Olympic medal for women's athletics*

*

Violet Webb, who has died aged 84, was the first woman to win an Olympic medal for Britain at athletics, as part of the 4 × 100m relay team which took bronze at the 1932 Games in Los Angeles.

Athletics for women had entered the Olympic programme in 1928, amid some controversy. Baron Pierre de Coubertin, founder of the modern Olympics, was strongly against women taking part in sport. 'This does not mean that they should not participate in any sports,' he opined, 'yet not in public. At the Olympic Games their primary role should be like in the ancient tournaments – the crowning of the (male) victors with laurels.'

As a result of the very limited women's involvement – they were invited to compete in only five events – the British female athletes decided to boycott the Amsterdam Games in 1928, the first year they were eligible to enter. Four years later they relented, and at Los Angeles Violet Webb and her team-mates constituted the first British Olympic women's athletics team. 'People thought it was terrible that we should want to compete,' Violet Webb remembered. 'But that was just stupid. Athletics was my life, so I just did it.'

The journey to Los Angeles was first by ship to Canada; other passengers included the Prime Minister, Stanley Baldwin, and the Cabinet. The athletes then continued by special train. 'When it stopped, we got off and ran up and down the platform. I hurdled a few dustbins.' In Los Angeles, the women's team stayed at the Chapman Park Hotel, while the male athletes were installed in the first ever purpose-built Olympic village, complete with a high wall to keep out female competitors. Violet Webb managed to glimpse such film stars as Jimmy Durante and Mary Pickford.

She reached the final of the 8om hurdles, finishing fifth. Then, when the sprinter Ethel Johnson injured her leg in the heats of the 4 × 100m relay, Violet Webb was called in as replacement for the final and ran the second leg. The British team won the bronze medal in 47.6 seconds; the Americans took gold. 'When you see people standing on the rostrum and you see their tears, I can understand that,' Violet Webb said later. 'If you're proud of your country, you do feel that way.'

One of seven children, Violet Webb was born on 3 February 1915 in Willesden, north London, and was educated locally. Her father Charles Webb was an athlete, and seeing the potential in young Violet, he built her a flight of eight hurdles which were kept at Paddington recreation ground. Fashioned from wood, the hurdles did not fall over if an athlete struck them. 'They were formidable,' Violet Webb recalled. 'I jumped high over them, as it hurt when you hit the solid barrier. I broke my arm on those awful hurdles once. It didn't deter me – I just went straight back again.'

She joined the Ladies Polytechnic Club in Regent Street, where she excelled. At her first international, against Germany in August 1931, she won the 8om hurdles and the relay, bringing her to the attention of the Olympic selectors. After the 1932 Olympics, Violet Webb competed in the Women's World Games (at first known as the Women's Olympics until the International Olympic Committee objected), which had been started in 1921 by the Frenchwoman Alice Milliat in response to the lack of women's involvement in the Olympics. At the last Women's Games in 1934, Violet Webb was invited to take the Olympic oath on behalf of all the competitors. She also competed in the 1936 Olympics in Berlin, where she remembered the arrival of Hitler at the Olympic stadium: 'You'd have thought God was coming down from Heaven.' There she finished fourth in the semi-final of the 80m hurdles. Independent observers judged her to have finished third – which would have meant a place in the final – but the officials disagreed. Undeterred, she came back to equal the world record of 11.7 seconds at a post-Olympic meet in Wuppertal.

Soon afterwards, she retired and married Harry Simpson. They had two daughters, one of whom, Janet, went on to international honours, competing in three Olympic Games between 1964 and 1972. At the Tokyo Games she followed her mother by winning a bronze in the relay.

29 May 1999

FANNY BLANKERS-KOEN

Dutch sprinter known as 'The Flying Housewife' who was voted the greatest female athlete of the last century

*

Fanny Blankers-Koen, who has died in Holland aged 85, was the only woman to have won four gold athletics medals at a single Olympics, a haul matched in the history of the Games by just two other competitors, Jesse Owens and Carl Lewis; in 1999 the governing body of track and field sports, the IAAF, voted her the greatest female athlete of the 20th century.

The 1948 Olympics, held in London, were the first to be staged since those at Berlin 12 years earlier. Fanny Blankers-Koen had represented the Netherlands there as a teenager, but had not made much of a mark in her two events – the high jump and the sprint relay – and, with the onset of war, had believed that her athletics career was over. This feeling was reinforced by the effects of the malnutrition she had suffered as the Dutch starved under Nazi occupation, and by the birth of her son and her daughter.

Nonetheless, she continued to train in secret under the eye of her coach and husband, Jan Blankers, a former triple jump champion whom she had married in 1940; and in 1943 she set two unofficial world records, in the long and high jumps. Encouraged by this, she returned to competition, and in 1946, in Oslo, claimed the European titles at 100m and in the 80m hurdles.

Fanny Blankers-Koen arrived at the White City stadium in London as the holder of six world records, yet found herself dogged by criticism. The manager of the British team dismissed her as being too old, at 30; while in Holland there were many who believed that she would be better employed looking after her children. Her detractors might have been even more vocal had they known that she was already in the early stages of a third pregnancy. She secured her first victory with ease, winning the 100m by three metres in 11.9 seconds. Two days later she lined up for the final of the 80m hurdles as favourite, but hit the fifth flight as she caught up with Britain's Maureen Gardner, lost her stride and finished in a dead heat with Gardner and the Australian Shirley Strickland. She thought that she had lost to the Briton, her training partner, and believed her fears confirmed when the band began to play *God Save The King*. This, however, was for George VI, who was just taking his seat, and a few moments later she heard the Dutch anthem. Blankers-Koen had won in 11.2 seconds (the same time as Gardner), a new world record.

By now, however, Fanny Blankers-Koen – a strongly-built yet rather shy blonde – was indeed beginning to miss her children; and when her husband went into the dressing room before the 200m semi-finals, he found her in tears. She told him that she hated the event – the distance was being run by women for the first time at an Olympics – and that she wanted to go home. He sympathised with her, but said that she would later regret her decision if she quit. 'Jan was right,' she remarked later. 'I had a good cry and felt much better.' Indeed, so good did she feel that, in the heat, she set a new Olympic record of 24.4 seconds, a time she almost equalled when she later won the final by seven metres on a soaking wet track.

The last of Fanny Blankers-Koen's four golds came in the sprint relay, and was claimed by her in dramatic fashion. Running the anchor leg, she received the baton in fourth place, but blasted past her opponents to snatch victory for Holland. She had won all four medals in just eight days. More remarkably still, it is probable that she would have won six golds had she not been confined by the rules of the time to competing in just three individual events. She did not enter either the long or high jumps, which were won by performances that were inferior to her own world records.

Fanny Blankers-Koen, who had been nicknamed 'The Flying Housewife' by the British press, returned to Amsterdam to be greeted by vast crowds. 'All I did was run fast,' she said in some bewilderment. Her critics were silenced and the nation showed its appreciation of her victories by presenting her with a new bicycle – so that she would not have to run so much.

The daughter of a government official, she was born Francina Elsje Koen at Baarn, Holland, on 26 April 1918. As a child she enjoyed swimming, gymnastics and fencing, and took up athletics only at 16, at her father's suggestion. As an 18-year-old at the Berlin Games, she finished sixth in the high jump and came fifth with the relay team. The highlight for her, however, was securing Jesse Owens's autograph. Almost 40 years later, at the Munich Olympics, she reminded him of this, telling him: 'My name is Fanny Blankers-Koen.' 'You don't have to tell me that,' said Owens, 'I know all about you.' 'Imagine,' she recalled later with her usual modesty, 'Jesse Owens knew who I was.'

In 1952 she was selected for the Helsinki Olympics, but although early on she reached the hurdles final, she was troubled by a large carbuncle, and pulled up after hitting the first two flights. She then decided to withdraw from the Games.

Fanny Blankers-Koen retired from competition in 1955, having set 16 world records in eight disciplines, including the pentathlon and the shot, and having won five European and 58 national titles. In 1960 she managed the Dutch team at the Rome Olympics.

She lived in Amsterdam (where a statue of her was erected), enjoying tennis and getting out on her bicycle until recently, when she began to suffer ill health. She refused to be jealous of modern athletes such as Marion Jones, who secured a multi-million-dollar sponsorship contract after taking two golds at the Sydney Olympics in 2000. 'She trains twice a day,' Fanny pointed out. 'We only trained twice a week.'

26 January 2004

MATRIARCHS AND MUSES

*

ENID HATTERSLEY

Lord Mayor of Sheffield who transformed the cultural life of the
city and inspired her son's career

✽

Enid Hattersley, who has died aged 96, was one of the group of
Labour politicians who in the post-war decades turned Sheffield
from one of England's grimiest cities into a modern industrial
centre; as chairman of the Libraries and Arts Committee, she
developed the city's museums and art galleries to the point where
they gained an international reputation. A kindly but formidably
persistent woman, Enid Hattersley was also the driving force
behind her son, Roy (now Lord) Hattersley, who served on the
city council with both his parents before making his name
nationally, ultimately as deputy leader of the Labour Party. Until
her death, she remained the strongest influence in his life.

Enid Hattersley kept a remarkable secret from her son until he
was into his fifties: that his father, who died an atheist, had been
a Roman Catholic priest and had renounced the Church to
marry her. The secret was closely guarded; friends were mys-
tified that this august, well-read man should occupy a mundane
clerical post in the Health Service.

Enid Anne Brackenbury was born at Shirebrook, Nottinghamshire, on 19 September 1904, the daughter of a coal
merchant; she claimed to have been 'born into the Labour
Party', though she had to wait until she was 14 for her membership card. She kept house for her invalid mother, although she
had by then married a miner called John O'Hara. When she was
27, however, Fr Frederick Hattersley (always known as Roy, his
second name) called to order winter coal for his presbytery. After
a brief courtship conducted perforce in secret, they decided to
marry. The Church put him under intense pressure not to

renounce his vows and even to return once he had burned his boats; Enid Hattersley told her son after his father's death that a 'wicked and ridiculous' bishop had been sent to 'take your father back'. After O'Hara's death, they eventually married in Worksop, Shirebrook being too disapproving. By the time their son was born, the Hattersleys had moved to Sheffield, settling in Wadsley village. Roy Hattersley senior was conscripted into the police force, and Enid Hattersley became active in Hillsborough Labour Party, working for the re-election of A.V. Alexander, First Lord of the Admiralty in Churchill's coalition. As she still had her mother to care for, it was 1960 before she was elected to the council.

Enid Hattersley spent 20 years on its Libraries and Arts Committee, chairing it from 1968 to 1980. She served four years on South Yorkshire County Council, and chaired the governors of Sheffield's first purpose-built comprehensive school. Enid Hattersley embodied the socialist belief that the people in post-war Britain would embrace excellence in culture if they were given the fullest access to books, art, music and drama. If those targets were not achieved in Sheffield, it was not for want of her efforts: under a series of talented directors, notably Frank Constantine, the city's museums and galleries developed fine displays of classical and modern art. Among the initiatives Enid Hattersley pioneered was one for people to borrow spare pictures from the galleries at a nominal fee. She also oversaw the birth of Sheffield's Crucible Theatre. The council had a considerable say in its design, not necessarily for the better; one councillor contested plans for its 'thrust stage' on the grounds that 'I'm not paying 8s 6d to see Hamlet's backside'. She had mixed feelings about its greater success as a venue for snooker.

Her influence on cultural life extended well beyond Sheffield. She was active for many years in regional arts organisations, and in 1979 as chairman of the Yorkshire Museums Service was instrumental in persuading Kirklees council not to sell its finest works of art, among them a Francis Bacon and a Henry Moore.

As a politician Mrs Hattersley – like her husband, who, though chairman of the council's Health Committee, was firmly in her shadow – was on the Right of the party. As such, she found the politics of the council increasingly difficult from the mid-1970s when Peter Walker's local government shake-up sidelined Labour's core of aldermen and opened the way for young militants. She survived for a while by concentrating on her promotion of the arts, but every so often took a stand. Most memorably, she foiled an attempt by Left-wingers in 1974 to stage a late-night debate on the perceived evils of the Pinochet regime in Chile by talking on her own committee's minutes for so long that most of the councillors went home. Next morning the *Sheffield Morning Telegraph* carried a front-page cartoon of a street-trader with a three-legged donkey demanding to see Mrs Hattersley. She was not amused. Her penchant for loquacity was not confined to council meetings. Any caller greeted by her habitual reply of 'Hattersley, Airedale Road' knew they were likely to be on the phone for at least an hour, generally without being given the opportunity to say why they had rung.

Enid Hattersley's civic career was crowned in 1981 by her installation as Lord Mayor. She carried out her engagements regally, and rallied the city when the destroyer Sheffield, the 'Shiny Sheff' as it was known to every Sheffielder, was sunk with heavy loss of life during the Falklands War. She immediately opened a fund for the families of those killed and wounded, prompting the Ministry of Defence to set up its own South Atlantic Fund.

Her husband died in 1973.

22 May 2001

DORIS THOMPSON

'Queen Mother of Blackpool' who was chairman of its Pleasure
Beach and rode its roller-coasters aged 100

*

Doris Thompson, who has died aged 101, was the chairman of Blackpool Pleasure Beach; popularly known as the Queen Mother of Blackpool, she reigned over an amusement park covering more than 40 acres of the town, and visited by more than seven million people a year, making it Europe's most popular tourist site after EuroDisney and the Vatican. The Pleasure Beach was founded by her father, Alderman William Bean, in 1896, and she pre-dated its oldest surviving ride by one year. This was Sir Hiram Maxim's Captive Flying Machine, opened on August Bank Holiday 1904. Maxim (inventor of the gun) used the ride to demonstrate 'captive flight' and to raise new capital.

Doris Thompson was a great aficionado of fairground rides: her father took her on her first tour of American amusement parks in 1924. At home in Blackpool, she continued to go on all the rides well into her nineties. From the charming Edwardian River Caves, to the wooden dippers and roller-coasters of the 1920s and 1930s and the high-tech rides of the 1980s and 1990s, she had seen them all built and tried them all out: 'When in my late seventies I tried out the Revolution Ride, I remember thinking then that perhaps I was getting too old to be going upside down.' Twenty years later, however, she was still being photographed at the grand openings of all the big rides, happily trying them out, while younger men turned pale at the thought: 'My last trip was on the Avalanche with the Bishop of Blackburn. I don't think we've seen him here since,' she reported blithely, in her early nineties.

Doris Thompson was a living archive for the Pleasure Beach and an astonishingly lively source of myth, and the sea changes she witnessed in the visitors to her amusement park reflected the profound shifts in British social structure – and culture – during the past century. In the pre-war years, the mill and factory workers who poured into Blackpool every summer on specially chartered trains always wore their best clothes – jacket and tie and boaters for the men, with the women all in hats: 'They kept them on with long pins and luck.'

As the rides became faster and roller-coasters were introduced in the 1920s, it was not always easy to maintain due decorum. When, in 1994, the lake through which the Log Flume runs underneath the Big Dipper was drained, among all the purses, wallets and jewellery that had been shaken out of passengers on the ride, there was found a large collection of dentures, toupées and glass eyes.

Doris Thompson's savvy father instinctively knew how to treat his customers. When he charged a whole shilling for a ride (to pay for the Big Dipper, built at a cost of £25,000 in August 1923), there was an outcry, so he built his customers a gleaming mahogany and marble pay desk and splendid entrance hall with an Italian terrazzo floor, reasoning that they would feel happier parting with their money in style. As the *Manchester Guardian* put it in 1922: 'It is the Earthly Paradise of a shrewd, hard-working people, who must take their pleasures on a big scale.'

While the clothes became more casual over the years, there was an increasing number of middle-class visitors in the late 1980s and 1990s, and Doris Thompson appeared on a programme about the conundrums of the British class system: here was a family of fairground ride owners, among the richest people in Britain, public school and Oxbridge-educated for three generations. Doris Thompson herself gave short shrift to those who knocked either the Pleasure Beach, or Blackpool, for being vulgar or unsophisticated, and she was never slow to point out the ways in which creative talent and innovation could flourish in seaside resorts.

She was born Lilian Doris Bean at Great Yarmouth on 12 January 1903, the daughter of William Bean, a businessman, and Lilian Crossland, who came from a Yorkshire family living in the town. It was there that Bean first set up his Patent Bicycle Railways, based on a contraption which he had seen while visiting Coney Island, New York, to transport the staff of an armaments factory across a river. It did not do as well as he had hoped, however, so he transferred it to Blackpool and thus laid the foundations of the Pleasure Beach, established, as he claimed, to 'make adults feel like children again and to inspire gaiety of a primarily innocent character'.

Doris Bean was educated at Malvern Ladies' College and was never expected to work. 'I think my father was the sort of man who thought he really didn't want a lot of women mixed up with the business at all, and he didn't have any women working in the office until the First World War,' she said. However, when he died suddenly, at the age of 60, in 1929, he left his entire estate, including all the holdings in the Pleasure Beach companies, to his daughter. Doris was then 25 years old and living in London with her husband, Leonard Thompson, whom she had married the previous year. He was working for the Swedish Match Company at the time, but it was decided that he should take over the running of the Pleasure Beach and Doris, the major shareholder, was made director.

For the best part of 50 years, her husband continued the work of her father, introducing new rides, such as the roller-coaster and the Grand National (the first twin-track roller-coaster in Europe), and rebuilding the park several times over, in an effort to keep up with changing tastes. The most ambitious building programme took place during the 1930s, when the architect Joseph Emberton (who designed the Royal Corinthian Yacht Club at Burnham in 1931, and Simpson's of Piccadilly) was commissioned to give the Pleasure Beach a modern style. Doris Thompson's contribution to this was the provision of a fully equipped crèche for babies and toddlers, also designed by Emberton and opened in 1936. Unfortunately, this building did not survive the Second World War. The architect's masterpiece was the fully air-conditioned circular Casino, a building far in advance of anything in Britain at the time. It was opened on 26 May 1939, the day Doris Thompson was appointed as the youngest ever magistrate to the Blackpool bench.

While she had naturally always taken an interest in the Pleasure Beach and supported her husband's work – 'I read all the notices to see what's going on and whether there's anything that needs doing. I take a woman's interest; especially where hygiene is concerned,' she once commented – it was not until her husband died in 1976, that, at the age of 73, she became a force in the Pleasure Beach in her own right. Although she had remained the major shareholder and been a director since her father's death, she had never been called upon to fill an executive role. Now she was appointed chairman (a function she had previously fulfilled in local and charitable organisations), while her son, Geoffrey, became managing director. Doris Thompson now became more than just a figurehead, and she relished this more active role. She came into the office every day to sign cheques, listen to problems and dispense advice, and to preside over a directors' lunch. Her son's three children, who became closely involved in the running of the Pleasure Beach, especially valued her wise advice and no-nonsense approach. She also proved adept at PR, and a bright-eyed photograph of her with a queasy-looking celebrity by her side, and a ready quip, could be guaranteed at the opening of each new ride.

When the 235ft Pepsi Max Big One opened in 1994, at the time the world's tallest and fastest roller-coaster, she was 91 and admitted that her family were worried it might give her a heart attack, although she gamely declared: 'I've been riding these things all my life, it doesn't worry me in the slightest.' Three years later she went up with the pop group Boyzone for the official opening of 'PlayStation: The Ride'. She was catapulted up a 210ft tower at 80mph and back. As she got off, she was heard to say: 'That's the closest I've been to heaven so far.'

She was appointed MBE in 1969 and OBE in 2003. On her 100th birthday, she rode the Spin Doctor ride, more than 120ft high.

One of her daughters predeceased her, killed in an air crash, and her son Geoffrey died just a few days before his mother. She is survived by her daughter.

25 June 2004

LORNA WISHART

Femme fatale who was muse to both Laurie Lee and Lucian Freud

*

Lorna Wishart, who has died aged 89, was a ravishing beauty who broke the hearts of both Laurie Lee and Lucian Freud and inspired some of their best work. She had two brothers and six almost equally striking sisters. Of these, Kathleen became the mistress and later wife of Jacob Epstein and Mary the wife of the South African poet Roy Campbell. Another sister married a French fisherman – 'like Jean Marais, only better looking' – while another managed to seduce her idol T.E. Lawrence before retiring to a cottage with a lady named Philip de Winton. But Lorna was loveliest of all; tall, lean and feline, with dark hair and enormous deep blue eyes, she exerted an extraordinary seductive power over men. She was, as her daughter Yasmin later described her, 'a dream for any creative artist. . . savage, wild, romantic and completely without guilt'.

The writer Laurie Lee, who met her in 1937 on a beach in

Cornwall, never stood a chance. He was playing his violin and Lorna beckoned him over, saying: 'Boy, come and play for me.' 'She was married and had two young children,' wrote Lee in *As I Walked Out One Midsummer Morning* (1969). 'She was rich and demandingly beautiful, extravagantly generous with her emotions but fanatically jealous and one who gave more than she got in love.' Lee soon found himself caught up in a delirium of passion with her. He wrote at the time, 'I am in another world, drugged and oblivious to the actual conditions of my life.'

To impress her, Lee went to fight in Spain as a Republican volunteer, albeit briefly – Lorna soon engineered his return. She then left her husband, Ernest Wishart, and her children and set up home with Lee in a small flat in Bloomsbury. She returned to her husband in 1939, after bearing Lee's daughter, Yasmin, who was brought up as part of the Wishart family; she only learned Lee was her real father when she was 21. Lorna's affair with Lee continued nonetheless. Hunched in a caravan or the back bedroom of a Bognor semi, Lee would wait in misery ('Oh the hopeless acid in the mouth, the fear, the madness, the anger') for her to roll up in her Bentley, in dresses with 'seductive rows of buttons', showering him with gifts of champagne, goose eggs and 'an eddying fragrance of irresistible passion' – only for her to race back hours later to her life of domesticity and chic.

Most of Lee's early poetry, collected in *The Sun My Monument* (1944), concerns his affair with Lorna. Gradually, through her connections with editors such as Stephen Spender, Lee had his work published in magazines, including *Horizon*, and his reputation grew. They continued to see each other until 1943, when she fell for the painter Lucian Freud, then 20, whom Lawrence Gowing described as 'fly, perceptive, lithe, with a hint of menace'. 'This mad, unpleasant youth appeals to a sort of craving she has for corruption,' Lee wrote in his diary. 'She goes to him when I long for her.'

Lee was almost suicidal: P.J. Kavanagh recalled seeing him sitting at a typewriter all day typing 'Lorna, Lorna, Lorna . . .' After his rejection, he lost his youthful optimism and drifted away from writing poetry. He wore her signet ring until his dying day. Freud too fell under her spell, describing her as 'the first person I was really caught up with'. He captured her feline, almost atavistic quality in *Girl with Daffodil* (1945). In time Freud too disappeared from the scene. Bizarrely, with Lorna Wishart's encouragement, Laurie Lee later married one of her nieces, while Freud went on to marry the other.

She was born Lorna Garman on 11 January 1911, the daughter of a wealthy, brutal doctor and his Irish wife. Strictly brought up and unhappy at boarding school, she jumped over the school tennis net with glee when she realised – aged 12 – that the death of her father meant she had to leave. At 14 she met Ernest Wishart, a Cambridge law student. Wishart was a Communist, but a rich one. His father, Colonel Sir Sidney Wishart, had extensive estates in Sussex. Lorna married at 16 and had her first son, Michael, at 17. After leaving Cambridge, Ernest Wishart formed a Marxist publishing company, Wishart & Co (later Lawrence and Wishart). Despite her affairs, it was Wishart to whom Lorna always returned and who ultimately gave her the stability she needed.

Her children were brought up surrounded by artists and writers, and Michael became a talented painter. He recalled his mother leaning over his bed 'dressed for dancing in clinging sequins which sparkle like her vast ultramarine eyes . . . a sophisticated mermaid'.

After leaving Lucian Freud, Lorna Wishart converted to Roman Catholicism and returned for good to her husband's Sussex home where she sculpted and cultivated a garden. Lorna Wishart's husband died in 1987 and Michael in 1996. She is survived by her younger son and by Yasmin.

15 January 2000

DAPHNE LADY ACTON

*Catholic convert who built a church in Africa and was described
by Evelyn Waugh as 'the most remarkable woman I know'*

*

Daphne Lady Acton, who has died aged 91, was an important
figure in the circle of Roman Catholic converts which came to
intellectual and social prominence during the middle third of the
last century; she was also a missionary in Africa and matriarch of
a clan of Biblical proportions.

Described by Evelyn Waugh as 'a tall, elegant beauty of strong
and original intellect', the young Lady Acton formed a particularly fruitful friendship with Monsignor Ronald Knox, the
former Catholic chaplain to Oxford University. While he prepared her for reception into the Roman Church, she provided
him with the opportunity to carry out his translation of the
Bible, employing him from 1939 to 1947 as private chaplain at
Aldenham Park, her husband's family seat in Shropshire. The
tranquillity this arrangement afforded him was jeopardised
when, on the outbreak of the Second World War, he was joined
at Aldenham by 55 evacuee convent girls plus their attendant
nuns. Lady Acton, however, rigidly enforced a zone of silence
around his study, and Knox emerged from the war years with his
translation of the New Testament complete and work on the
Old well advanced.

After Aldenham was sold and the Actons moved to Southern
Rhodesia, their farm at M'bebi became a popular staging post
for aristocrats and Catholic notables travelling in sub-Saharan
Africa. Guests included Lady Acton's cousin 'Bobbety' (the 5th
Marquis of Salisbury and a leading Tory politician); David
Stirling, founder of the SAS; and Evelyn Waugh, who paid two
extended visits. In a letter written to Ann Fleming in 1958,

Waugh described life at M'bebi: 'Children were everywhere, no semblance of a nursery or a nanny, the spectacle at meals gruesome, a party-line telephone ringing all day, dreadful food . . . ants in the bed, totally untrained black servants (all converted by Daphne to Christianity, taught to serve Mass but not to empty ashtrays). In fact, everything that normally makes Hell, but Daphne's serene sanctity radiating supernatural peace. She is the most remarkable woman I know.'

She was born Daphne Strutt in London on 5 November 1911, the second and only surviving daughter of the 4th Baron Rayleigh and the former Lady Hilda Clements, daughter of the 4th Earl of Leitrim. She was brought up at Terling Place in Essex, surrounded by Strutt farmland. Although she received no formal education beyond that provided by governesses, she grew up in a climate of great intellectual confidence and curiosity. In 1894, her grandfather, the 3rd Baron, had discovered the gas argon in his laboratory in the west wing of Terling Place, an achievement which earned him the Nobel Prize for physics, and, ultimately, the Chancellorship of Cambridge University. Daphne's father, too, was a distinguished scientist, who eventually became President of the Royal Institution and Professor of Physics at Imperial College, London. The political atmosphere at Terling Place was scarcely less rarefied. As a teenager, Daphne spent hours playing tennis with her paternal grandmother's brother, the former Prime Minister Arthur Balfour. From a sporting perspective, these sessions were less than satisfactory: his age dictated that she hit the ball straight to him, a feat which, to his chagrin, she was not always able to perform.

After coming out as a debutante, Daphne Strutt became engaged to be married to the 3rd Baron Acton, grandson of the liberal Catholic historian best known for his dictum that 'power tends to corrupt, and absolute power corrupts absolutely'. Some members of her family viewed the prospect with dismay, a stance given context by the 3rd Lord Rayleigh's recollection that, as a child, he had confided in a playmate that 'my Mama once saw a Roman Catholic!' Daphne's father made it a condition of his consent to the match that Lord Acton agreed to forego a Catholic wedding and refrained from raising any children according to his faith. Thus, the couple married at Chelsea Register Office, in November 1931. Lady Acton now took up residence at Aldenham Park, near Bridgnorth, a large William and Mary house with a private chapel and the unusual feature of an upstairs lavatory that produced hot water when flushed.

Although she took to the role of chatelaine with ease, beneath the surface she was acutely uneasy about the conditions under which Lord Acton had agreed to marry her. This manifested itself in indecision about her first two children's religious upbringing. When her second child, Charlotte, was born in 1934, her first daughter, now almost two, had yet to be baptised. When Charlotte contracted pneumonia at the age of just three months, Lady Acton surrendered to her conscience and asked her husband to baptise the dying baby, which he did, in the bath. This tragedy was the catalyst for the sequence of events which led to her conversion.

Her first point of call was Stamford Dingley, the Berkshire house of Lord Acton's sister Mia Woodruff and her husband Douglas, editor of the Catholic periodical *The Tablet*. It was there, in the summer of 1937, that she met Ronald Knox, whom the Woodruffs had lined up as a potential candidate to take over her instruction. Knox was dreading the prospect: Lady Acton had been represented to him as a formidable bluestocking. In the event, he was captivated by her. Knox became a frequent guest at Aldenham and Lady Acton was duly received into the Catholic Church.

As international tensions mounted, Lord Acton approached the nuns of the Assumption Convent School in Kensington Square with a proposal that they evacuate to Aldenham with their senior pupils. In return, they were to feed his family and educate his elder daughter. When war broke out, he went to fight with the Shropshire Yeomanry, leaving Lady Acton to manage a household stretched to the seams. She also had to contend with three pregnancies, a rapidly decaying roof and a 960-acre farm, all of which she managed with admirable composure. After the Second World War, Lord Acton felt increasingly frustrated with a tax regime at odds with his expanding family. In 1947 he sold Aldenham and bought, unseen, a farm in Southern Rhodesia. There he raised a herd of Jersey cattle, and pursued interests in business and horse racing. Lady Acton did not share his love of the Turf, although she did own a handful of horses, the best of which was called Devil's Choice. Instead, she directed her energies towards the compound at M'bebi, attending to the medical, educational and spiritual needs of the African farm-workers and their families. Her proudest achievement was the construction of a church on the farm, partly financed by a cousin who sponsored her to give up smoking. It was consecrated in 1962.

M'bebi was known for its atmosphere of racial harmony. Certain sections of the white community grumbled that the Actons spoiled the Africans who worked for them, but they maintained their liberal approach. Lady Acton also made the then remarkable decision to send her youngest son to St Ignatius, the Jesuit School outside Salisbury that had hitherto catered exclusively for black pupils. Lady Acton was a vehement opponent of Ian Smith's Unilateral Declaration of Independence in 1965. In a gesture of solidarity with Sir Humphrey Gibbs, the displaced Governor of Southern Rhodesia, she affixed a toothpaste carton bearing the provocative legend 'Gibbs SR' to her car, and drove into Salisbury displaying it. Despite prophecies of retaliatory vandalism, she returned from shopping to find the car unscathed.

For some years following UDI, the Actons were peripatetic. They settled first on a property nearer the capital, then emigrated to Swaziland before retiring to Majorca in the 1970s. During the following decade, Lady Acton returned to England to live first with her brother Charles, then with her eldest brother, Lord Rayleigh, at Terling Place, and then with her sister-in-law Mia Woodruff in Oxfordshire. She lived out her remaining years with her third daughter in Birmingham. From time to time she would write to her friend Lord Longford to chastise him for boasting about his numerous descendants. As she liked to remind him, she could easily trump him with her 62.

Lady Acton is survived by five daughters and five sons; her husband died in 1989.

22 March 2003

GRETA VALENTINE

Beautiful bohemian mystic whose charms mesmerised Aleister Crowley, the black magician, in the 1930s

*

Greta Valentine, who has died aged 91, was one of the last survivors of the circle around Aleister Crowley, the black magician and self-styled 'wickedest man alive'; but Crowley was not the only older man over whom she was to exercise an irresistible fascination.

It was as Greta Sequeira that she entered into London life in the 1930s. She soon plunged into the noisy Café Royal set of bohemians, loving the company of artists and the excitement of party-going. At the Café Royal, Crowley was known as The Magus. He soon became her close friend and confidant, openly declaring his love for her. When they met in 1936 she was studying anthroposophy, the mystical teachings of Rudolf Steiner, whose school she attended. Her own interests stopped short of traditional occultism. Nor did she share Crowley's interest in drugs. But she did tease and flirt with him. He was excited by her approaches but found her difficult to handle.

Greta Sequeira was iron-willed, but witty and cultured, and her classic beauty ensured that she commanded attention. She adored fast cars – driving a white Packard convertible – and she courted danger. Crowley inscribed a book of his poems: 'To Greta, whom I love, but I'd love much more if she were not so elusive.' His letters, bearing such sentiments as, 'What is life without you, but dust and ashes?' would arrive at her London home in Hyde Park Crescent bearing the purple wax seal of Ankh-af-na-khonsu. (It was at her house that Crowley and Greta Sequeira's friend Frieda Harris developed *The Book of Thoth*, an essay on the Tarot of the Egyptians published in 1944.)

Crowley found that some of Greta Sequeira's friends were more susceptible than she to the philosophy he preached and the excitement it offered. One of her friends was to bear his child. Such relationships left Greta Sequeira bemused and worried. In August 1938 Crowley followed her to Cornwall where she had already formed a warm attachment to Lamorna Birch, the land-scape painter and senior Academician. His appearance made some impression at the Lobster Pot restaurant in Mousehole. They sat sharing a bottle of Chablis at a table by the window. She was then aged 31, dressed in a loose-fitting cotton frock, with her golden hair hanging at shoulder length. Crowley was 63, tweedy, flabby and very bald. After lunch they walked in the sunshine along the cliff path. 'Wooed Greta on the cliffs,' Crowley wrote in his diary for that day. 'She is a comedian. Will come one day and snatch.'

Greta Mary Sequeira was born on 27 June 1907, the daughter of an English doctor of Portuguese descent. She was educated in England and on the Continent. Her family took holidays in Cornwall where her friendship with Lamorna Birch and his wife blossomed. At the time of their first meeting Birch was in his mid sixties, and at the peak of his reputation. But she was in her twenties, and Birch had daughters of her age. Over the years Lamorna Birch inscribed pictures for her with various sentiments of affection, and wrote her letters in extravagant language. She was Birch's companion in London during the season, accompanying him at studio parties and at the private views of the Royal Academy summer exhibitions. Birch would send her coded messages in his pictures. Swans in a painting, for example, were a symbol of his love for her. Greta Sequeira described their friendship as 'a form of Pre-Raphaelite love, not at all physical but a love energised through our shared joy of art and poetry'.

Her generous instincts were demonstrated just before the Second World War. She drove to Germany and faced considerable danger attempting to help Jewish doctors escape. She continued this self-appointed task right up to eve of war, helping several to a safe refuge in England.

At about this time Birch introduced her to Ranald Valentine. When news spread some time later that they were to marry, Crowley was wounded. 'Dear child,' he wrote, 'I knew you would be up to some mischief the minute my eye was off you. . . . You might have told me. I shouldn't have taken any actual measures to stop you. And you would certainly have got a No. 1 epithalamium. All the same, give me a week or so notice and you shall have an ode for your divorce.' The Valentines had houses in London and Coupar Angus, Tayside. She enjoyed holding parties in London a comfortable distance from 'all that ghastly formality in Scotland'. During the private views at Burlington House the Valentines rented suites for entertaining at the Park Lane Hotel. Ranald Valentine ran a company in Dundee making greetings cards and calendars, and he was always on the look-out for painters whose work he could reproduce. Their parties were a lively mix, and guests included Alexander Fleming, the discoverer of penicillin, Willard Garfield Weston, the biscuit magnate,

Barbara Hutton, the Woolworth heiress, Sir Robert Watson-Watt, the inventor of radar, and Enid Blyton.

Lamorna Birch introduced Greta Valentine to George Cross, the property developer known as 'Mr Edgware'. Cross also owned the Compton Chamberlayne estate near Salisbury, where he entertained Birch and such painters as Harold and Laura Knight.

In her quiet moments Greta Valentine wrote poetry and painted. Encouraged by Birch, a leading fly fisherman of his day, she took up fishing. By 1945 Ranald Valentine had become Birch's patron and his regular fishing companion in Scotland. Birch was given a small studio at the house in Coupar Angus where he gave Greta and Ranald painting lessons. She aspired to be a portrait painter and her first sitter was Birch himself. 'He kept jumping up from his chair to look at the picture, and grumbling a lot,' she recalled. 'But really his only concern was that I was using the oil paint too thinly.' The truth was that Birch disliked having his portrait painted, by anyone.

Greta Valentine believed friendship implied complete commitment on both sides, and this sometimes pushed her relationships to breaking point. At the end of her life she struggled to cope with blindness and physical incapacity but found solace in the friendship of a small circle of friends who shared her spiritual ideals. She co-operated enthusiastically in the writing of a biography of Lamorna Birch, *A Painter Laureate*, by Austin Wormleighton (1995). At that time she was living in a studio on a Sussex farm where she slept in the same room as the cheap plywood coffin she had commissioned for her own funeral.

Ranald Valentine died in 1956.

24 November 1998

ELISABETH FURSE

*One-time Communist whose bohemian bistro in London
attracted politicians, diplomats and aristocrats*

∗

Elisabeth Furse, who died yesterday aged 92, was a former
Communist, wartime resistance worker and London bistro proprietress, whose Slavic warmth and ardent personality attracted
a wide circle of devoted friends. These included diplomats, MPs
(among them one former Foreign Secretary), journalists, students and miscellaneous aristocrats who would happily crowd
around the table in her cluttered basement flat in Belgravia to eat
dubious food off jumble sale china. Reviewing her autobiography in 1993, her old friend Lord Owen told of 'a life almost
inconceivable for most of us to imagine in its fortitude, frailty
and overall zest'. Its dominant and compelling theme was the
conjunction of grandeur and poverty. She was princess and peasant at the same time.

She was born Louise Ruth Wolpert on 30 August 1910 at
Konigsberg (later called Kaliningrad) in what is now the Baltic
Sea enclave of the Russian Federation. Her father was a Russian-
speaking Latvian Jew and a wealthy textile merchant; her
mother, also Jewish, a German-speaking Lithuanian from a
family of rich corn merchants. Louise was nicknamed 'Lisl' by
an aunt, from which she derived Elisabeth, the name she adopted
for herself. Her childhood was privileged but loveless. Her
mother told her: 'You are not beautiful, nor are you pretty, but
you have charm, good teeth and good legs. You may make it.'
This she did, but on her own terms. Her vivacious character
found its means of expression as a teenager when she joined the
Communist Party. 'I told the comrades I was the daughter of a
grocer, and I left my family and my home. I gave up the

Chippendale, the Gobelins, the Meissen, the Bohemian glass, the Persian carpets and my own room. I went out, literally penniless, into the world. My father very wisely cut me off. I was, and have remained ever since, a self-made poor. This is quite different from having been born into poverty or having been forced into it. I have no envy of the rich. I chose my condition with my eyes open, and by hard work and determination I have managed to remain poor when circumstances were against it.'

In her early twenties, she was tasked with collecting money in France and England to help political refugees in Germany, mainly Party members, escape the Nazis. Soliciting support for the cause, she met many of the leading artists and writers of the time: Picasso, Braque, Giacometti, Thomas Mann, André Gide and H.G. Wells. In such figures she instinctively looked for the real individual beneath the public persona.

Her first marriage, in 1934, was a marriage of convenience, intended to give her a new nationality and with it legal residence outside Germany, when her activities with the Communists put her at risk of arrest and execution by the Gestapo. She married Bertie Coker, a journalist and fellow Communist.

She left the movement in 1934, long before Stalin's excesses disillusioned his supporters in the West, and moved to London, where she was offered a job as interpreter and companion to a Russian actress. That engagement led to a formal job as a cinematic continuity girl. In later years she was very proud of her ACTT (Association of Cinematograph, Television and Allied Technicians) membership card, with its early membership number, 35. The card entitled her to free admission to cinemas in London, and she would always make her distinguished status known to amused box office staff when claiming her free tickets.

Her second marriage was to Peter Haden-Guest, son of a Labour MP. He was 22, an aspiring ballet dancer, and still an undergraduate at Oxford. Their alliance was sealed in a cinema, where they had the following dialogue:

'Where shall we go for our honeymoon?' he said.

'Italy.'

'No, Spain. How many children shall we have? I think four.'

'No, six.'

After a pause, he said: 'I'm serious. I intend to marry you.'

His mother didn't approve, and stopped his allowance, but they eventually married anyway. 'He brought me back to elegance and fun and life,' she wrote: the perfect antidote to the ascetic rule of 1930s Communism. Their son, Anthony Haden-Guest, now a successful journalist based in New York, was born in 1937.

Elisabeth was in France, and separated from Peter Haden-Guest, when war broke out. She spent part of 1940 in the Brittany château of the Forbes family, where she recklessly fell in love with a German officer, one of a group who had commandeered the house. Pretending to be American, she was allowed to remain in the house with her infant son and his nanny, until an indiscreet remark brought catastrophe. At dinner with the Nazi officers, who up until then had shown the courtliest manners to her, she remarked that Churchill, a friend of the family that owned the house, had often dined at the table at which they were sitting. Their response was to burn down the house and send Elisabeth and her child to an internment camp.

The following year, while being transferred to another camp, she escaped from her German escorts. Disguised as a widow, she fled from occupied France with Anthony, giving him fragments of sleeping pills when they travelled by train to prevent him from speaking English. She made her way to Marseilles, where she joined MI9, a branch of British Military Intelligence engaged in helping British soldiers and others opposed to the Germans to escape Occupied France. When her group was betrayed by an informer, she was held in squalid conditions in a women's prison in a castle overlooking the harbour at Marseilles. During negotiations over her release, occasioned by her status as daughter-in-law of an MP, she would smuggle out messages from other prisoners in condoms hidden in her vagina.

She returned to London, where she found that her high profile and indiscretions, such as the one made before German officers at the Forbes house, made her unfit for further intelligence work. She spent the rest of the war in the comparative safety of rural England, on the Devon estate of the family of her third husband, Pat Furse. They married in 1945, and Elisabeth continued her career in the film industry. In 1952 Elisabeth and Pat took the lease of a small, 'beautifully shabby' workman's cottage at Bourne Street, near Sloane Square. Pat was an artist, and they sold pictures and antiques from the house. Elisabeth worked as a continuity girl. When, by the end of 1953, commitments to her three small children had grown to make location work impractical, she and Pat started a small bistro in the house.

Based on the French idea of the bistro as a sociable yet intimate annexe to the home, Elisabeth's bistro attracted a diverse and dynamic crowd. Neither the decor nor the food were of high quality. She despised hygiene. Clement Freud, then a Liberal MP, was so upset by Elisabeth's cooking that he took her aside and trained her to cook a steak and an omelette. Her attitude to food was formed in years of poverty and wartime imprisonment. After the bistro closed in 1970, she held court at her house in Chapel Street, Belgravia, at a long refectory table given to her by the industrialist Jeremy Fry. This table was usually covered with papers and a manual typewriter on which she would pound out blunt letters telling people exactly what she thought of them. These communications invariably arrived in a reused envelope, addressed in her Germanic scrawl. Her house in Chapel Street, and its heterogeneous community of lodgers (mostly students), was immortalised in fictional form in 1991 by the novelist Sam North, whose superb novel *Chapel Street* contains a character – a Mrs Gorse – who was clearly based on Elisabeth.

In the early 1980s, her friendship with David (now Lord)

Owen, allied to an apostate Communist's distrust of the far Left, which was then in the ascendant in the Labour Party, inspired an early enthusiasm for the short-lived Social Democratic Party, of which Owen was leader. *Harper's & Queen* described her as 'the mother of the SDP'. Lord (Robert) Skidelsky and the chess player Nigel Short, then both SDP supporters, also became her friends.

In 1993 her autobiography, *Dream Weaver*, was published, with a title suggested by her son, Johnny, who felt it expressed her talent for self-invention. The book gathers together the cycle of anecdotes that formed her colourful life story, all her adventures and love affairs. It was ghost-written by the *Harper's & Queen* writer Ann Barr, and Elisabeth affected indifference towards it. It is, perhaps, the only book ever written whose author claimed to be completely unaware of its contents.

Her zeal for politics remained as strong as ever in her later years. In 1991 she went to Maastricht to follow the treaty negotiations at first hand, somehow obtaining a press pass for the purpose. With her crutch and her wheeled shopping basket, she stood out as the oldest member of the press corps, and was interviewed during quiet moments by younger colleagues, with whom she shared her forthright views on human affairs. Her last political enthusiasm was for Jimmy Goldsmith's movement for a referendum on British membership of the EU. That he, too, was a 'Bistro boy' certainly helped focus her interest.

She is survived by two sons, Anthony Haden-Guest and John Furse, and three daughters, Katya Chelli, Anna Furse and Sara Furse.

15 October 2002

ADVENTURESSES

*

PAMELA HARRIMAN

English adventuress who set her cap at the rich and powerful and ended up as a millionairess and American ambassador in Paris

*

Pamela Harriman, the American ambassador in Paris who has died aged 76, was proudly described by her second husband as 'the greatest courtesan of the century'. From obscure, if aristocratic, beginnings in Dorset, she became in turn Winston Churchill's daughter-in-law, the lover of the some of the world's richest men, a powerful Washington hostess, a multi-millionairess and finally a successful diplomat. All this, and much more, Pamela Harriman achieved through the clear-sightedness with which she marked down her quarries, the ruthlessness with which she pursued them, the seeming indifference with which she shrugged off criticism, and the courage and energy with which she accepted reverses and marched on to new conquests. She was never guilty of self-pity.

Red-haired, but with a tendency to dumpiness, Pamela Harriman was far from being an overwhelming beauty – though 'the best facelift in the world' (as friends described an event which she herself refused to acknowledge), together with her undimmed vitality, made her an exceptionally stunning 70-year-old. Her secret lay in her ability to make any man at whom she set her cap feel that he was the sole object of her attention. Women tended to be less impressed. Yet part of her skill was to subsume her own ambitions in those of her conquests. 'She's interesting because she has fantastic taste,' Truman Capote considered, 'but she has no intellectual capacities at all. She's some sort of marvellous primitive. I don't think she's ever read a book or even a newspaper except for the gossip column. Pamela's a geisha girl who's made every man happy.'

The talent ran in her family. She was born Pamela Beryl

Digby at Farnborough, Kent, on 20 March 1920, the first of four children born to Edward Kenelm Digby, who succeeded as the 11th Lord Digby two months after her birth. Pamela's mother was a daughter of the 2nd Lord Aberdare. 'Something in all the Digbys caused them to win renown by being at odds with society,' wrote the biographer of Sir Kenelm Digby (1603–65). The rogue gene was still active in the 19th-century when a Jane Digby became one of the great adventuresses of her time, leaving a trail of husbands and lovers from Bavaria to Syria. Pamela Digby was much struck by Jane Digby's career; at first, though, she did not seem destined to emulate it. She spent her infancy in Australia, where her father was military secretary to the Governor-General. She learnt to talk by mimicking a loquacious white parrot, the first fruits of a talent which would later be practised on Sir Winston Churchill.

At Cape Town on the voyage home from Australia, the three-year-old Pamela sank her teeth into the calf of a black man on the quay, on the theory that he was made of chocolate. Thereafter she was brought up at Minterne Magna, the family home in Dorset. By chance, in the early 17th century it had been bought by John Churchill, grandfather of the 1st Duke of Marlborough.

Pamela Digby's father's interests were hunting and horticulture (especially carnations). Though Pamela became an excellent horsewoman, her boredom was relieved only by the visits of fox-hunting Americans, who appeared to her as the epitome of glamour. She was sent away to Downham School in Hertfordshire, before being 'finished' in Paris – an episode later inflated into 'postgraduate work at the Sorbonne'. She also went to Germany where, she claimed, Unity Mitford introduced her to the Führer. In 1938 Pamela Digby returned to do 'the season'. 'She was very plump and so bosomy that we all called her "the dairy maid",' one of her contemporaries remembered. 'She wore high heels and tossed her bottom around. We thought she was quite outrageous. She was known as hot stuff, a very sexy young thing.' On coming out she was taken up by Lady Baillie, whose Leeds Castle set was a rival to that at Cliveden. Pamela Digby was delighted to be drawn into the ambit of men of power and influence.

In 1939 she met Randolph Churchill, and notwithstanding dire warnings on every side married him three weeks later. Nine years older than she, he already had a reputation as an alcoholic roustabout, and it did not help that he insisted on reading Gibbon aloud to her during their honeymoon. Fidelity he never even attempted. Worse, his capacity for accumulating debts left her constantly short of money, breeding in her two enduring characteristics: insatiable avarice and a dislike of English men which eventually came to embrace the entire country.

Nevertheless, she established excellent relations with her parents-in-law, Winston and Clementine Churchill, and while Randolph was away lived at 10 Downing Street and Chequers. Her alliance with the Prime Minister was sealed by the birth of young Winston in October 1940. As Pamela Churchill's marriage deteriorated, she amused herself with American servicemen; Sir Charles Portal, the British Chief of Air Staff, was also much struck. But she did not confine herself to the military; her American admirers included William Paley, the president of CBS, Jock Whitney, who would later be American ambassador to London, and the broadcaster Ed Murrow. Her most notable conquest was Averell Harriman, President Roosevelt's Lend-Lease envoy, and 28 years her senior. Their liaison was encouraged by Lord Beaverbrook, who gave her money for clothes, and condoned by Winston Churchill, who saw Pamela's potential as a conduit of information between the Allies. The affair ended when Harriman was sent as ambassador to Moscow in 1943. By this time her attitude to Randolph had become vitriolic. 'Panto [Pamela] hates him so much that she can't sit in a room with him,' recorded Evelyn Waugh in

May 1942. And Harold Nicolson noticed Randolph's 'little wife squirming' in embarrassment as she listened to him in the House of Commons.

They were divorced in 1946, though Pamela always remained loth to relinquish the name of Churchill. For a while she worked for Beaverbrook on the *Evening Standard*'s 'Londoner's Diary', but her journalistic career did not survive her conquest of Prince Aly Khan. In 1948 she moved to Paris and pursued an affair with Gianni Agnelli, heir to the Fiat empire. But though she nursed him back to health after a serious car crash, and even joined the Roman Catholic Church (which duly produced an annulment for her), he would not contemplate marriage. When she became pregnant she had an abortion. She became a friend of the Greek shipping magnate Stavros Niarchos, and the lover of the French banker Elie de Rothschild. But de Rothschild, like Agnelli, preferred to finance her as a mistress rather than indulge her as a wife. 'They just don't want to marry her,' Truman Capote gleefully observed.

By the late 1950s the British establishment regarded her as a scandalous figure. In 1956, when the Queen Mother was on a visit to Paris, Lady Jebb, the ambassador's wife, found it impossible to invite Pamela Churchill to lunch at the embassy. Pamela Churchill did not repine; she turned to America, where she settled on Leland Hayward, a theatrical impresario and the producer of *The Sound of Music*. He had been married five times (though only to four women); and in 1962 the number increased to six. Though he turned out to be less than colossally rich – and such fortune as he possessed was speedily diminished by her taste for interior decoration – the marriage was a success. Pamela Hayward looked after her husband devotedly as his health failed. When he died in 1971, she moved speedily into action. Spurned by Frank Sinatra, that August she found herself – whether by chance or design – sitting next to her old flame Averell Harriman (now 79, recently widowed and one of the richest men in

America) at a Washington dinner party given by Katharine Graham, editor of the *Washington Post*. The opportunity was not wasted; they were married at the end of September 1971. In December Pamela Harriman became an American citizen.

Averell Harriman was a pillar of the Democratic Party, to which Pamela, though instinctively conservative, now conformed. Their house in Georgetown, Washington, became the unofficial heart of the party in exile during the years of Reagan and Bush. Pamela Harriman proved herself an incomparable hostess and fundraiser, and invitations to her parties became as prized as those to the White House. Though still no intellectual, she began to acquaint herself with foreign policy issues, and accompanied Harriman on trips to the Soviet Union. In consequence, when Raisa Gorbachev visited America in 1987 she had tea with Pamela Harriman rather than Nancy Reagan.

Harriman had died in 1986, leaving her a fortune and a leading position in the Democratic Party. Her choice for the 1988 nomination was Al Gore; in the event she had to make do with Michael Dukakis, who caused her considerable alarm on his visit to her house by threatening to slip off a narrow podium into her proudest possession, Van Gogh's *White Roses*.

In 1992 Pamela Harriman gravitated to Bill Clinton, who delighted her by picking Gore as Vice-President. After his election President Clinton appointed her the American ambassador in Paris, the post once held by Benjamin Franklin and Thomas Jefferson. Her energy and social adroitness ensured her success in Paris. Although she was embarrassed by two failed spying operations, she helped America and France to reconcile their differences over trade in audio-visual and farm products, thus making possible the successful conclusion of a GATT deal. Impressed by her accomplishments, the French government cited her 'passion, ardour and intelligence' in appointing her a Commander of the Order of Arts and Letters in the *Légion d'honneur*.

But Pamela Harriman had become embroiled in controversy

over the management of trusts which Harriman had left her, and from which his two daughters drew income. At first all went well, but between 1989 and 1993 $21 million of the trust money was poured into a hotel and conference centre in New Jersey that failed. In 1994 the Harriman heirs, whom Pamela Harriman had treated with disdain, instituted a lawsuit alleging that she had squandered the family funds. A settlement was reached at the end of 1995, but the cost was evidently considerable: Pamela Harriman sold three of her paintings (a Picasso, a Renoir and a Matisse) for $11 million, as well as one of her two houses in Georgetown.

In April 1996, after three years in Paris, she told the *Washington Post* that she was 'ready to go back to Washington. It's been nice, but there's a limit to how long you can live a public life. You're on most of the time.' In May, though, the American embassy in Paris 'categorically denied' that her resignation was impending.

6 February 1997

K'TUT TANTRI

Scots-born writer and broadcaster who operated under various pseudonyms, fell for a Balinese prince, and as Surabaya Sue broadcast propaganda for Indonesian guerrillas fighting the Dutch

*

K'tut Tantri, who has died aged 99, was variously a journalist, hotelier, guerrilla fighter and aspiring film maker. She was known throughout an extraordinary career by several names; but her best-known persona was that of 'Surabaya Sue', the romantic rebel who made propaganda broadcasts on behalf of Indonesian nationalists in their fight for independence from the Dutch after the Second World War. From a rebel camp in the town of Surabaya in East Java she provided for Western consumption an Indonesian version of the nationalist struggle, summoning up in her Scottish accent the shades of such heroes as Washington, Jefferson and Tom Paine.

Barely five feet tall and plump, with heavy-rimmed glasses and red-auburn hair – sometimes dyed black, as red hair was thought by the Balinese to be the sign of a witch – K'tut Tantri was a complex, passionate and difficult woman. Her account of her time in Indonesia, *Revolt in Paradise*, published in 1960 and translated into a dozen languages, is a lurid and unreliable romance set in exotic locales and describing heroic deeds, revolution, spying and adventure. A fascinating exercise in self-mythology, it leaves her past foggy and herself an enigma. A different picture emerged in a study published this year by Timothy Lindsey, *The Romance of K'tut Tantri and Indonesia*.

She was born Muriel Stuart Walker in Glasgow on 18 February 1898 of Manx parents. When her stepfather was killed in the First World War, mother and daughter left Britain for California, settling in Hollywood, where Muriel Walker made a living writing about film stars for British magazines. In 1932, inspired by a film called *Goona-Goona* about the island of Bali, she packed supplies of painting materials, abandoned her husband and took ship for the Dutch East Indies.

Bali between the wars was a paradisal destination whose elegant, refined culture was beginning to be exploited by Westerners, who saw it as an untouched Eden in which to live out a romantic tourist aesthetic. Muriel Walker arrived in Bali under the name Mrs Manx, after her parents' birthplace. According to her autobiography, she was adopted, in best Hollywood tradition, by one of the island's rulers, the Raja of Bangli, and given the names K'tut, meaning 'fourth-born child', and Tantri – 'teller of tales'. She certainly exaggerated the romantic aspects of her life in Bali, but undoubtedly she found a soul mate in Anak Nagung Nura, the Raja's princely son. Whether he proposed marriage, as she claimed, is unclear. By

1936, though, her relationship with the Raja had deteriorated, not least because the rumours, true or not, of a sexual relationship with Anak Agung Nura had made a bad impression on the Dutch colonial authorities and embarrassed the royal court.

K'tut Tantri then embarked on a business partnership with an American couple, Bob and Louise Koke, starting a hotel on the then-unspoiled Kuta beach. With thatched huts and a relaxed, simple style, the hotel presented a Western version of an island paradise. But K'tut Tantri soon fell out with the Kokes, and eventually the two parties ran separate hotels within a stone's throw of each other.

As K'tut Tantri grew to love the Balinese, so she came to dislike their Dutch masters, while the Dutch saw her easy relations with the Balinese as weakening white authority. She managed to ride out scandalous rumours of immorality and had a deportation order overturned. Her day of triumph came in 1941 when, with war imminent in the Pacific, Duff Cooper, Britain's Minister of State for the Far East, flew in from Singapore with his wife Diana. Having booked in at her hotel, Duff Cooper declined the official Dutch hospitality and enjoyed a royal junket with 'Mrs Manx', as she was still then known to Westerners. Diana Cooper approved of the 'jungly grass houses', and the party given in their honour on Kuta: 'Nothing lovelier could there be.'

By then K'tut Tantri liked to think of herself as Indonesian rather than British or American, and when the Japanese invaded Bali in March 1942, it was her connections with the Raja that saved her from internment. By her own account (in a period of which the facts become elusive), she then secretly took documents, arms and two cars from Java to Bali, under the noses of the Japanese, and then proceeded to work dangerously with an underground nationalist movement. But the many inconsistencies in K'tut Tantri's story suggest that it may have been partly invented to cover collaboration with the Japanese. In any case, disaster followed for K'tut Tantri when the Japanese discovered her American background and imprisoned her as a spy. She told later of being tortured, made to walk naked down the street, and suffering mock-execution by firing squad. After two years of solitary confinement she was reduced to skin and bone. The exact details of when, where and for how long she was imprisoned by the Japanese are unclear. But the details she gives in her book tally with the stories of other female Western prisoners, and several women who met her soon after the war were convinced of her story. Corroboration was found years later in the form of a handful of playing cards, stashed in her belongings, made from dried oblongs of palm leaf, pin-pricked and painted with dried mud: the makeshift playing cards made by internees of prison camps.

When, immediately after the war, the nationalists declared independence against the British and Dutch forces, K'tut Tantri threw in her lot with their guerrillas in East Java, and broadcast from the rebel headquarters. Though she used the name K'tut Tantri, the Allies gave her the sobriquet 'Surabaya Sue', and it was under this name that she became, briefly, famous. She was a radical supporter of Sutomo, the guerrilla leader, and worked for him as an interpreter in interviews with Western journalists. K'tut Tantri was called by the revolutionary government to Jogjakarta, central Java, to broadcast on their radio station, and was then invited to write a speech for Sukarno, the President. She became friendly with Sukarno, who introduced her to a huge crowd as 'the one and only foreigner to come openly to our side'.

But relations between K'tut Tantri and the Indonesians were to slide into mutual disenchantment. She became weary of war, while they began to find her views too extreme, and feared that she would become an embarrassment to them. Out of favour with the Republic, K'tut Tantri seems to have done some spying for the British in Singapore, winning permission in 1947 to visit

Australia. Her reputation as a revolutionary and her lack of a recognised passport made it difficult for her to travel internationally, but after Australia she was able to make a journey to the United States. She soon returned to Indonesia, and for most of the 1950s worked for the Indonesian Ministry of Information and as a journalist.

Revolt In Paradise was an immediate success when published, attracting almost unanimous critical praise. K'tut Tantri spent most of the rest of her life trying in vain to have the book turned into a film. Negotiations with Hollywood fell through mainly because of her fierce determination not to depart from the book's storyline, and in particular her insistence that the relationship with her Balinese prince be portrayed as platonic and decorous, and that there should be no kissing, smoking or swearing in the film.

She spent her last days in Sydney, an Australian citizen, formally named K'tut Tantri by deed poll, still iron-willed but reclusive. Her husband, Karl Pearsen, died in 1957.

21 August 1997

PATRICIA COCKBURN

Irish aristocrat who charmed tribes of homicidal pygmies during her explorations in equatorial Africa

*

Patricia Cockburn, who has died at Cork aged 75, was an accomplished horse-woman, an intrepid traveller and, unwittingly or otherwise, a Comintern agent and revolutionary. As a child she witnessed the murder of the Chief of the Imperial General Staff; among her many adult achievements, she made a language map of Central Africa, charming whole tribes of

homicidal pygmies in the process, and survived a volcanic erup-
tion. She was also a talented artist and the wife of Claud
Cockburn, the celebrated journalist who died in 1981. The vol-
cano and the pygmies, she always thought, had been apt training for life with Cockburn, whom she supported towards the
end of his life by dealing in ponies and making shell pictures on
black velvet.

She was born Patricia Evangeline Anne Arbuthnot on St
Patrick's Day 1914 at Rosscarbery in Co. Cork; her mother had
intended to name her Kawara Finnbaragh, but was thwarted at
the christening by the Bishop of Cork.

Her father was Major J.B. Arbuthnot, a merchant banker
whose family had arrived in West Cork from Scotland at the end
of the 18th century; a versatile man, he combined his banking
with service in the Scots Guards and the authorship of the original 'Beachcomber' column in the *Daily Express*. Her mother's
family were the Blakes of Galway. From Lady Blake, her grandmother, who had irritated even Charles Stewart Parnell with the
intensity of her patriotism, Patricia inherited a romantic Irish
nationalism – but she was never nonsensical about it.

In a characteristically implausible but entertaining bit of history Claud Cockburn later wrote that, as a child, 'Patricia
hunted half the day and in the evenings, supine on a board for
reasons of deportment, lay drinking Madeira wine and reading
The Golden Bough.' She was educated in the ordinary aristocratic
manner by governesses and in due course was presented at
Court. The family camped for a while at Myrtle Grove, the
Blake residence at Youghal, which had once been the redoubt of
Sir Walter Raleigh.

As bankers, the Arbuthnots had not been ruined by the Land
Acts and could afford to rent a London house in Grosvenor
Square. On 22 June 1922 Patricia was walking home from school
when she saw the CIGS, Sir Horace Wilson, shot dead on his
own doorstep in Eaton Square – most likely, it now emerges, by

agents of the newly-independent Irish Free State. Her father told her to keep quiet about it, in case she were shot too, and for years she did so. After a hunting accident on her 16th birthday her parents sent her to recuperate in Algeria, where she made friends with Clare Sheridan, the sculptor and courtesan (then living with a local Arab potentate) and acquired a fondness for travel. In 1932 she married Arthur Byron, by whom she had a son who died in infancy and with whom she travelled in Asia, the Pacific, North America and Africa. He was rich and handsome, but could not keep her attention.

Shortly before the 1939–45 War she undertook an exploration of Equatorial Africa on behalf of the Royal Geographical Society, who wanted a language map of the pygmies and other tribes living there: 'I'm hopeless at languages. That's probably why the RGS asked me to do it.' The pygmies were at first frightened of her, but soon recovered their composure. Her not unintentionally hilarious account of her meetings with these peoples – and of the hapless colonial authorities, British, French and Belgian, supposedly in charge of them – is contained in her picaresque autobiography, *Figures of Eight* (1985). She was characteristically scathing of liberally-inclined persons whose enthusiasm for African wildlife exceeded their concern for African human beings. She said there was not much point preserving leopards so that they might eat people; and she wore with pride a leopard-skin coat, the pelts taken from animals that had crossed her own gunsights.

In 1940, after the dissolution of her first marriage, Patricia married Claud Cockburn. Cockburn's tale has yet to be fully told and probably never will be, but he was certainly an unashamed Communist agent. Before her marriage she had always had plenty of money; after it she was cut off without a penny. She fell in utterly with her husband's politics and diverged from them neither when he was a member of the Communist party nor when, belatedly, he resigned from it. In his absence she edited *The Week*, the cyclo-styled scandal sheet which invented the Cliveden Set, applauded the Nazi-Soviet pact and was the precursor of *Private Eye*. In 1968 she published a lively history, *The Years of The Week*.

No criticism of Cockburn or herself ever ruffled Mrs Cockburn, nor had they any purposeful enemies. After the 1939–45 War they moved to a dilapidated house on the outskirts of Youghal. They had a 30-year lease, which they thought would never run out. When it did Mrs Cockburn spoke scornfully of the American policeman who inherited it ('Who does this Californian cop think he is?') and took with her to their new home above Ardmore Bay several lorryloads of topsoil, thinking herself quite in the right as she had mulched it.

The Cockburns' finances were precarious, but their hospitality was always unstinted and the gossip that flew around their dinner table was never less than vigorous. Both displayed a patrician disdain for filthy lucre, and paying the rent was never a priority. In true bohemian fashion the family never went without luxuries, though they might lack the occasional necessity. In his attempts to keep the duns from the door, Claud wrote film scripts and novels, as well as copious journalism, ably assisted by his wife. Learning from the Irish tinkers she traded with, she became one of the most skilled horse-copers in Co. Cork.

The Cockburns had three sons, Alexander, Andrew and Patrick, who were properly educated and then became journalists.

11 October 1989

SHOE TAYLOR

Butcher's daughter who sought, and found, adventure as a hippy
before becoming the devoted mistress of Jonathan Guinness

*

Shoe Taylor, who has died aged 58, became the long-standing mistress of the eccentric politician, businessman and writer Jonathan Guinness (now Lord Moyne) after an eventful decade during which she pursued the life of a wandering hippy. Her story was told in 1989, when Guinness (best known for his vigorously right-wing views – he was chairman of the Monday Club in the early 1970s) published an account of her life in a doomed attempt to forestall tabloid gossip about his polygamous relationship with Shoe, with whom he had three children, and his second wife Suzanne, with whom he had two.

Susan Mary Taylor (known as 'Shoe') was born over her father's butcher's shop at Oldham, Lancashire, on 26 July 1944. As a child, she helped out in the slaughterhouse: 'The slaughterer slit the carcass down the middle, and pushed the steaming insides, or rops, towards me. My job was to pick them up, pull each part away from the slime which holds it together and put it in the rops bucket, separating the large intestines from the small, the stomach from the throttle.' Meanwhile, her father told her: 'Don't forget the maggots.' It was not work for a beautiful young girl with dreams of glamour, but there was romance amid the offal: one 14 February, her father gave her mother a Valentine's gift consisting of a raw sheep's heart pierced with a meat skewer.

After leaving school aged 14, Shoe drifted from job to job, working as a nursing cadet, delivery van driver for her father and eventually setting up in business as a hairdresser. But the rops bucket never seemed far away, and she longed to escape. After seeing *The Sound of Music*, it 'became obvious' that her destiny lay in Austria, even though she knew nobody there and had not a word of German. Accordingly, aged 21, she hitchhiked across Europe hoping to meet a version of the von Trapp family, thus becoming perhaps the only person in the world to have been inspired to adopt an alternative lifestyle by Julie Andrews. Instead, she charred for a princess and became a hippy, embarking on a vagabond life of hitching and busking her way round squats and communes in Europe, north Africa and Asia, risking her health with drugs while trying to improve it with macrobiotics, eastern mysticism, alchemy and magic.

In Britain, she joined 'love-ins' and 'Legalise Pot' rallies and associated with Alan Ginsberg, Felix Topolski and Venetia Stanley Smith; in Beirut, she became a circus performer, riding a hermaphrodite elephant called Sally; in Munich, she danced in the chorus of *Hair*. She also worked as a tea lady for the Beatles at Apple Studios and performed topless as 'the world's strongest woman' with a burlesque circus act from Paris. She sat at the feet of a guru in India; worked as a geisha in Japan (where her form was used as a mould to make dummy western women for shop windows), and spent a summer on the Spanish island of Formentera where she got high and learned to play the tom-toms.

Shoe Taylor survived several brushes with the law – and with death. In Tunis she was jailed, then deported, for taking cannabis through customs; she did two stints in Holloway for the same offence. Following the hippy trail to Marrakesh, she met Jean François, a young Frenchman who 'read the *Bhagavad Gita* and the *Tibetan Book of the Dead* and was on a serious spiritual search'. Looking for the best hash cakes in Morocco, he took her to Rabat, where they were kidnapped – and she gang-raped – by five Arab men.

By the time she met Jonathan Guinness in 1978, Shoe Taylor had become a bulimic recluse living in a stone hut in the foothills of the Pyrenees, reduced to scrounging around restaurants and guzzling leftovers which she would then immediately vomit. She turned up at a St Sebastian's Day party which Guinness was giving at his house in the Costa Brava village of Cadaques; they met again at a local art exhibition and struck up a conversation. She was 'good-looking with her high cheek-bones, balanced features and bold, brown-eyed gaze,' Guinness recalled. 'She strode like an athlete. She looked wild, but only up to a point because she was in fact quite tidy. Her gipsy appearance owed more to the casting department than the car-avan site.' Guinness immediately realised that they had some-thing in common when she told him she had done time in Holloway. He informed her that his mother (the former Diana Mitford, later Lady Mosley) had been a political prisoner during the war. This was a test, as he later explained, to make sure that Shoe Taylor was non-political. She passed with flying colours: not only had she never heard of Diana's husband, the British fas-cist Sir Oswald Mosley, but, Guinness recalled, 'she didn't even know that Britain does not suppose itself to go in for political prisoners. I liked this.'

He sent her a copy of his mother's autobiography, *A Life of Contrasts*, and they began a correspondence, she writing to him as 'Dear Ear', as if he were 'the reeds to which the barber whis-pered King Midas's secrets'.

As a result of her bulimia (which she had developed after the gang rape), Shoe Taylor had lost all her teeth, replacing them with a temporary set of 'big men's ones with a gold eyetooth so that the rest would seem more real'. Although Jonathan Guinness was twice married and had several children, he and Shoe began an affair. She bore him three more children and eventually moved to Cornwall as his mistress. Guinness paid for her upkeep while remaining married to Suzanne, his wife since 1964. Shoe's affair with the Guinness heir was a society rumour for years before he published her warts-and-all biography, *Shoe: an Odyssey of a Sixties Survivor*, in 1989. He claimed that it was intended to forestall a tabloid smear, but the book only fuelled his reputation for eccentricity, while revealing Shoe's rackety past in explicit and often gynaecological detail. The experience would have been humiliating for most women, but not for Shoe, who gamely undertook publicity photographs with her children, as well as with Jonathan (both standing on their heads). She drew strength from her lover's devotion, shaking off her addiction to drugs and her bulimia, though not her enthusiasm for new age therapies. Earlier this year, after having surgery and chemotherapy for breast cancer, she was to be found belting out Beatles hits through a battery-powered megaphone in the foyer of the Adelphi Hotel in Liverpool – part of a 'free-thinking' therapy she had discovered.

By this time, Jonathan Guinness had succeeded his father as Lord Moyne. In 2000 he was declared bankrupt and disqualified from serving as a director for five years as a result of his dealings with a company wound up by the High Court in 1997; two years ago he was acquitted of embezzlement by a Swedish court. He and Shoe helped to make ends meet by selling magnetised wristbands as a treatment for arthritis. They remained devoted to each other. Her son and two daughters survive her.

16 August 2003

BAPSY, MARCHIONESS OF WINCHESTER

Colourful Indian-born third wife of a marquess who sued Eve Fleming for 'enticing' her husband

*

Bapsy, Marchioness of Winchester, who has died in India aged 93, became the third wife of the 16th Marquess of Winchester in 1952, when he was in his 90th year, and spent much of the next decade engaged in public squabbles with her husband's friend Eve Fleming.

An enthusiastic self-publicist, Lady Winchester was prone to circulating documents extolling her own virtues. One described her as 'a great and gracious lady . . . an unofficial ambassador for India . . . recognised for her beauty and grace . . . for her wealth and fabulous jewels'. Another listed the many heads of state who had received her, including Calvin Coolidge, the King of Afghanistan, King Farouk of Egypt and Emperor Haile Selassie.

Lady Winchester ensured that even her marital disputes were widely broadcast. While she was wintering in India in 1953 her husband went to Nassau to visit Eve Fleming, the mother of Ian Fleming. Lady Winchester followed him, and stalked the pair, rather in the manner of the native lady, forever staring, in Somerset Maugham's short story *The Force of Circumstance*. According to Ivar Bryce, a neighbour, 'There was almost always an overweight Indian lady clad in a dingy sari, pacing the main road . . . occasionally pausing to raise and shake her fist towards the main house.' She wrote vitriolic letters to her husband: 'May a viper's fangs be forever around your throat,' she raged, 'and may you stew in the pit of your own juice.'

Lady Winchester claimed that Eve Fleming had made Lord Winchester a prisoner, and forced him to stay in courier rooms at hotels while she took comfortable suites. When Bapsy Winchester saw her rival press the Marquess's left thigh in 1954 she sued her for enticement. The litigation continued in various forms over the next four years, and in 1957 the case came before Mr Justice Devlin at the High Court in London. Lady Winchester proved a temperamental witness, sometimes talking ceaselessly, at other times stubbornly mute. When in communicative mood she claimed that her husband had at first worshipped the ground she walked on, and then 'murdered' her. At one point the judge became so exasperated that he threatened her with a night in prison. Lady Winchester's counsel told the court that his client had been portrayed as 'a sort of mixture of Jezebel, Sapphira and Mrs Malaprop'. In fact, he said, she was 'a wronged woman distraught . . . like Dido – with a willow in her hand upon the wild sea banks and wafting her love to come again to Carthage'. The court found against Mrs Fleming, but to Lady Winchester's fury the verdict was later reversed in the Appeal Court.

Lord Winchester and Mrs Fleming retired to Monte Carlo, with Lady Winchester still in pursuit. He died in 1962, just short of his 100th birthday.

Bapsybanoo Pavry was born at Bahrat, India, in 1902, the daughter of Khurshedji Erachji Pavry, who she claimed was High Priest of the Parsees in Bombay; Lord Winchester maintained that his father-in-law was merely the priest of a fire temple. Young Bapsy was educated at Columbia University, New York, and in 1928 was presented at court to George V. In 1930 she published a book, *Heroines of Ancient Iran*, for which she was awarded the Iranian Order of Merit 25 years later. In 1947 she was a delegate at the Unesco Paris Peace Conference.

When she married in 1952 she circulated a document claiming that she was the first non-European ever to become a marchioness. The younger son of the 14th Marquess, who was born in 1801, Montagu Paulet had succeeded as 16th Marquess in 1899, when his elder brother was killed in the South African War. 'Monty' Winchester's first two wives died in 1924 and 1949 respectively, without children. When he died in 1962 the marquessate passed to a kinsman. From then on Lady Winchester divided her time between London and Bombay, escorted by her brother Dasturzada, Dr Jal Pavry. In London the pair lived at the Mayfair Hotel, and doggedly solicited invitations to public functions. When her brother died in 1985 Lady Winchester put out a statement that she had 'received messages of sympathy from all over the world'. She was a member of the Council of World Alliance for International Peace through Religion, and in 1989 made an endowment to Oxford University, in memory of herself and her brother, for the study of international relations and human rights.

Lady Winchester wrote hundreds of letters to celebrated figures, and usually received replies from their secretaries. But her extensive archives, presented to the City of Winchester between 1974 and 1995, did include such triumphs as Christmas cards from King Olav of Norway, a reproduction of a portrait of herself by Augustus John, and photocopies of thank-you letters from George Bernard Shaw.

9 September 1995

SUSAN TRAVERS

Englishwoman who abandoned life as a socialite to become the first female member of the Foreign Legion

*

Susan Travers, who has died in Paris aged 94, was the only woman to have joined the French Foreign Legion; English by birth, she came to regard the Legion as her true family and played a key part in the breakout by its troops from Rommel's siege of the desert fortress of Bir Hakeim in 1942.

When war came in 1939, Susan Travers was living in the South of France, where she had grown up, and she joined the Croix Rouge, the French Red Cross. Hitherto she had led the rather inconsequential life of a socialite, but the challenges that now faced her gave her a purpose for the first time. Although her dislike of blood and illness made her a less than ideal nurse, she soon realised her ambition to become an ambulance driver, and in 1940 accompanied the French expeditionary force sent to help the Finns in the Winter War against the Russians.

France fell to the Nazis while she was in Scandinavia, and so she made her way to London, where she volunteered as a nurse with General de Gaulle's Free French forces. She was attached to the 13th Demi-Brigade of the Légion Étrangère (about half the Legion had stayed loyal, the others throwing in their lot with Vichy) and sailed for West Africa, where she witnessed the abortive attack on Dakar. She was then posted to Eritrea and took on the hazardous job of driving for senior officers. The desert roads were often mined and subject to enemy attack, and she survived a number of crashes, as well as being wounded by shellfire.

Her dash and pluck quickly endeared her to the legionnaires, who nicknamed her 'La Miss'. For her part, she admired the Legion's code of '*honneur et fidelité*', and formed good friendships with many of her comrades, among them Pierre Mesmer, later Prime Minister of France. She also enjoyed several romantic liaisons, notably with a tall White Russian prince, Colonel Dimitri Amilakvari, but none of these proved lasting. Then, in June 1941, her world was transformed. The cause was Colonel Marie-Pierre Koenig, her commanding officer, whose new driver she became. Although he was married, they quickly fell for each other – he wooing her with roses when she was in hospital with jaundice – and although it was impossible to show affection for one another in public, they enjoyed a happy few months together while posted to Beirut. This idyll was ended when their unit was attached to 8th Army and, in the spring of 1942, sent to hold the bleak fort of Bir Hakeim, at the southern tip of the Allies' defensive line in the Western Desert. At the start of May, Italian and German forces attacked in strength, Rommel having told his men that it would take them 15 minutes to crush any opposition; 8th Army hoped the fort would last a week. Instead, under Koenig's command, the 1,000 legionnaires and 1,500 other Allied troops held out for 15 days, and Bir Hakeim became for all Frenchmen who resisted the Nazis a symbol of hope and defiance.

With all ammunition and – in temperatures of 51°C – all water exhausted, Koenig resolved to lead a breakout at night through the minefields and three concentric cordons of German panzers that encircled Bir Hakeim. Susan Travers was to drive both him and Amilakvari. The attempt was swiftly discovered, however, when a mine exploded, and with tracer lighting up the night sky and tank shells hurtling towards her, Susan Travers took the lead. Determined to get both her passengers to safety, she pressed the accelerator of her Ford to the floor and burst through the German lines, blazing a trail for the other Allied vehicles to follow. Although her car was struck by a score of bullets, and on one occasion she drove into a laager of parked panzers, she reached the British lines.

Of the 3,700 Allied troops who had been at Bir Hakeim, more than 2,400 escaped with her, including 650 legionnaires, and Koenig became the hero of France. Susan Travers was awarded the *Croix de Guerre* and the *Ordre du Corps d'Arme* for her feat. With Koenig's career in the ascendant, he ended his affair with Susan Travers soon afterwards, much to her grief. Nevertheless, she remained with the Legion through the fighting in Italy and France until the end of the war, acting as both a driver and a nurse to the wounded and the dying. By May 1945 'I had become the person I'd always wanted to be' and, not wanting any other life, she applied to join the Legion officially. She took care to omit her sex from the form, and her application was accepted. She was appointed an officer in the logistics division, and so became the only woman ever to serve with the Legion.

Susan Travers was born in London on 23 September 1909. Her father, a naval officer, had married her mother for her money and the union was not an especially happy one. Susan's childhood was comfortable but over-strict, and she had her most enjoyable times away from her parents with her grandmother in Devon. She was sent to school at St Mary's, Wantage – an experience which she did not remember fondly – but during the First World War her father had been put in charge of marine transport at Marseilles (where his own father had once been British Consul), and in

1921 he decided to move the family to Cannes. The Riviera was starting to become fashionable, and Susan quickly took to the way of life there. Inspired by the deeds of a neighbour, Suzanne Lenglen, she also became a fine tennis player.

Being a girl, she had been more or less ignored by her father and her only brother, and by her late teens had developed a craving for male company: 'Most of all,' she wrote later, 'I wanted to be wicked.' Sent to a finishing school in Florence, she succumbed at 17 for the first time to the blandishments of a man, a hotel manager named Hannibal. By her own admission, she spent the next decade in a rather vapid, if enjoyable, round of skiing and tennis parties all over Europe, thinking nothing of travelling to Budapest or Belgrade for a week's entertainment. With her gamine figure, striking features and blue eyes, she was a constant and willing object of male attention, heedless of her father's reproach that she was '*une fille facile*'. It was a careless approach to life brought to an abrupt halt by the onset of conflict in 1939.

After the War she served for a time in Indo-China, but resigned her commission in 1947 to bring up her children from her marriage that year to a Legion NCO, Nicholas Schlegelmilch. He contracted an illness in the tropics in 1949 and, after spending 18 months in hospital, was never the same person as before. Nevertheless, they remained together; after his death in 1995 she continued to live in France.

In 1956, Susan Travers was awarded the *Médaille Militaire* in recognition of her bravery at Bir Hakeim. The medal was pinned on her by Koenig, by then Minister of Defence. Forty years later, in 1996, she was given the Legion's highest award, the *Légion d'Honneur*, in recognition of her unique part in the force's history. She published a memoir, *Tomorrow To Be Brave*, in 2000.

Susan Travers is survived by two sons.

23 December 2003

MARION WILBERFORCE

*Early aviatrix who flew a calf from Hungary and was one of
only 11 women to fly a Lancaster bomber*

*

Marion Wilberforce, who has died aged 93, was one of the band
of intrepid early aviatrices. She gained her pilot's licence in 1930
and bought her first aircraft, a Moth, seven years later. For tax
purposes the aircraft was classified as a 'farm implement', and was
used to ferry poultry and Dexter cattle. She once flew a calf back
from Hungary. Until she was obliged by law to do so, she refused
to instal a radio in her aircraft. To indicate that she wished to
land, she would circle and waggle her wings. She navigated by
features in the landscape, and would break her journey to ask the
way or read a signpost.

She was among the first eight women recruits to the Air
Transport Auxiliary in 1940, by which time she had 900 flying
hours to her credit. The ATA's role was to ferry aircraft to oper-
ational airfields. Initially, because of some prejudice among male
members, women were permitted to fly only non-operational
aircraft. But the desperate shortage of able male pilots meant that
by mid-1941 she was piloting Hurricanes and Spitfires as a
matter of course. She qualified to fly twin-engined bombers,
and in 1944 was one of only 11 women trained to fly the four-
engined Lancaster. On some days she would ferry as many as
four different aircraft, some of which went on to South Africa,
some to Ceylon, some to Russia; aircraft which she had ferried
were used in the attack on the Gestapo headquarters in Oslo in
1942. By mid-1943 she had clocked up some 1,800 flying hours
for the ATA; and by the end of the war she had flown most of
the 130 types of aircraft it ferried.

Among her colleagues was Amy Johnson, the celebrated pilot

who later drowned in the Thames. Wilberforce considered Johnson to have been a poor flyer prone to panic, though publicly she remained loyal to her memory.

She was born Marion Ogilvie-Forbes on 22 July 1902. Her father, John Ogilvie-Forbes, 9th Laird of Boyndlie in Aberdeenshire, was a dour figure who studied for the Anglican priesthood but was received into the Roman Catholic Church by Cardinal Newman. He was later Privy Chamberlain to four Popes. Boyndlie House, the family seat, was an austere granite edifice, cluttered with family portraits which had long overwhelmed the available hanging space. Young Marion was educated by a series of French governesses, and at the Convent of Jesus and Mary, Stony Stratford. She obtained a preliminary certificate in bee-keeping, and from the age of 12 bore some responsibility for the management of her father's estate. At 14 she was collecting rent from the tenants. She read agriculture at Somerville College, Oxford, and also obtained a certificate of merit in jiu-jitsu. (When she was in her eighth decade she was aggrieved at her inability to 'sort out' a burglar at her home.) She paid for her flying lessons by working for a country sports magazine in Bedford Square, where she shared an office with her pet Austrian grass snake. Encouraged by her uncle to dabble in the stock exchange, she used the profits to buy her first aircraft. She remained a successful, if idiosyncratic investor, scanning the index for company names that had a pleasing ring to them.

Several suitors were rejected because of their lack of knowledge of horses. But she did marry, in 1932, Robert Wilberforce, a respected solicitor and a descendant of the anti-slavery campaigner. Their protracted courtship almost came to nothing when Robert resolved to test his vocation as a monk at Ampleforth Abbey. After six months he decided against it; Marion was waiting to collect him at the abbey gate.

Though somewhat formidable on first encounter, Marion Wilberforce was kind, with a vigorous sense of humour; she liked to tease, and usually took a contrary line in argument. There were certain areas of absolute privacy in her life and she had a room, dubbed 'the Kremlin', from which even her husband was banned.

At one of her houses in Essex she bred pigs, always calling the runt of the litter Malcolm after her brother of that name. She had little faith in doctors, and where possible would take her medicines from the vet, claiming that a horse was sick. Marion Wilberforce began hunting in 1933, and from 1962 to 1982 was on the committee of the Essex Union Hunt, becoming the only woman Master of Fox Hounds in the hunt's 236-year history. She was a fearless rider, and hunted into her eighties, when her bones no longer healed so fast. She made a good combination with her husband, who was so short-sighted towards the end of his hunting career that he could not see beyond his horse's head.

There were no children of her marriage but Marion Wilberforce found consolation in the Child Emigration Society ('Empire Settlement through Child Colonisation') set up by the South African Kingsley Fairbridge; the society gathered orphaned or 'destitute' children from industrial cities in Britain and settled them throughout the Dominions. Marion Wilberforce took a particular interest in the Fairbridge Farm Schools and was for many years chairman of the Child Care Committee, charged with choosing children to send to Australia. In the 1930s she made a 9,000-mile trip over Australian dirt tracks to visit old Fairbridgians.

She gave up flying when she was 80 and sold her Hornet Moth to an Aberdeen sheep farmer. In subsequent years she would sometimes sink into a reverie while driving a motor-car, and meander gently across the road, her arms resting on the steering wheel, as though she were back in the cockpit.

When her husband died she returned to Boyndlie to stay with her brother Malcolm, then a widower. The house was dilapidated, the paint peeling, the gardens overgrown and the family chapel derelict. She and 'the runt' lived happily amidst the decay, meeting in the Red Room at 5.45 pm for a noggin. When their hearing failed Malcolm rigged up a car horn for a doorbell; Marion refused to wear hearing aids, claiming they caught on the branches of trees.

After an initial panic she bore her final decline stoically. Several times she inquired, 'Am I dead yet?' and 'How long have I been dead for?' Her last words before she finally lost consciousness were, 'I've been dead for a while now. Doesn't feel any different.'

6 January 1996

BLUESTOCKINGS

*

REAR-ADMIRAL GRACE HOPPER

American computer expert who coined the term 'bug' and was
known as 'the first lady of software'

*

Rear-Admiral Grace Hopper, the US Navy computer expert who has died at Arlington, Virginia, aged 85, was known as 'Amazing Grace' and 'the First Lady of software'. A mathematician 'from the days when they were still interested in arithmetic', Hopper helped develop Cobol, the automatic programming language which first launched computers as a universal instrument in the 1940s. She was also credited with coining the term 'bug' to describe the problems which plague computers and their programs. The appellation derived from an incident in 1945, when Hopper was a lieutenant assigned to the Bureau of Ordnance computation project at Harvard. A breakdown in one of the circuits of the Mark I computer was discovered to have been caused by a two-inch moth, which had become trapped in the system; the insect was duly removed with tweezers.

Under yearly special exemptions, Hopper stayed in uniform long after the retirement age of 62 to work on the US Navy's computer programs; when she finally retired in 1986 she was the oldest active-duty officer in America. She was studiously modest, though, and would claim that her inventions were merely the fruit of a natural laziness, which prompted her constantly to search for an easy way of doing things.

A slight, vigorous, and occasionally contrary woman, Hopper believed in giving her 'kids' (as she referred to her junior staff) complete creative freedom. At the Pentagon she earned a reputation as something of a radical, and reserved a withering contempt for anyone who submitted to the dictates of bureaucracy. 'The only phrase I've ever disliked is, "Why, we've always done it that way,"' she would observe, in her soft Southern drawl. 'I always tell young people, go ahead and do it. You can always apologise later.'

A self-professed 'old-fashioned patriot', she wore full beribboned uniform at every opportunity, and was wont to sport a filterless Lucky Strike between her unpainted lips. This somewhat eccentric appearance, combined with her pioneering spirit, invited many a hapless interviewer to inquire about her feminist views. Hopper, who was delighted to be named the First Computer Sciences Man of the Year in 1969 (she regarded 'man' as a generic rather than a genetic term), gave her interlocutors short shrift on this point. 'I'm thoroughly in the dog-house with the women's liberation people,' she remarked. 'They once asked me if I had ever met prejudice, and I said I've always been too busy to look for it.'

Grace Murray Hopper was born in New York City on 9 December 1906. Her grandfather, a civil engineer, was commissioned to lay out a section of the Bronx, and young Grace spent many happy afternoons trailing around after him to hold the measuring stick.

She became fascinated by geometry and maps, and once said that she would have gone into civil engineering herself, had there been a place for a female engineer when she graduated from Vassar in 1928. She went instead to Yale, where she took a doctorate in mathematics, and in 1931 returned to Vassar to take up a teaching post. Hopper acquired her computing skills during the Second World War. After joining the Naval Reserve in December 1943 she was posted to the computer laboratory at Harvard, where she was confronted with an amazing new toy: the first large-scale digital computer in America, the Mark I. She never looked back.

After demobilisation Hopper was informed that she was too old (at 40) to join the Navy proper, so, keeping her place in the Reserve, she joined a company that was building the Univac I, the first commercial computer. That company later merged into the Sperry Corporation, and it was there that Hopper worked on the programming idea that led to Cobol. In 1966 Hopper retired from the Reserve, but a year later was recalled, this time to active duty, to the Naval Data Automation Command (NDAC), where she was briefed to impose a standard on the Navy's many computer languages.

In 1975 an Act of Congress was required to allow the Navy to promote her to captain, as she was still theoretically on the retired list; and in 1983 she received a special presidential appointment to the rank of rear-admiral. Hopper soon became head of the NDAC, and spent two tireless decades working at the Pentagon, where she had four computers at her disposal. What she liked above all, though, was teaching, and whenever possible she would delegate her duties and set off on lecture tours. She was an inspired speaker, with a brilliant knack of adapting her software idiom to suit her audience's level. And she was not above playing the disingenuous neophyte herself. Once, during a computer conference at Llandudno in North Wales, she astonished a reporter when she leapt out of an amusement arcade and waved a handful of hot pennies under his nose. 'D'you know,' she beamed, 'there's some much better computers here, and they pay out real money,' then scuttled off to play another fruit machine further down the pier.

Besides computers, Hopper enjoyed needlework – she was particularly fond of creating intricate *petit point* dragons. She was also a keen amateur genealogist. 'Amazing Grace' remained an immovable optimist. She once expressed a desire to live until she was 94 so she could attend the 'splendid parties' that would abound in 1999. 'Then maybe I'll retire to a mountain top with a computer and send messages to everyone telling them where they are going wrong.'

Hopper won many awards, including five service medals, and was a member of 27 societies. But she claimed to be most proud of being the only woman, and the first American, to be elected a distinguished fellow of the British Computer Society.

She married, in 1930, Vincent Hopper; the union was dissolved in 1945.

7 January 1992

CYNTHIA LONGFIELD

Intrepid traveller and naturalist who searched the world for dragonflies

*

Cynthia Longfield, who has died aged 94, was the author of *The Dragonflies of the British Isles* (1937), part of Frederick Warne's *Wayside and Woodland* series – the first book on the subject to achieve a wide popular readership. She herself represented a late flowering of the Victorian tradition whereby a passionate interest in natural history flourished under the shelter of ample private means. Her expertise was beyond dispute, but throughout her life she retained the verve of an enthusiast following a beloved hobby. Thus, although she won the respect of scientists with the papers in which she set forth the taxonomy of dragonflies – notably of the genera *Ortherum* and *Ceriagrion* – she also delighted, however alarming her imperious figure, to answer the questions of the veriest beginner at the Natural History Museum.

Cynthia Longfield was born in London on 16 August 1896. The seminal event in her early career was her participation, in 1924, in the St George scientific expedition to the Pacific, which brought together a band of natural historians prepared to share the cost of chartering the ship. Many of them later achieved distinction in their particular fields, none more so than two of the women – Evelyn Cheesman, who had been hired to marshal the scientific material, and Cynthia Longfield, who was one of the sponsors. These two struck up an acquaintance, and planned further expeditions together, although, being both strong individualists, they decided in the end to work alone. Longfield travelled widely and intrepidly in Africa. 'I find machetes so useful in the jungle, don't you?' she would casually remark. On another occasion, hunting for dragonflies in South America, she bumped into the Paraguayan army on its way to invade Bolivia – and later surprised the Bolivians with this intelligence.

Longfield brought back much material for the Natural History Museum. From 1948 to 1957 she was an Honorary Associate of the Museum.

When William Collins' great series, *The New Naturalist Library*, became established as an authoritative compendium of modern knowledge, Cynthia Longfield was asked to contribute a volume. She recruited two able young men, Philip Corbet and Norman Moore, to share the task, and the resulting book, *Dragonflies* (1960), quickly sold out, changing hands at a high premium until it was reprinted.

Cynthia Longfield was a vice-president of the Royal Entomological Society of London and served for some years as a council member. Without her the British Dragonfly Society, founded in 1983, might never have existed, so it was only right that she was elected its first honorary member. Likewise, the splendid books which are now appearing on dragonflies owe much to her pioneering work. She was recently rewarded by the discovery in Ireland of a species new to Britain.

12 July 1991

ELSIE WIDDOWSON

*Nutritionist whose work on chemical composition of foodstuffs
resulted in Britain's healthy wartime diet*

*

Elsie Widdowson, who has died aged 93, was one half of the scientific partnership, with Professor Robert McCance, whose work on the chemical composition of foods formed the basis for the austerity diet promoted by Lord Woolton, Minister of Food during the Second World War. The diet, which included such ingredients as dried eggs and 'Woolton Pie' (made from vegetables and breadcrumbs), has since been acknowledged as the healthiest diet the British population has ever had.

The partnership between Elsie Widdowson and Robert McCance was to last 60 years, ending only with McCance's death in 1993. It began in 1933 in the kitchens at St Bartholomew's Hospital, where Elsie Widdowson was learning about large-scale cooking as part of a postgraduate diploma in dietetics; McCance, a young doctor, was investigating the chemical consequences of cooking as part of research into the treatment of diabetes. Elsie Widdowson had completed a doctoral thesis on the chemistry of ripening and stored fruit, and she realised that some of McCance's research results must be incorrect – and told him so. McCance was so impressed that he asked her to work with him in his laboratory and, at Elsie Widdowson's suggestion, the pair began to work together on tables showing the chemical composition of foodstuffs in the British diet.

In 1940, their results were published by the Medical Research Council in *The Chemical Composition of Foods*, a comprehensive digest containing some 15,000 nutritional values and listing cooked as well as raw foods. 'McCance and Widdowson', as the book was soon dubbed, ran into six editions and became known as the dietician's bible.

With the Second World War under way, McCance and Elsie Widdowson turned their attention to rationing. They constructed an experimental diet based on bread, cabbage and potatoes, all of which were in relatively plentiful supply and which they believed contained all the necessary nutrients for national survival. Using themselves and fellow scientists as guinea pigs, they lived on the diet for three months, at the end of which they decamped to the Lake District for some vigorous fell walking to test their physical fitness. The experiment was pronounced a resounding success and the diet was subsequently promoted by the Ministry of Food. Further research on the importance of calcium in preventing rickets led to the statutory inclusion of chalk in bread-making flour. After the war, they were approached by the Army who were worried that their cadets at Sandhurst were not gaining weight as they should and were wondering whether it was because they were not getting enough 'good red meat'. Elsie Widdowson and McCance were able to show that the problem was not a lack of meat, but that the cadets were not eating their bread ration, preferring cakes and pastries.

Elsie May Widdowson was born in London on 21 October 1906 and educated at Sydenham County Secondary School and Imperial College, London, where she read Chemistry. After graduating, she joined a group at Imperial College's Department of Plant Physiology under Helen Archbold (later Professor Helen Porter) studying the chemistry of ripening and stored fruit. Subsequently, she researched the metabolism of the kidneys under Professor E.C. Dodds at the Courtauld Institute of the Middlesex Hospital. It was Dodds who suggested that dietetics might be a rewarding field of research and persuaded her to take a postgraduate diploma at King's College, London.

When McCance became a Reader in Medicine at Cambridge

in 1938, Elsie Widdowson became a member of his team at the Department of Experimental Medicine. Before the war they conducted experiments to investigate how the body metabolises certain elements, using themselves as guinea pigs. By injecting themselves with iron, for instance, they discovered that the amount of iron in the body is regulated not by excretion but by controlled absorption. Not all their experiments went according to plan. While researching strontium, they injected strontium lactate into their veins and, when nothing happened, decided to increase the dose. Less than an hour later they began to feel extremely ill, with intense headaches, raging fever and aching backs and limbs. Nevertheless, they were able to show that the body rids itself of strontium slowly and that about 90 per cent of it is excreted through the kidneys.

Before the war, Elsie Widdowson had begun to research the composition of the human body at various stages of development. She continued this work after the war, using bodies dissected by the pathologist at Addenbrooke's Hospital, Cambridge, and backing up her research with comparative studies of animal species including pigs, rats, cats and guinea pigs. She discovered that the human new-born infant is exceptional in being 16 per cent composed of fat, whereas most species contain just one to two per cent. This led her to begin examining the feeding of new born babies. Her research took her to Canada to study the nutrition of baby seals during their first few days of life on the ice off the Labrador coast, and how bear cubs survive while their mothers are hibernating. During the 1970s, she became involved in analysing the composition of breast milk, as a template for the design of modern infant feeding formulae.

In the spring of 1946, she and McCance toured Holland, Germany and Denmark as part of a study of the nutrition of communities which had suffered during the war. This work launched an experimental programme which continued for the next 25 years on the effects of nutrition on growing and adult human beings. In the course of this work, Elsie Widdowson discovered that she could undernourish pigs so severely from ten days of age that by one year they weighed only three per cent as much as their well nourished litter-mates. When the pigs were allowed to gain weight, she found that the longer they had been undernourished, the sooner they stopped growing. Yet the malnourished pigs were still able to breed healthy full-sized litters.

In 1966 Elsie Widdowson became head of the Infant Nutrition Research Division at the Dunn Nutrition Laboratory, Cambridge. From 1972 until her retirement in 1988, she worked in the Department of Investigative Medicine at Addenbrooke's Hospital. She was president of the Nutrition Society from 1977 to 1980, and of the Neonatal Society from 1978 to 1981. Intellectually extremely sharp, Elsie Widdowson was also a kindly, down-to-earth woman with an engaging smile. She took an almost maternal interest in her students and their families; some of them even called her 'Mum'.

To her own diet, she took a refreshingly robust attitude: 'I eat butter, eggs and white bread which some people think are bad for you but I do not,' she said in 1992. Her longevity she attributed to 'good genes', her father having died aged 96 and her mother aged 107.

She was appointed CBE in 1979 and was made a Companion of Honour in 1993.

22 June 2000

DAME OLGA UVAROV

*Russian child refugee who became the first woman president of
the Royal College of Veterinary Surgeons*

*

Dame Olga Uvarov, who has died aged 91, arrived in Britain as
a child emigrée from the Russian Revolution, qualified as a vet
and went on to become the first woman president of the Royal
College of Veterinary Surgeons.

Olga Nikolaevna Uvarov was born in Moscow on 9 July 1910,
the daughter of Nikola Uvarov, a prosperous lawyer who traced
his descent back to a Tartar count ennobled by Tsar Ivan the
Terrible in the mid-16th century. The family had an estate at
Ouralsk, in the Urals, and as news came of the Bolsheviks' suc-
cesses in 1917, Olga's father put her, her three brothers and their
mother Elena into the charge of two of the family's coachmen
and sent them by carriage to what he hoped would be the relative safety of the country. Having soon sold their horses and a
few pieces of jewellery to survive, they then fell prey to a typhoid
epidemic. Olga's mother, after nursing her children back to
health, died; her father – with whom the children had been
briefly reunited in hospital – was brought before a revolutionary
tribunal and shot. For months Olga and her brothers lived
together as best they could in one room, foraging for food and
witnessing horrors they would never forget. But they had an
uncle in London, the entomologist Sir Boris Uvarov, who heard
that they were still alive.

The American Red Cross found the children for Sir Boris,
but such was the cost of getting people out of Russia at that time
that he could afford only to pay the costs for a single passage.
After much heart-searching, he elected to save Olga. Weeks
later, Olga was given a Red Cross label marked 'Orphan No 7'

to hang round her neck, and was told to pack a basket with a change of clothes and something to eat. From food parcels previously sent by her uncle she took a dozen Oxo cubes wrapped in gold paper. An ignorant official, suspecting the cubes were real gold, insisted on dissolving every one.

Having reached Moscow once more, Olga had to wait another six months until, shaved and disinfected, she was escorted to Estonia and put on a ship for England. Sir Boris was horrified by the state of his waif-like niece when she arrived in England; she was without hair or fingernails, and was suffering from malaria. Olga, for her part, would remember being amazed that the English could leave their washing out on the line without it being stolen.

After schooling, Olga Uvarov commenced her studies at the London Royal Veterinary College, where she won the college's Bronze Medals for Physiology and Histology and qualified in 1934. The veterinary profession of those days had changed little in outlook since the *Veterinary Journal* of 1889 reported that women vets were not expected to treat horses, but to follow 'the lighter labour of alleviating the sufferings of sick lap-dogs'. The horse remained the focus of veterinary attention, and women trainees were rare. In 1934, only 34 women were registered by the Royal Veterinary College, and the first of these, a Miss Cust, had had to wait 32 years after qualifying before its portals were opened to her.

Olga Uvarov began her career as an assistant in a general mixed practice, and then in 1944 set up her own small animal practice in Surrey, with clients including an RSPCA clinic and a greyhound stadium. Then in the early 1950s she switched to work in the pharmaceutical industry, becoming head of the veterinary advisory department of Glaxo Laboratories from 1967 to 1970.

She believed passionately in the care of animals and in their use to help conquer human diseases, but only provided the strictest welfare conditions were observed. Subsequently, she worked in the technical information service of the British Veterinary Association, serving for two years (1976–78) as the BVA's Adviser on Technical Information, a post that combined practical work with research and administration.

Olga Uvarov was president of the Society of Women Veterinary Surgeons from 1947 to 1949, and of the Central Veterinary Society in 1951–52. She was awarded the Victory Gold Medal of the Central Veterinary Society in 1965. She was elected to the council of the Royal College of Veterinary Surgeons in 1968, and became a fellow in 1973. She took over as the first woman president of the Royal College of Veterinary Surgeons in 1976. In later years, she was much in demand as a member of parliamentary and other committees concerned with veterinary matters, and as a speaker at international veterinary symposia. She also found time to write more than 40 scientific papers on veterinary pharmacology and therapeutics.

Away from her work, Olga Uvarov had a deep interest in literature and the arts, especially ballet. She also loved flowers, and was delighted when an orchid-growing friend named a new hybrid in her honour – the golden yellow cymbidium orchid 'Olga Uvarov', officially registered in 1976.

Having devoted her life to the care of animals, Dame Olga was saddened when animal rights activists attacked her bungalow and forced her to move. Her last years were spent in a nursing home at Hatch End, north London. She read avidly, without spectacles, and particularly enjoyed the *Daily Telegraph*.

She was appointed CBE in 1978 and DBE in 1983.

20 September 2001

LORNA SAGE

*Writer and professor of English Literature whose memoir of a
bleak childhood in post-war provincial Britain brought
comparisons with the Brontës*

*

Lorna Sage, who has died aged 57, had been Professor of English
Literature at the University of East Anglia since 1994, and was
also a literary journalist and a critic; but she was perhaps best
known as the author of *Bad Blood* (2000), a memoir of her childhood which won this year's Whitbread Award for Biography.
The book gave an unsparingly intimate and grimly humorous
account of growing up in post-war provincial Britain. It was also
an examination of the powerful forces that determine the shape
of a life – genetic inheritance, family secrets, even landscape.
Indeed, so Gothic-seeming were some of the characters in *Bad
Blood* that the events it related appeared to belong more properly
to the 19th century, and, since the setting was a vicarage in bleak
countryside, more than one reviewer drew comparisons
between Sage and the Brontës.

She was born Lorna Stockton on 13 January 1943, but traced
the pattern of her life to the appointment, ten years before, of
her grandfather, an Anglican clergyman, to a parish in rural
Flintshire, north Wales. With her father away on armed service,
Lorna grew up in her grandparents' house, and was witness to a
marriage that had become a relationship of mutual hatred. Her
grandfather 'was good at funerals, being gaunt and lined and
marked with mortality. He had a scar down his hollow cheek,
too, which Grandma had done with the carving knife one of the
many times when he came home pissed and incapable.' From this
theatrical, womanising figure (who would later take up with one
of his granddaughter's teenage friends), Lorna inherited the two

dominant and competing instincts of her early life – boys and books. Her Christian name, chosen by her grandfather (a frustrated writer), had been taken from *Lorna Doone*.

Her intelligence won her a place at a school over the border in Whitchurch, Shropshire, where she and her parents went to live in that symbol of post-war hope, a new council house. There her father ran a failing haulage business, while her fey mother retreated from the wreckage of her own ambitions into a life whose high point was the successful preparation of fish fingers. By 16, having evaded the incestuous attentions of an uncle, Lorna was longing to escape, and vowing never to have children. But already, without knowing that anything significant had happened, she was pregnant by a boy she had met at a school dance; she seemed to have succumbed to her grandfather's 'bad blood'. But she and the baby's father, Vic Sage, were married in 1959, and, against her parents' wishes, she kept her daughter. More remarkably still, she and her husband then both went up to Durham University, where they graduated with Firsts in English in 1964, and then found teaching jobs at the same university, East Anglia.

There *Bad Blood* ends. Lorna Sage, however, went on to an academic career as a lecturer at the university, and was twice dean of its School of English and American Studies, from 1985–88 and 1993–96. Having undertaken research on 17th-century poetry, her first writing was about Thomas Love Peacock, Thomas Hardy and George Meredith. Later she became interested in women writers, including Virginia Woolf and Edith Wharton. In 1983 she published a biography of Doris Lessing, and in 1992 a survey of post-war women novelists, *Women in the House of Fiction*. She also wrote a introduction to the work of Angela Carter (1994); but her most substantial scholarly legacy is *The Cambridge Guide to Women's Writing in English* (1995), which she edited, capably marshalling 300 contributors and 2,500 entries. She was a regular reviewer, too, for the *Observer*, *London Review of Books*, *New York Times* and *Times Literary Supplement*.

Her marriage to Vic Sage was dissolved in 1974. After the unexpected conception of their daughter, they had, she explained, shunned 'sexual intercourse. We thought – we hardly spoke about it, hardly needed to – that we'd find a way out of this impasse. But as time went by it was our secret sexlessness that cemented our intimacy. We were brother and sister.' They separated, and on a sabbatical in Florence, Lorna Sage met Rupert Hodson, an authority on Italian houses and gardens and a gifted pianist. They married in 1979, and thereafter she divided her time between Norwich and Florence.

She is survived by Rupert Hodson, and by the daughter of her first marriage.

13 January 2001

CRESSIDA RIDLEY

Asquith's granddaughter who turned her sharp intellect not to Liberal politics but to neolithic archaeology and made notable discoveries in Greece

*

Cressida Ridley, who has died aged 81, was a granddaughter of H.H. Asquith, the Liberal Prime Minister, and inherited her full share of that family's remarkable brainpower; she herself, though, came to concentrate on archaeology rather than politics. Her most important excavation, between 1971 and 1973, was on a 6th to 3rd millennium BC site near Servia, in the Haliakmon Valley in northern Greece. The work, carried out before the area was flooded as part of a hydro-electric scheme, has provided a vast range of information about life in neolithic Greece – there were even two-storey houses.

Cressida Ridley could seem formidable, and Greek labourers

who were inclined to male chauvinism soon learned the error of their ways. They might also find their Greek corrected. Equally, archaeologists who worked with her developed the highest admiration for her scholarship, and for the rare mixture of horse sense and imagination that characterised her interpretation of finds. Their principal memory, however, is of what tremendous fun they had with her, and of the help and encouragement she gave them. She was a woman held in the great esteem, but in still greater affection. On site her co-workers discovered with some frustration that, no matter how early they rose, it was impossible to prevent Cressida Ridley from tackling the routine chores before them. In necessarily primitive conditions, she made sure that everyone else was more comfortably installed than herself – even if there were rules to be observed. 'My dear,' she told one young assistant, 'never put lovers in the same trench.' On the other hand she also held that 'dogs pull together better when there's a bitch among them'.

These Cressida-isms, always spontaneous, often went to the heart of the matter. 'If you can foretell the future and do something about it,' she remarked apropos of astrology, 'then you can't foretell the future – and if you foretell the future and can't do anything about it, why bother?' Her own faith rested on the premise, integral to the Liberal tradition, that human affairs are infinitely susceptible of improvement through the application of reason and experience. She had the greatest respect for science, only partially satisfied by her archaeological studies. If she could be born again, she said towards the end of her life, she would be an oceanographer. Her seriousness of purpose, however, was never solemnly expressed. Frances Partridge wrote of 'the combination of a pale, handsome and intelligent face with spontaneous gaiety'. For all her brilliance, Cressida Ridley loved simple pleasures: singing, the pantomime, collecting dreadful postcards.

Nothing human was alien to her. Well read across a vast range of subjects, she also possessed a remarkable memory. One moment she might be discoursing on an 18th-century *Ode to Indifference*, explaining how the meaning of that word had changed; the next she might be addressing the problem of football hooligans. Cressida was highly perceptive about character, however absent-minded she might appear. A natural teacher, she had a special gift for talking to and listening to the young. Yet her high spirits and intellectual virtuosity had been maintained throughout a long widowhood which might have undermined a less indomitable spirit.

She was born Helen Laura Cressida Bonham Carter on 22 April 1917, the eldest child of Sir Maurice 'Bongie' Bonham Carter, who was Asquith's private secretary between 1910 and 1916, and of Violet, Asquith's only daughter by his first wife Helen Melland. Winston Churchill was one of her godparents. Three more children followed: Laura, who would marry Jo Grimond; Mark, who won Torrington for the Liberals in 1958 and was later Chairman of the Race Relations Board; and Raymond, who is the father of the actress Helena Bonham Carter. From the age of about nine Cressida Bonham Carter spent much time at Stockton in Wiltshire. Until she was 15 she was educated mainly by governesses, with a short spell at a *lycée* in Paris; then in 1932 she went to school in Vienna, where she was befriended by Sir Ernst Gombrich's family. Gombrich's mother Leonie, who had studied harmony with Anton Bruckner, taught her the piano.

By the time Cressida returned to Britain in 1935 she had travelled widely in central Europe and had become fluent in German as in French. Philip Toynbee remembered visiting her and her sister in Wiltshire that summer. Cressida and Laura, he recalled, 'amiably diverged from the preoccupations of their parents by taking little interest in politics. They preferred books and pictures, cricket and riding – and the books and pictures which they preferred were more advanced than those with which their parents were at home.' Cressida, in fact, had been spotted reading

Plato at the age of ten. Yet her parents showed no disposition to send their brilliant daughter to university – even though Lady Violet Bonham Carter was one of the most politically advanced women of the day.

But nothing could prevent Cressida Bonham Carter from gravitating towards intellectual company. In 1939 she married Jasper Ridley, a close friend of Isaiah Berlin, who was soon equally struck by Cressida; in 1953 Berlin would dedicate *The Hedgehog and the Fox* to Jasper's memory. Cressida Bonham Carter and Jasper Ridley enjoyed only a couple of months in their flat in Mecklenburgh Square before the outbreak of the Second World War. Jasper Ridley joined the 60th Rifles, and in 1942 was captured by the Germans in North Africa and sent to an Italian prison camp. Cressida for her part, worked as an auxiliary nurse at the Royal Free Hospital, and then in psychological warfare at Woburn, when she was billeted with Hugh and Dora Gaitskell, who named their daughter Cressida in her honour. Meanwhile Jasper Ridley, who had been moved northwards when the Allies landed at Salerno, escaped from a train. For several weeks he was hidden by an Italian schoolmaster, but at the end of 1943, having heard a wireless report of his brother-in-law Mark Bonham Carter's successful escape to the Allied lines in the south, he determined to emulate him.

Six months later Cressida Ridley was informed by the Red Cross that he had been killed in a minefield. The next day she received a letter which he had written to her and left with the Italian schoolmaster.

In 1945 Cressida moved to the Glebe, in Stockton, where she brought up her son Adam, who had been born in May 1942. During the 1950s she did some freelance translating, and at a neighbour's request, bent her mind to developing more efficient methods of farming.

The presence of so many archaeologists in the area inspired a new interest, and in 1961, the year her son went up to Balliol, she entered the Institute of Archaeology at London University to study the archaeology of prehistoric Europe. Two years later, without having taken a first degree, she attained a postgraduate diploma, coming out top in her year. This achievement was rewarded by a scholarship to the British School of Archaeology in Athens. Subsequently she worked on a number of digs in Greece and elsewhere, before starting her excavations in the Haliakmon Valley in 1971. Thereafter she returned annually to Greece, spending six to nine months every year studying her finds, as well as joining other excavations. Her last visit was in 1993, after which hip troubles prevented further physical exertion although her mind remained as sharp as ever.

With her Liberal loyalties, Cressida Ridley could hardly approve of her son Adam leaving Lord Rothschild's Think Tank in 1974 to join – and in 1979 to direct – the Conservative Research Department. But she did not always succeed in disguising her pride in her son's position as chief adviser to the Chancellor of the Exchequer, Sir Geoffrey Howe. Adam Ridley's knighthood, in 1985, presented a similar dilemma. 'I don't approve,' she remarked on hearing the news, 'no, not really.' By that evening, however, she had risen to a 'Goodnight, Sir Adam', and she made quite certain that she did not miss the investiture.

The first volume of the book about Cressida Ridley's excavations, *Servia – A Rescue Operation*, which she wrote with Ken Wardle and C.A. Mould, will be published shortly.

18 June 1998

MARJORIE COURTENAY-LATIMER

*Curator whose enthusiasm led to the discovery of a prehistoric
fish thought to be extinct*

*

Marjorie Courtenay-Latimer, who has died aged 97, was a
museum curator whose persistence led to the discovery that the
coelacanth, a prehistoric 'fossil fish' which had been assumed to
have been extinct for 70 million years, was alive and well in the
sea off South Africa. On 22 December 1938 she was working at
her desk at the East London Museum in the Eastern Cape prov-
ince, struggling to reassemble a fossil dinosaur which she and a
friend had excavated in Tarkasand, when she was telephoned by
the manager of the local trawler fleet. He informed her that
Captain Hendrik Goosen, a local trawlerman who sometimes
provided her with specimens for her museum, had arrived in port
with a catch she might want to look at. Though initially tempted
to stay and complete the work she was doing, she went down to
the quayside and inspected the pile of fish lying on the trawler's
deck: 'I picked away at the layers of slime to reveal the most beautiful fish I had ever seen . . . It was five foot long, a pale, mauvy
blue with faint flecks of whitish spots; it had an iridescent silver-
blue-green sheen all over. It was covered in hard scales, and it had
four limb-like fins and a strange puppy-dog tail.'

She did not know what it was – her speciality was birds not
fish – but she knew that it was unusual. So she and her native
assistant, Enoch, transported the 127lb fish back to the museum
in a taxi. She searched through various textbooks, but could find
nothing resembling the fish, though she was struck by its curious structure, its head plates, fin formation and the absence of
blood or slimy discharge from its mouth, nose or body. The
chairman of the museum dismissed her find as 'nothing but a

rock cod', but she remained determined to preserve the animal until she could get someone to identify it properly. It was high summer and the weather was sultry, so she and Enoch pushed the fish to the local hospital mortuary on a small handcart. The mortuary refused to put a 'stinking fish' in its freezer, as did the town's cold storage depot. By the time she reached the local taxidermist, the fish's bright blue scales had faded to a dusky grey. With the taxidermist's help, she wrapped it in formalin-soaked newspapers tied up with an old sheet belonging to her mother.

That done, she telephoned James Smith, a chemistry lecturer and friend of hers at Rhodes University in Grahamstown. Smith was away, so she left messages and then wrote to him, including a description and drawings, asking his opinion. But it was not until 3 January that Smith received her letter. Meanwhile, oil had started leaking from the fish and, fearful that it was in danger of rotting away, she asked the taxidermist to skin it and gut it. A few days later she received a wire from Smith which read: 'Save viscera . . . fish interesting.' But the message arrived too late and, by the time Smith arrived in East London on 16 February, the soft tissues had been thrown away. Only the skin and a few hard parts remained. Nevertheless, Smith immediately identified the fish: 'There was not a shadow of doubt,' he recalled. 'Scale by scale, bone by bone, fin by fin, it was a true coelacanth. It could have been one of those creatures of 200 million years ago come alive again.'

The discovery of the coelacanth, a representative of a family thought to have died out more than 70 million years ago, was hailed as 'the zoological find of the century'. Smith named the fish *Latimeria chalumnae* in honour of Marjorie Courtenay-Latimer and after the Chalumna River near which it was trawled.

Marjorie Eileen Doris Courtenay-Latimer was born more than two months prematurely on 24 February 1907, the daughter of a station master on the South African Railways. Although she had not been expected to live and was often ill as a child, she was a determined little character who showed a precocious interest in the natural world. Birds were her special interest, and as a child she spent long hours watching their nests, collecting feathers and eggs and studying their behaviour. Aged 11, she announced that she would one day write a book on birds.

At 15 she was sent to a convent where she came top of her class in everything but mathematics. She had always dreamed of working in a museum but there were no opportunities available, and in 1931 she decided to become a nurse. She secured a place on a training course in King William's Town but, three weeks before she was due to start, she was invited by a naturalist friend, George Rattree, to apply for the post of curator at a new museum being built in East London, of which he was a board member. 'I went to meet the board, which consisted of the mayor and all these old gentlemen,' she recalled. 'They asked me all sorts of questions about what I liked doing. Dr Rattree said, "Do you know anything about a platanna?" Now a platanna is a frog, and I said "Oh, yes", and told him chapter and verse.' Nine days later they offered her the job at a salary of £2 per month. She was just 24.

When Marjorie Courtenay-Latimer took over the museum, its exhibits consisted of a bottled piglet with six legs, six stuffed birds which were so riddled with parasites that she had to burn them, 12 pictures of East London and 12 prints of Xhosa War scenes. Consumed with doubts about how she was going to fill the museum, she gathered up some old evening dresses, china and jewellery belonging to her mother and stone implements which she had collected. These items, together with her mother's collection of beadwork dating back to 1858, and her great aunt Lavinia's dodo egg, formed the nucleus of her museum display. From the day it opened, the museum became her life. On weekends and holidays she would go out and collect wild flowers, shells, birds' eggs, butterflies, moths, insects and local ethnological material to add to the collection.

In 1933 she met James Smith for the first time, and he invited her to send him any fish she needed classifying. In November 1936 she and her parents visited Bird Island, off the East Cape coast, where she amassed a huge collection of sponges, seaweeds, sea shells and birds' eggs. She also went to sea in the trawler Nerine, making friends with Captain Goosen, who promised to save interesting fishes from the trawl nets for her attention.

After the discovery of the coelacanth, Marjorie returned to her duties as curator at the museum, at which the fish became the prize specimen. James Smith devoted the rest of his life to studying it, attempting to find more specimens and campaigning for its protection. It was to be another 14 years before another coelacanth was caught – this time off the coast of the Comoro Archipelago.

After her retirement from the museum, Marjorie Courtenay-Latimer went to live on a farm at Tsitsikamma for 15 years, and wrote a book about wild flowers in the local national park. She eventually returned to East London, to a small house next door to the one in which she had lived as a child. In her old age she took up sculpture and painting flowers on ceramic tiles. In 1988, aged 91, she was guest of honour at a ceremony held by the South African Mint to launch a commemorative gold coelacanth coin. She also received an honorary doctorate from Rhodes University in 1973 for her work and dedication to marine research, and was fêted at many scientific conferences for her 'scientific perspicacity'.

As a young woman, Marjorie Courtenay-Latimer was briefly engaged to a childhood friend, but she broke off the engagement because her fiancé 'didn't like my madness in collecting plants and climbing trees after birds'. Later she fell in love with the son of the owner of a local steel factory; but he died, and she never married.

19 May 2004

ENTERTAINERS

*

BERYL REID

Comic actress who spent 30 years in variety before hitting the big time

*

Beryl Reid, the actress, who has died aged 76, possessed a boisterous sense of comedy which sometimes disguised the fact that she was also a fine character actress. She spent her first 30 years as a stand-up comic in variety, pantomime and 'intimate revue', before switching to straight theatre, where she proved herself an accomplished actress in classical and modern comedy.

The turning point in her career was her appearance in 1959 in a revue sketch by Harold Pinter called *One To Another* (Lyric, Hammersmith, and Apollo). For the first time she was not playing to the audience with a view to raising laughs, but to the text with a view to raising tension. The American critic Harold Clurman saw her in the revue and called her 'a real artist and trouper with technical command'. This encouraged her to believe she had the makings of a serious actress, and in 1965 she achieved réclame in *The Killing of Sister George* by Frank Marcus. She played the bossy half in a disintegrating lesbian partnership, a radio actress about to be written out of the series. On tour, she recalled, the play was a disaster. 'Nobody had spoken about lesbianism on stage and it rather destroyed the people we were playing to.' One newspaper headline ran: 'Bath Not Ready For Sister George'.

In Hull, she remembered, 'people would barely serve us in shops, they were so horrified'. When the show opened in the West End, however, it sold out for five months and ran for over a year at the Duke of York's Theatre before transferring to Broadway. Beryl Reid won the American Tony award for Best Leading Actress. Having agreed to appear in the screen version directed by Robert Aldrich, she stipulated that she had no intention of appearing in a sex film. 'Robert Aldrich thought there should be some very sexy moments between George and Childie,' Beryl said. 'I completely disagreed.' The sex scenes were played by other actresses, though Beryl capitulated to the extent of kissing Susannah York, who played Childie McNaught. The film was given an X certificate. 'Robert Aldrich told the public that certain scenes had been cut in some cinemas but not in others,' Beryl Reid said. 'This was his gimmick for the film. People flew all over the place to see it. It was a tremendous success. They were waist-high in £5 notes in the box office in London.'

Beryl Reid was born at Hereford on 17 June 1920, the daughter of a Scottish estate agent. As a child she loved to make people laugh, and declared her theatrical ambitions at the age of four. She attended Withington and Levenshulme high schools, where she performed at club concerts. But she left school at 16 to work in a Manchester department store. One lunch hour she auditioned successfully as a soubrette and dancer with a seaside concert party, and made her professional debut in the North Regional Follies at the Floral Hall, Bridlington, in 1936. 'I knew nothing about how to take off make-up,' she recalled. 'I used Trex, rubbed all the goo off with a towel and sent it home to my mother for laundering.'

Beryl spent her early career touring the music hall circuit in variety shows and concert parties with such performers as Billy Bennet, Max Miller and George Formby. At the Palace Theatre, Attercliff, she said, 'The rats ate my knickers. You had to leave them in the dressing room at night and the rats always found them very tasty.'

During the Second World War Beryl Reid joined ENSA, and appeared on billings alongside 'Koringa', the French Hindu fakir who 'travelled with snakes and crocodiles'. She played in several Tom Arnold pantomimes, including *Cinderella* and *Mother Goose*, and toured with Harold Fielding's variety revue *Music for the*

Millions. In 1942 she joined the *Will Fyffe Show* and performed with the Dagenham Girl Pipers at the Glasgow Empire, the 'comedians' graveyard'. 'I got the bird and was booed off,' she remembered, 'Even Will Fyffe didn't go down well. One of the audience waited at the stage door after the show just to tell us we were rotten.'

After the war Beryl Reid continued to appear in pantomime and variety shows. She spoke with awe of the difficulties involved in performing 427 different sketches in 26 weeks. On radio she prospered in shows such as *Variety Bandbox*, *Henry Hall's Guest Night* and *Educating Archie*, in which she conceived the characters Monica, the ghastly schoolgirl, and Marlene, the Pride of the Midlands, celebrated for her enormous earrings and Brummie accent.

She eventually forsook her work in variety for intimate revue, a now defunct form of theatrical entertainment still in fashion after the war. It was in this kind of entertainment that, in 1951, she made her first London stage appearance, in *After The Show* at St Martin's Theatre. She was also in the series of *New Watergate* revues in 1954, and in *Rockin' The Town*, at the Palladium in 1956. After another revue, *On The Avenue* (at the Globe), shows with Jimmy Edwards and Tommy Cooper, and a further West End revue *All Square* (at the Vaudeville) came *The Killing of Sister George*. She played Mme Arcati in Noël Coward's *Blithe Spirit* (at the Globe, 1970), proving somewhat tetchier than Margaret Rutherford, the original creator of the part. She then acted Frau Bergmann in Wedekind's *Spring Awakening* and the Nurse in *Romeo and Juliet* (at the Old Vic, 1974), all to general approval.

In the Royal Court revival in 1975 of Joe Orton's *Entertaining Mr Sloane*, Beryl Reid was perfectly cast as the sinister-genteel Kath. Her briskness as Donna Katherina brought some consoling brightness to a dull production of Goldoni's street comedy *Il Campiello* at the National Theatre. In 1978 Beryl Reid triumphed as Lady Wishfort in the Royal Shakespeare

Company's revival of *The Way of The World* (at the Aldwych, 1978), once more proving a match for Margaret Rutherford's earlier interpretation, and all the better for being younger and more lurid. In Peter Nichols's *Born in the Gardens* she won a prize for the best comedy performance of 1980 as Maud, the mother of a drummer. Three years later came a startling Mrs Candour in Donald Sinden's revival of *The School for Scandal*.

Beryl Reid's film career had begun in 1940 with *Spare a Copper*, but it was 14 years before her next film, *The Belles of St Trinian's*. She made notable cameo appearances in *The Extra Day* (1956), *Two-Way Stretch* (1960), *The Dock Brief* (1962), *Inspector Clouseau* (1968), and *No Sex Please, We're British* (1973). On television she made an excellent impression as Mrs Knox, the Irish magistrate, in Channel Four's *The Irish RM* (1983), as Connie Sachs in *Tinker, Tailor, Soldier, Spy* (1979), and as the grandmother in the *Adrian Mole* series. For again playing the character of Connie Sachs in *Smiley's People* (1983), she won a prize for best television actress.

In 1984 Beryl Reid published an autobiography, *So Much Love*. One of the few revelations in the book was that she had once put off some visitors with the startling announcement: 'I'm afraid you can't come in. I'm in bed with somebody I don't know very well.' She later said: 'Of course, I wasn't, but it was the first thing which sprang to mind.' In 1984 she published a book about cats, *Cats' Whiskers*, and two years later, *Beryl, Food and Friends*.

She was appointed OBE in 1986. She married first, in 1951, Bill Worsley, whom she was soon describing as having 'the temperament of a U-boat commander'. They were divorced in 1953. The next year she married Derek Franklin; this marriage was also dissolved.

14 October 1996

IRENE THOMAS

*Former chorus girl and pub pianist who became BBC Brain of
Britain and a mainstay of Round Britain Quiz*

*

Irene Thomas, who has died aged 81, was an omniscient panellist on television and radio quiz programmes from the 1960s
onwards; she was the only woman to become both 'Brain of
Britain' and 'Brain of Brains'. For 22 years she was a member
of the team representing London in Radio 4's *Round Britain
Quiz*. Contestants were expected to display general knowledge,
spot allusions and solve brain teasers such as: 'A Roman one
added to an alternative was a dedicatee of Beethoven's. Adding
nothing gives the French recipient of a theologian's amatory
epistles. Explain.' Irene Thomas could usually be relied upon to
come up with the answer (here: I; else; Elise; Eloise) in less than
a minute.

Witty and charming, she exuded an air of erudition and many
who met her assumed that she must have had a first-rate education. Lord Quinton, sometimes the question master on Round
Britain Quiz, was astounded by her knowledge: 'I thought she
must go home every night to read Encyclopaedia Britannica.' In
fact, far from being well educated, Irene Thomas had left school
at 15. She attributed her success to a highly retentive memory
and to a magpie's instinct for 'jewels of information which lie
about everywhere'.

She was born Irene Roberts Ready at Feltham, Middlesex, on
28 June 1919, the only child of a former bandsman in the King's
Royal Rifles who had entered the Army as a nameless orphan.
Her mother, a former court dressmaker, was the daughter of a
village blacksmith. Little 'Reen' was greedy to learn and taught
herself to read long before she went to school; by the age of ten

she was absorbing everything she could find, from *Jane Eyre* to her grandfather's copy of *Diseases of the Horse*. She learned the piano from the age of eight and by 13 was playing with a semi-professional concert party called 'The Mayfairs'. At the County School, Ashford, she loved exams and was assured by her teachers that she was certain to win a scholarship to Oxford; but there was no question of her going to university at all, since her upkeep would have been far beyond her parents' means. Instead, at 15, she joined the Inland Revenue as a clerk.

Shortly after the outbreak of the Second World War, she married Wesley Baldry, but the marriage did not endure and they were divorced in 1949. During the war she served in the National Fire Service until being invalided out in 1944.

Having had singing lessons, in 1946 she was taken on as a member of the embryonic opera company at Covent Garden. For three years she sang in the chorus, and took a small solo role in *The Magic Flute*. She absorbed the atmosphere of the Opera House and left with a phenomenal knowledge of music which was to prove invaluable to her in her quiz career. At Covent Garden she had met another singer, Eddie Thomas (brother of the novelist Gwyn Thomas), and in 1950 they were married. Lean times followed, and for several years she made ends meet by playing the piano and singing in pubs. Later she joined the chorus of the ice pantomimes at Wembley, which in turn led to 15 years' work as a session musician with George Mitchell. She provided the backing for films and detergent commercials, and appeared as a sequinned chorus girl in *Saturday Night at the London Palladium*.

In 1959, she underwent successful surgery for cancer. While convalescing, she saw an advertisement for Mensa, took the test and discovered that she had an IQ of 159. This encouraged her to take part in the radio programme *What Do You Know?* (later *Brain of Britain*), which she won in 1961. She then applied for the *Round Britain Quiz*, but was turned down. Undeterred, the next year she defeated two other Brains of Britain to take the title 'Brain of Brains'.

She then began to make appearances on television and radio quizzes, including *Ask Me Another* (on which she won enough kitchen cupboards to equip a barracks), and *Sale of the Century*, on which she won prizes worth more than she had ever earned in a year. But it took seven years of patient letters to the BBC before she was allowed to appear on *Round Britain Quiz* in 1967. 'I had almost lost hope of disturbing the monastic calm of the Quiz with the presence of an ex-chorus girl,' she recalled. From 1973, when the programme returned after several years off the air, she became a permanent member of the London panel. By the time the programme finally came to an end in 1995, she was, with John Julius Norwich, its most senior contestant.

During the 1970s and 1980s, Irene Thomas appeared on numerous radio quiz shows, including *The Gardening Quiz* (though she had no garden). In 1974 she was question master on *Who Said That?* and in the same year, with Roy Hudd, presented *The 60-70-80 Show*, an educational television series aimed at retired people. She wrote a regular column for *Woman and Home* magazine and in the late 1990s became a panellist on the radio quiz show *X Marks the Spot*.

Irene Thomas was a firm believer in the value of good manners and in 1986 became patron of the Polite Society (now the Campaign for Courtesy). She published a memoir, *The Bandsman's Daughter*, in 1979.

She is survived by her husband.

3 April 2001

ELSIE WATERS

Partner in a famous sisterly comic double-act

*

Elsie Waters, the comedienne who has died aged 95, played Gert to her sister's Daisy in the celebrated double-act which flourished during the heyday of Variety in the 1930s and 1940s. Never raucous or suggestive, they appealed to wireless and theatre audiences because they were so much more polite than most comedians of the day. As two ordinary charladies, Gert and Daisy dispensed gentle cockney humour as they gossiped about boyfriends, husbands and relations, occasionally breaking into song. Gert had a boyfriend named Wally, and the state of their engagement was a staple topic of their chat: Daisy was more forthrightly married, to the less genteel Bert.

In spite of its banal content, their material – which was all their own – was once threatened with censorship. The offending dialogue went thus:

'How's Bert?'
'He's got lumbago.'
'Has he had it before?'
'No, he always gets it behind.'

When the Birmingham Watch Committee heard that such ribaldry was coming its way, it demanded the deletion of those lines. The sisters replied that they had played it the week before at a Command Performance before King George and Queen Mary and 'they didn't complain.' This proved sufficient answer.

Elsie Waters was born at Bromley-by-Bow in 1896, the second of six children, all of whom were sent to the Guildhall School of Music and to elocution lessons. Elsie's younger brother later became the actor Jack Warner, who played Dixon of Dock

Green for 20 years. Elsie and Doris began their career with charity concerts at the houses of friends. Elsie played the violin and Doris the piano. In those days Doris told the funny stories and Elsie hardly spoke at all.

Their big break came after a church hall concert. The parson, impressed by their amiable act, rang a firm of booking agents and suggested they look at the sisters.

'I don't know why they booked us, I'm sure,' Elsie used to say. 'They put us on first turn at the Alhambra! Imagine it! All we could hear was people coming into their seats.' Afterwards Elsie placed the following announcement in the *Sunday Referee*, a newspaper used by theatricals to promote their wares: 'Elsie and Doris Waters, all last week, first turn, three times daily, at the London Alhambra – thereby disproving the old saying "You can only die once".'

Chastened, they returned to private functions, and in 1929 began to make gramophone records. Their light-hearted songs were hardly sensational, but for a while the sisters filled each two or three-minute side of a record without much difficulty. One day, they decided to do a talking record. Everyone loves a wedding, they reasoned, so that was the subject they chose. Doris wrote a tune, Elsie the words, and they both thought up some jokes. All they needed were names. 'I'll call you Gert because I like saying it,' said Doris. Elsie called her Daisy because 'there is always a Daisy in a group of Cockney women'. Their first 'patter record' came out in September 1930.

Daisy: 'It reminds me of my brother's wedding. He got
     married last week.'
Gert: 'What, 'Arry?'
Daisy: 'Yes.'
Gert: 'No!'
Daisy: 'Yes!'
Gert: 'No!'
Daisy: 'Don't say "no" when I'm telling you "yes!"'

Gert: 'How did he come to meet her?'

Daisy: 'He didn't – she overtook him.'

Gert: 'Is she nice?'

Daisy: 'No, I don't like her much – first time she come in the place, she upset a cup of tea all over our clean table cloth and we hadn't even read it.'

The script may now have lost some of its freshness; but ten days after the record's release, the sisters' recording manager announced: 'You've struck oil.'

Gert and Daisy had a ring of realism, and during the Second World War they reached the height of their popularity with sketches about food rationing, absent husbands and the like, which they performed down the Underground in the Blitz. The sisters' dribbling Cockney gossip made little impression on television, but they continued working on the stage – their last engagement was a South African tour in 1973. They were inseparable until Doris died 12 years ago.

Elsie and Doris were appointed OBE in 1946. Forty years later Elsie received the Burma Star at the Burma Star Association's reunion, for having entertained the troops of the 'Forgotten Army', and Doris was included posthumously in the award. They were also honoured when a pair of elephants at the zoo were named after their alter egos.

15 June 1990

FRIEDA PUSHNIK

Freak show artiste with Barnum and Bailey

*

Frieda Pushnik, who has died in California aged 77, was among the last surviving freak show artistes to have worked for the

Barnum and Bailey Circus. A botched appendectomy on her pregnant mother had severed all four of Frieda's limbs before birth. Yet Frieda showed true grit in adapting to her circumstances and carried her sideshow performances beyond the realm of mere oddity. She was billed as the 'Armless and Legless Wonder', and her act, consisting of five-minute demonstrations of such skills as writing, typing and sewing, was performed by holding implements between her one small stump of an arm and her chin. All the while, she would amuse the audience with her repartee.

She was never resentful of her condition, nor demeaned by her status as a sideshow freak. When an interviewer asked her whether she thought it acceptable to exploit disability for entertainment, she replied, with a characteristic snap: 'If you're paid for it, yeah.'

Frieda Katherine Pushnik was born at Connemaugh, Pennsylvania, on 10 February 1923. Early on, her mother insisted she try to do everything for herself, and through sheer force of will she taught herself all kinds of skills. Aged nine, she was discovered by Robert L. Ripley, the founder of Ripley's 'Believe it or not!' sideshows. In 1933, she appeared at the World's Fair in Chicago, billed by Ripley as 'The Little Half Girl'. Accompanied by her mother and sister on tour with Ripley's, Frieda would present her short act several times an hour for 16 hours a day. At the World's Fair, more than two million people paid to see her. She toured with Ripley for six years and then in 1943 joined the Ringling Brothers and Barnum and Bailey Circus, travelling with them for the next 13 years.

After retiring in 1956, she and her mother went to live with Frieda's sister Erma and her husband, who built her a specially adapted house. She always enjoyed recalling her days as a sideshow star.

24 April 2001

KYRA VAYNE

*Soprano who performed with Gigli and Gobbi in the 1950s but
then endured 40 years of obscurity before finding fresh celebrity*

*

Kyra Vayne, the soprano, who has died aged 84, achieved a
celebrity in her last years that had obstinately eluded her in her
prime during the 1950s, when she had sung with Gigli, Gobbi
and Janet Baker.

The resurgence of interest in Kyra Vayne began in the early
1990s, when an Austrian label issued two discs of her recordings
made between the 1940s and the 1970s. These revealed a voice
of uncommon beauty which had been used intelligently in a
wide variety of repertory. Part of the music had been recorded
privately, the rest by the BBC. Some opera-lovers were astonished that such a talent had been so neglected, for Kyra Vayne
had latterly worked as a secretary in a bank and was living on
income support in a small flat in London, kept company only by
her cats. She was rapidly taken up by the media, interviewed in
newspapers, and invited to appear on *Desert Island Discs*. In 1999,
she published her autobiography, *A Voice Reborn*.

This purported to tell the story of an artist to whom the fates
had been unkind, and who had suffered from the machinations
of those central to both her professional and her private life.
But those old enough to remember her performances on the
stage were more cautious in their appraisal than her new
generation of admirers. They recalled a singer of somewhat
limited acting ability who, though possessed of a natural voice
that might have taken her further, was also a difficult person
with whom to work. Certainly this was the experience, too, of
some of those who had to deal with her after her late re-emer-
gence from obscurity. The only indisputable merit of her

sudden stardom was that at least it had brought her the attention she had so long desired.

She was born Kyra Knopmuss in St Petersburg on 29 January 1916. Her parents were both of Russo-Germanic stock, offshoots of the Baltic nobility. At the start of the Russian Revolution her father was an army officer and director of the Imperial horseshoe factory. While he was working there one day, the Bolsheviks came to arrest him. He exchanged clothes with his chauffeur and left by the back entrance, expecting his driver to be arrested in his place, and then released when the Bolsheviks realized their mistake. Instead, the revolutionaries stormed the building and shot dead the man they took to be Maxim Knopmuss.

For a few years the family were able to continue living in their large apartment on the Nevsky Prospekt. Kyra recalled with a shudder her father's attempts to teach her to swim by forcibly submerging her in the icy River Neva. But in 1924, with the death of Lenin and the advent of Stalin, the Knopmusses decided to leave Russia for England, where Kyra's father found a job as a banker, although he soon lost all he had in the stock market crash of 1929. Quite out of her element, Kyra was sent to a school at Honor Oak, south London, where an eccentric schoolmistress taught the girls algebra while trimming her toenails.

Kyra did not discover that she could sing until she was 16, when she began appearing with a Russian Orthodox church choir. She then had voice lessons with Horatio Davies and the soprano Mignon Nevada, paying for her tuition by appearing in touring shows such as *Balalaika*, *Choo Chin Chow*, and *Show Boat*.

When war came, Vic Oliver, the radio comedian, who was looking for someone who could sing Russian gypsy songs, signed her up for his programme. According to her account, he exploited her talents while paying her very little, and she was glad to move on to entertaining the troops with ENSA. She changed her stage name first to Vronska, and then to Vayne in deference to anti-Soviet feeling. While at Aldershot in 1941, she was invited to audition for the new Russian Opera Company. She made such an impression that she was engaged to sing the lead mezzo role of Khivria in a production of Mussorgsky's rarely heard *Sorochintsy Fair*, to be conducted by Anatole Fistoulari at the Savoy Theatre, London. The staging was extremely well received and further engagements followed.

After the war she was able to begin her international career, and in Spain in 1949 she enjoyed success in Rimsky-Korsakov's *The Invisible City of Kitezh* as Fevronia, a role that might have been written for her Slav-tinted lyric soprano. In 1953, she had another success at the Maggio Musicale, Florence, in Dargomizhsky's *The Stone Guest*, and the next year in Rome was Tosca, the role for she became best known. She also sang with Carlo Bergonzi in *La Forza del Destino* and in 1955 sang Santuzza to Beniamino Gigli's Tirridu in the tenor's last appearance, a performance of *Cavalleria Rusticana* at Recanati, his birthplace.

Kyra Vayne later appeared in London with the Welsh National Opera, although with only intermittent success. Covent Garden never called on her talents. Then in 1957 her manager Eugene Iskoldoff committed suicide, and this blow, together with numerous other vicissitudes (many of them, by her account, involving grasping men), left Kyra destitute. For eight years she worked as a secretary, occasionally fulfilling engagements such as singing Stravinsky's *Les Noces* alongside Janet Baker. However, in 1965 she decided to retire completely from opera. She gave away her piano, sold her stage jewellery to the Royal Opera House, and thereafter worked both as a secretary and as a restorer of ceramics. This allowed a personality that was always somewhat self-absorbed to contemplate such questions as (she recorded in *A Voice Reborn*) 'Why did I never become a megastar?' She was inclined to believe this was due to her low self-esteem.

Her rediscovery began when the Russian section of the World Service found some tapes of her old performances. Soon, compact discs of these recordings were in considerable demand. The last act of what had been a rather topsy-turvy life came when she was invited to sing at the Bolshoi Theatre, Moscow, on Millennium Eve. To her credit, although she relished the attention, Kyra Vayne remained sanguine about her new fame. 'Suddenly I'm spoken of as one of the great voices,' she said. 'I just scream with laughter when I hear this. It's idiotic.'

She never married.

15 January 2001

PORTLAND MASON

Film star's daughter said to have smoked when she was only three and to have had a couture dress at four

*

Portland Mason, who has died aged 55, was the daughter of the film star James Mason, and used to be routinely described in the press as 'the world's most precocious child'.

Born in Los Angeles on 26 November 1948, Portland Mason's early years were spent in Hollywood, where her parents' house, built in the 1920s by Buster Keaton, was appointed with every luxury. When she was two she was allowed to go to bed at midnight. She was presented with her first couture evening gown when she was four. At six she appeared on television dressed in furs, diamonds and stiletto heels. In 1956, when she was seven, she accompanied her parents on a visit to London, prompting the *Daily Express* to observe that she already owned a mink coat and that she had a 'Mamie Eisenhower fringe to her coiffured hair'. James Mason himself remarked at the time: 'We want Portland to be able to do what she likes, how she likes, and when she likes. That way we feel she will achieve a personality of her own.'

The child's mother, Pamela (Kellino) Mason, added that their daughter was already working on her memoirs: 'We are doing it by just letting her talk into a tape recorder. I am prompting her with questions like, "What do you think of divorce?"' When Portland was only three, her father had introduced her to cigarettes. His master plan was that they would cause her to cough, thus encouraging her to avoid smoking in her later years. When, a short time afterwards, a friend asked Mason for a progress report, the screen star replied: 'Well, she's now up to two packs a day.'

In December 1958 it was reported that Portland had celebrated her tenth birthday by going shopping in Los Angeles for bras and a girdle. Meanwhile, she attended the El Rodeo School in Beverly Hills, being delivered every morning by a Rolls-Royce and collected in the afternoon by a white Cadillac. Her favourite scent was Arpège. Whether all this added up to an accurate impression of Portland Mason's character is doubtful. She went on to drama school and then tried modelling, and by the time she was 18, and living in London, a journalist who interviewed her found her 'surprisingly unspoilt, somewhat shy and unassuming'.

By now she was already a veteran of a number of films. Aged seven she had starred in a picture called *The Child* (1954), directed by her father. She had appeared on television; played Gregory Peck's daughter in *The Man in the Gray Flannel Suit* (1956); and had had parts in two films starring her father, *Bigger Than Life* (1956) and *Cry Terror* (1958). At one stage it looked as though she might even secure the part of Lolita in Stanley Kubrick's 1962 film of Nabokov's novel, but the role was taken by Sue Lyon. In 1966 she was in *The Great St Trinian's Train Robbery*, and two years later had a part in *Sebastian*, which starred Dirk Bogarde. She also appeared on the British stage: in 1967 she was at the Vaudeville in London, playing Hester in *A Woman of No Importance*. She later became a scriptwriter, and made her home in California.

In 1964 Portland Mason's parents' marriage was dissolved after 22 years. Her father died 20 years later, leaving a second wife, the actress Clarissa Kaye. There then began a bitter dispute over his estate between Clarissa and Mason's two children, Portland and her younger brother Morgan (the film producer, married to the singer Belinda Carlisle). Mason had left everything to Clarissa, leaving his children to, as he put it, 'stand in line' for their inheritance. They decided to contest the will. Even the disposal of James Mason's ashes became a matter of dispute. Clarissa had refused to hand them over to the children, preferring to keep them in an urn on the mantelpiece at the house she had shared with Mason at Vevey, overlooking Lake Geneva. After her death in 1994, it was discovered that the ashes had been transferred to a safety deposit box. In 1999 a Swiss court finally ruled that the ashes should be given to Portland and Morgan. In November 2000 brother and sister were finally able to scatter their father's ashes beneath his marble monument in the cemetery at Vevey. A few months after this ceremony, Portland Mason suffered a serious stroke.

Recently she had been working on a book about her father. She is survived by her husband, Rob Schuyler.

3 June 2004

BEATRICE LILLIE

Theatrical comedienne who delighted in comic chaos both on and off the stage

*

Beatrice Lillie, otherwise Lady Peel, who has died aged 94, was a theatrical entertainer of genius. Her credits stretched from revue in the 1920s, when she sang Noel Coward's *Poor Little Rich Girl*, to the musicals *Auntie Mame* and *High Spirits* in the 1950s and 1960s, when she also scored a success as a villainous Chinese madam in the film *Thoroughly Modern Millie* opposite Julie Andrews and Carol Channing. Along the way she toured the world with her brilliant one-woman show, *An Evening With Beatrice Lillie*.

Like the accepted wit who has only to say: 'Pass the mustard, please,' to set the table guffawing, Miss Lillie was never anything but funny on or off stage. She had a reputation as a prankster, and in 1951 ordered a live alligator from Harrods and sent it to Noël Coward with the message: 'So what else is new?' But Miss Lillie was no actress. Nature did not intend her to create any character except her eccentric own. If she tried her hand at legitimate drama or indeed any show where the lines were presumed to be sacrosanct, she only caused chaos. Whatever success she had in such circumstances was usually won at the expense of the play and her fellow-players (not to mention the director). Yet her kind of chaos was apt to be more enjoyable than anybody else's order, and was relished for its wrecking effect in musicals like *Auntie Mame* and *High Spirits*.

It was in revue or as a solo turn that 'Bea' Lillie won the affection of theatre-goers the world over, to the extent of becoming a cult with her ability to demolish social pretence. An inflected eyebrow, a furtive sniff, a sotto voce growl or a steely grimace (her repertoire of grimaces was limitless) were her favourite weapons. Words hardly mattered as she chattered incoherently because the pulling of faces, shooting of glances, the under-the-breath murmurs and the disdainful corners of the mouth expressed all she had to say. And because she seemed incapable of taking anything or anyone seriously, least of all herself, she enjoyed adulation on both sides of the Atlantic for over half a century, though it was in America where her scatty and spontaneous comedy was most appreciated.

From being one of André Charlot's discoveries in the 1920s, and sharing the limelight with Gertrude Lawrence, she veered

into variety and musical comedy, but it was not for acting, singing or dancing that she was revered. It was for clowning, and this
she brought to a peak in the 1950s with her much-travelled one-
woman show. She had the gift of making everything she did look
fresh, however often she had done it. Her impishness revelled in
being inexplicable. The cropped hair tightly hidden by a pink
fez, the long cigarette holder as something to toy with, the tendency to bang her head inexplicably but repeatedly against the
proscenium arch: these were beyond rational explanation, like
much of her humour.

Her art, though eluding, had something of the amiable air of
a game of charades. She had a trick of seeming to ignore the
audience so that her private fantasies might be indulged as if
unperceived. It was, however, the unexpected and impromptu-
seeming side of her fooling which made it so different, summed
up perhaps by the story of a pigeon which flew by chance into
her apartment. 'Any messages?' she asked blandly.

She made many film appearances (including *Around the World
in 80 Days*) and something of her garbled, mimic's joking came
through, as it did in her work on television. But her off-the-cuff,
buttonholing fun required a playhouse or cabaret in which to
flourish. Rarely did she need to drag topical events into the spray
of light, larky satire. To set the house on a roar she had merely
to come up with a warbled complaint about the 'wind round my
heart', or to muse upon a hostess who had ordered a dozen
double-damask dinner table napkins, or to attack the proscenium
arch with her head, or to moralise on a friend called Maud
whom she accused of being 'rotten to the core'.

The daughter of a school-master from Co. Down, Beatrice
Gladys Lillie was born in Toronto in 1894. Reputedly expelled
aged eight from the church choir for making faces while singing
hymns, she left school at 15 to move to England with her mother
and sister. At 16 she sang in the bill at Chatham music hall and
later that year appeared at the London Pavilion in *The Daring of*

Diane and at the Alhambra in the revue *Not Likely*. It was the celebrated Anglo-French producer Charlot who perceived and encouraged the Canadian girl's unusual style. She worked in shows with titles like: *Now's The Time, Samples, Cheep, Tabs, Oh Joy, Bran-Pie, Now and Then, Pot Luck* and (her first legitimate role) *Up In Mabel's Room*.

In 1920 Miss Lillie married Robert Peel, great-grandson of the famous Victorian statesman Sir Robert Peel. He was a Guards officer who resigned and became a sheep farmer and racehorse owner. In 1925 when her father-in-law died and her husband succeeded to the baronetcy, Bea Lillie became Lady Peel. 'Get me', which was one of her catchwords, was applied on more occasions than that when social posturing needed puncturing. Sometimes, however, the title landed her in difficulties as when her routine about a suburban snob down on her luck ('I always had my own 'orses') was taken literally by an embarrassed Mid-Western audience. Unbeknown to Miss Lillie she had been billed as 'Lady Peel'.

In 1928 she appeared in Coward's revue *This Year of Grace* in New York and four years later played the nurse in Shaw's *Too True To Be Good*, but she never looked at home off the light musical stage. Nor was she ever off it for long.

During the 1939–45 War she toured the world, entertaining the troops for ENSA. Her husband had died in 1934, and in 1942 their only child, the 6th Baronet and an Ordinary Seaman, lost his life when the destroyer *Tenedos* in which he was serving was attacked by Japanese dive bombers. After the War she returned to the West End in the revue *Better Late* (at the Garrick, 1946). Then came summer shows, and tours, in America. In the 1950s *An Evening With Beatrice Lillie* set the seal on her popular but subtle art. She appeared in the *Ziegfeld Follies* of 1957 on Broadway, and in 1958 took over the title role in Patrick Dennis's *Auntie Mame* from Greer Garson in New York before playing the same part in London. At the Edinburgh Festival in

1960 she returned to her revue form in *A Late Evening With Beatrice Lillie*.

In the mid-1970s she suffered a stroke and became bedridden. In 1977 she was brought back to England from New York to be nursed. She died at her home in Henley-on-Thames.

21 January 1989

VICTORIA KINGSLEY

Collector of songs who could chant in Gaelic and accompany herself on an instrument made from the carapace of the hairy armadillo

*

Victoria Kingsley, who has died aged 100, acted with travelling players and collected folk songs from around the world. She believed that the only way to learn such music was at source: 'I always preferred to learn from people rather than books. I felt I learnt about the inside of the song along with getting to know the person who taught me.'

She had become interested in music while at RADA in the 1920s, but it did not become her life's work until the 1930s. She went to Spain to study with Emilio Pujol, the classical guitarist and editor of early music, and returned home with many Catalan tunes. She also became interested in Hebridean songs and spent time on Barra to learn enough Gaelic to sing them authentically, without accompaniment.

In 1949, she travelled through South America, giving concerts and collecting songs in Uruguay, Brazil and Argentina. She rode with gauchos, listened to shoeshine boys sing while tapping out accompaniments with their brushes, and was taught cuca rhythms by a Chilean dressmaker. She added coffee-pounding songs and a ritual chant to the Afro-Brazilian god of thunder to her repertoire. Among the musical instruments she acquired and played was a charango (a ten-stringed instrument which uses the carapace of the hairy armadillo as a sounding box). The next year, she managed to attach herself to a party of ophthalmic surgeons visiting India and embarked on a five-month concert tour of the subcontinent, broadcasting on radio and being hailed as 'the cultural ambassadress from Britain'.

By now she had acquired a considerable reputation at home and gave recitals at the Wigmore Hall, Royal Festival Hall and Cecil Sharp House that drew large audience and won praise from the critics. But the audiences were not always large. 'Masterly recital by Victoria Kingsley – but very few heard her,' ran one dispiriting headline in a Cambridge newspaper.

In 1952, she set off on a world tour, taking in the United States, Mexico, Honolulu, Australia, New Zealand, India and Ceylon. She cheerfully told reporters: 'I shall earn my living as I go. If I run short of dollars, I'll try and earn a bit as a home help.'

From every trip she brought back new material, and although some critics complained that her voice lacked power, all agreed that she was able to put across a song in any language. She presented her one-woman show, *Mosaic*, at the Edinburgh Festival for three years running in the 1960s. The *Daily Telegraph*'s Peter Clayton called it 'the strangest event' of the 1966 Fringe. 'Miss Kingsley sings, recites, dresses up as a statue, whistles and plays lute, guitar, charango and drum in a bewildering collection of items ranging from songs by Thomas Campion to Argentinian folk songs.'

She was born Hilda Victoria Parker on 23 May 1900, the daughter of the owner of the Penketh Tannery Company, Warrington. Her father believed that the best education was to be had in Scotland, and Victoria followed her sisters to St Leonard's School in Fife. She soon tired of life as a young unmarried woman, but turned down a proposal of marriage from the manager of a local cinema. At a summer school in Greek dancing at Oxford, she met a woman don who suggested that she should come to the University. On the strength of this recommendation (and her prowess at hockey), Victoria Parker matriculated in 1920. A bout of mumps led to a disappointing Third in Finals, but she was in the first batch of women to be awarded a degree by Oxford. She also won her hockey Blue.

While at Oxford she saw a production of *Romeo and Juliet* and was so disgusted by the performance of the leading actress that she determined to go on the stage. She got into RADA and turned out to be the only pupil in a production of a Shakespeare play who was prepared to perform a song. The play was directed by Claude Rains, who suggested an unauthentic piano accompaniment for the song. But she decided instead to buy a guitar and a book explaining simple chords. Within ten days she was singing and playing on stage.

On leaving RADA, she took the stage name of Victoria Kingsley and went into repertory, enjoying some success in a London production of *Dracula*. During the early 1930s she set up a travelling theatre company with her former professor of Mime and Gesture, Suzanne Stone.

The Noah's Ark Theatre toured the country, with the players sleeping in tents and putting on shows in theatres, schools and village halls. Audiences were promised 'A Programme of Unusual Variety comprising Acting, Singing, Dancing and Mime'. An evening's entertainment might include extracts from the medieval miracle play *Noah's Flood*, Fielding's burlesque *Tom Thumb*, the Victorian ballad *Villikins and His Dinah*, Chekhov's *The Bear*, Wilde's *The Florentine Tragedy* and 'costume renderings of Shakespearean sonnets', interspersed with Flemish folk songs and Japanese dances.

Victoria Kingsley designed and made many of the sets, costumes and masks, all of which were transported in the dicky seats of the company's motor cars. Her passion, however, was international folk music, and when the Ark hit the rocks she began travelling to gather songs. She lost no chances to widen her repertoire. When a West Indian company put on a ballet in Westbourne Grove, west London, she persuaded them to teach her drumming. When she followed the Brazilian singer Olga Coelho to Paris, she took the opportunity to study there with the flamenco player Aliro Diaz.

After retiring from the concert platform, she concentrated on writing. She had long been a member of the Society of Women Writers and Journalists, serving on its committee. But the stories she wrote and illustrated for her great nephews and nieces failed to find a publisher, and she was unable to interest the BBC in her television adaptation of George Meredith's *The Egoist*.

In later years, Victoria Kingsley became a keen member of the Highgate Poets, and issued several pamphlets of whimsical and satirical *Relevant Rhymes*.

She never married.

4 October 2000

EVA GABOR

Starlet who specialised in jewels, mink and matrimony

*

Eva Gabor, who has died in Los Angeles aged 74, was the youngest of three Hungarian-born sisters, all actresses by profession and celebrities by instinct. Magda, Sari (Zsa Zsa) and Eva Gabor shared a predilection for jewellery, mink and matrimony, notching up 19 husbands between them. Five of these husbands belonged to the petite (5ft 2in) Eva, who was given to addressing all and sundry as 'dahlink'. 'Hello, Mr President, dahlink,' she greeted Lyndon Johnson.

But she never appreciated being mistaken for her sister Zsa

Zsa. 'I'm much tinier,' she would say, 'and thinner.' She also took pride in having worked for her living: 'unlike my sister, I have never accepted alimony.' No less beautiful than Zsa Zsa, Eva often appeared the lighter spirit. She revelled in the role of exotic emigrée, and insisted that her mink should be the same colour as her hair and her pets.

On one occasion she tried to smuggle one of her Yorkshire terriers through Customs by hiding it under her jacket. 'It was ridiculous, really,' she recalled. 'I was staring deep into the eyes of the official and trying to distract him but he just said, "Miss Gabor, your mink is staring at me too."'

Arriving in Hollywood before the Second World War, Eva appeared over the next 25 years in numerous films without making much of a mark in any of them. Her chic and elegant performance in the remake of *My Man Godfrey* (with David Niven, 1957) was one of her few cinema roles to win good reviews. Her first notable success came on stage in 1950, when she landed the part of Mignonette, an acrobat turned maid in Richard Rodgers's musical *The Happy Time*. This led to a daily television programme, *The Eva Gabor Show*, and to a well received performance as Elena in a television production of *Uncle Vanya*. But another venture on the small screen, *Famous Women in History*, seemed to have put paid to her television career.

In 1956 she returned to the stage as a countess who destroyed her lovers in Frank Wedekind's *The Little Glass Clock*, but the production closed after eight performances. Two years later, in *Lulu*, her attempts to convey poignancy by pirouetting around the stage in ballet shoes evoked only mirth from the audience. On the other hand, Noël Coward, who directed Eva Gabor as Joanna in *Present Laughter* in 1958, described her as 'adorable to work with, no trouble and determined to be good'.

By the end of the 1950s Eva Gabor was principally employed as an advertising model. But in 1963 she took over from Vivien Leigh as Tatiana in the musical *Tovarich,* and two years later unexpectedly triumphed as Lisa Douglas, a glamorous city girl stuck on a farm in the television comedy series *Green Acres*. Eager to demonstrate how much more reliable she was than the temperamental Zsa Zsa, Eva worked on *Green Acres* from dawn to dusk five days a week for six years, obeying directorial whims without a murmur. Her industry was rewarded by a fortune in fees, later increased by re-runs. 'I was hurt,' she reflected, 'that people were so shocked when I gave a good performance, and that suddenly after 25 years I was discovered.'

Eva Gabor was born in Budapest on 11 February 1921. Her father was a former cavalry major who owned a jewellery business; her mother, who believed she had come down in the world, planned brilliant marriages for her daughters. 'I promise that you will all be rich and famous,' she told them, 'and you will all marry kings.' To that end, she urged her girls to acquire every accomplishment. 'When will you be able to do that?' she demanded when they saw a fire-eater at a circus.

By the age of four Eva was set on Hollywood. In the late 1930s, accompanied by her first husband, she arrived in the United States; and almost immediately – on the recommendation of a dentist who had been struck by her potential when extracting a tooth – gained a contract with Paramount. Eva learned English by attending the local cinema twice a day for eight months – though few were convinced by her claim that thenceforward she had to assume a Hungarian accent. She also divested herself of her first husband, who disapproved of Hollywood. Curiously she filed for divorce on the grounds that he had forced her into acting when she had wanted to settle down and have children.

Eva Gabor's first film was *Forced Landing* (1941), which she described as 'a B-picture only to those too lazy to go down the alphabet'. Subsequently she had parts in *The Wife of Monte Cristo* (1946), *Song of Surrender* (1949), *The Mad Magician* (1954), *The Last Time I Saw Paris* (1954), *Gigi* (1958), *Youngblood Hawke* (1964) and many others.

As her vision of Hollywood stardom faded, so Eva Gabor began to diversify into television and repertory theatre. It was her role as a French girl in a live broadcast of *L'Amour the Merrier*, that persuaded Richard Rodgers to cast her in *The Happy Time*.

Eva Gabor gave up acting in the 1970s. A student of the *Wall Street Journal*, she successfully formed a wig company, Eva Gabor International. She took a keen interest in horticulture, and became one of the biggest non-commercial orchid growers in the United States. In 1988 she came out of retirement to record the voice of an aristocratic mouse in the cartoon *The Rescuers*. She had also been heard in *The Aristocats* (1970). She published an autobiography, *Orchids and Salami* (1954).

Eva Gabor married first, in 1939 (dissolved 1942), Dr Eric Drimmer; secondly, in 1943 (dissolved 1950), Charles Isaacs, a property tycoon; thirdly, in 1956 (dissolved 1957), Dr John Williams, a surgeon; fourthly, in 1959 (dissolved 1973), Richard Brown, a former stockbroker; and fifthly, in 1973 (dissolved 1986), Frank Jameson, a businessman.

Men, she concluded in 1986, were a necessary evil, whatever the perils of matrimony. 'I could not possibly live without them, nor do I intend to. Sex is very good for pimples.'

6 July 1995

PAOLA BORBONI

Actress known as 'Paola of the scandals' who stunned 1920s Italy by baring her breasts on stage

*

Paola Borboni, who has died aged 95, was the *grande dame* of the Italian stage, whose willingness to shock earned her the soubriquet 'Paola of the scandals'. In 1925 she stunned the audience at one production by flagrantly baring her breasts, causing, a journalist noted, 'the use of more binoculars than at San Siro [the Milanese race course] in 50 years'. 'I was neither sensual nor vulgar,' recalled Borboni. 'I was just young and my bare breasts didn't bother anyone, not even Il Duce.'

In the course of a career that spanned eight decades, she appeared in hundreds of productions by playwrights ranging from Pirandello to Eugene O'Neill. She attracted headlines for her personal life as much as for her professional career. In 1972, aged 72, she married an actor more than 40 years her junior. Six years later he was killed in a car accident, in which Borboni's thigh was broken.

'After 90,' she recently observed, 'intelligent women reduce their sexual expectations.'

Paola Borboni was born at Golese, Parma, on 1 January 1900. Her father was an opera entrepreneur who squandered his wife's wealth on unsuccessful ventures. Paola made her stage debut at 16, and soon formed a company to perform the plays of Luigi Pirandello, at one point even selling her jewels to keep the troupe going.

After the Second World War Borboni appeared in a wide range of plays, and performed monologues which prominent Italian authors wrote specifically for her. In 1992, Mario Luzi, one of Italy's leading poets, wrote a one-woman play about Borboni's life; she was unable to perform it. Her last stage role was in 1994. She retired to a nursing home, where she liked to wear evening dress. After her death she lay in state, in an elegant black dress she had chosen 30 years before, in anticipation of the occasion.

27 April 1995

CORAL BROWNE

*Actress who excelled at duchesses and dragons and appeared in
a film about her real life encounter in Moscow with the spy
Guy Burgess*

*

Coral Browne, the actress who has died aged 77, was one of the
most elegant and sophisticated players of her time – notable
almost as much for her waspish wit and sexual candour off-stage
as for her allure on it. She will be remembered especially for two
films. In real life, on tour in Moscow, she had met the spy Guy
Burgess, and in Alan Bennett's brilliant treatment *An Englishman
Abroad* (1983) she recreated this incident, including some of the
original conversation. Burgess, who found solace in his exile by
continually playing the music of Jack Buchanan, asked Coral
Browne if she had known him. 'I suppose so,' the actress replied,
'I almost married him.' The other film, *Dreamchild* (1986), was
about Lewis Carroll. In it Miss Browne gave an affecting
account of the later life of Alice Liddell, who inspired Alice in
Wonderland.

On the stage Miss Browne excelled at playing duchesses or
dragons – or, above all, Edwardian women with a past. With her
striking dark looks, lustrous brown eyes, blitheness of spirit and
ability to remain poised in a crisis, she had tremendous stage
presence, which saw her safely through anything from light
comedy to Shakespearean tragedy, from farce to melodrama. As
for her off-stage persona, her irreverent witticisms, real and
apocryphal, became legendary. She had a deep, throaty voice and
impeccable timing. It is not difficult to imagine the effect of her
whispered but reverberating aside as a giant golden phallus was
unveiled at the end of Peter Brook's production of *Oedipus*:
'Nobody we know, darling.'

No less memorable was her description of her affair with Cecil Beaton during the Second World War. When doubters queried the photographer's romance with Greta Garbo, Coral Browne would indignantly defend his masculinity, recalling that 'Cecil was very passionate, and I should know. I've been under the bridges in my time. He asked me to lunch and then to dinner. But I really was extremely surprised when the great leap took place. I didn't even have time to say "Gosh".' Another story has her casting a lubricious eye over a young actor, only to be assured by a friend, David Dodimead, that the cause was hopeless. Undaunted, Coral Browne bet Dodimead £1 that she could gain her end that very night. Her friends waited anxiously for the outcome. 'Dodders,' the actress drawled when she saw him across a crowded room the next morning, 'I owe you twelve and sixpence.'

The only daughter of a restaurateur (who spelt his surname without an 'e') Coral Edith Browne was born in Melbourne, Australia, on 23 July 1913 and was educated at Claremont Ladies' College. Her theatrical career began by chance. Studying at art school, she was suddenly seconded to the Melbourne repertory theatre when the stage designer died. Shortly afterwards the actress playing a woman 'living in sin' in Galsworthy's *Loyalties* succumbed to sickness, and Miss Browne, still only 16, replaced her. At 18 she played Hedda Gabler, and by the time she was 21 she had appeared in a number of productions, including *Dear Brutus*, *The Quaker Girl*, *Hay Fever* and *The Apple Cart*.

As a 21st birthday present her father gave her £50 to visit London, on condition that she returned home as soon as it was spent. For a time it looked as though this promise might be kept.

With her theatrical experience, energy, looks – and an introduction to Marie Tempest – Coral Browne must have been disappointed to land nothing better than understudy to Nora Swinburne in a play called *Lover's Leap*. It was seven years before she made a real mark. Good parts in two successful American comedies, *The Man Who Came to Dinner* (1941) and *My Sister Eileen* (1943), resulted in leading roles in such celebrated revivals as *The Last of Mrs Cheyney* (1944) and *Lady Frederick* (1946). The period after the war, though, proved to have little to offer an actress whose trademark was elegance. For a time no new dramatists appeared, and when they did they showed scant interest in drawing rooms. The far-sighted Browne must have noticed the red light looming, for in 1951 she made her first appearance in Shakespeare, joining the Old Vic Company to play Emilia in *Othello* and Regan in *King Lear*, parts in which her fine voice and flamboyant manner won acclaim. This venture into the classics was interrupted when she landed a part in *Affairs of State* (1952), adapted from the French, which ran for 18 months. There followed a spell in New York, where she played Zabina in *Tamburlaine the Great*. Back with the Old Vic Company in 1956 she appeared as Lady Macbeth – she also toured America in that part – and as Helen in *Troilus and Cressida*.

In the 1957–58 season she played Gertrude in *Hamlet*, Helena in *A Midsummer Night's Dream* and Goneril in *King Lear*, and joined the Stratford-on-Avon company for another season as Gertrude. It was in that role that she undertook the fateful trip to Moscow, where she met Burgess. Back in London she appeared to great effect in *The Pleasure of His Company* (1959), making an unforgettable entrance in a superb creation by Molyneux ('I've just put on a rag'). Another American play, *Toys In The Attic* (1960), followed, and the next year she played in a French import, *Bonne Soupe*. By now she was equally in demand on Broadway, and when *The Right Honourable Gentleman* (1964), in which she played Mrs Rossiter, ended its run at Her Majesty's, she took the part over to New York.

Coral Browne's performance as Mrs Erlynne in *Lady Windermere's Fan* (1966) suggested that she would have made an admirable Lady Bracknell, but the nearest she ever came to such a role was in Edward Bond's *The Sea* at the Royal Court in

1973. In 1969 she appeared as the nymphomaniac wife, acting mainly in her underwear, in Joe Orton's *What The Butler Saw*, brilliantly balancing anxiety and poise. Her performance was rendered all the more effective by ribald interruptions from the gallery. Unable to retaliate, she took comfort in the elegant underwear which the management had allowed her to buy in Paris for the production: 'Going on stage in nothing but your undies on at my time of life you've got to be wearing something pretty and delicate, otherwise you'd look like old Frilly Lizzie or a can-can girl.' What promised to be a more likely role, that of the Countess of Warwick who threatened to publish love letters from Edward VII in *My Darling Daisy* (1970), proved in fact disappointing, but in Shaw's *Mrs Warren's Profession* (1970), and in two plays by Anouilh – *The Waltz of the Toreadors* (1974) and *Ardele* (1975) – she found parts well worth the acting.

Among her better known films were *The Ruling Class* (1972) and *The Killing Of Sister George* (1968) in which she played, to the great amusement of her friends, a lesbian. One observer noted that she twiddled with Susannah York's nipple as if trying to find Radio Three.

Browne was a Catholic convert. She was once standing on the steps of Brompton Oratory after mass when a theatrical queen bustled up with the latest gossip. She stopped him with: 'I don't want to hear such filth, not with me standing here in a state of fucking grace.'

Coral Browne was married twice. Her first husband was Philip Pearman, whom she married in 1950 and who killed himself in 1964. At his funeral, she looked into his grave and is reported to have said, 'See you later,' before departing to a waiting car.

She met her second husband, the film actor and art historian Vincent Price, whom she married in 1974, in a studio cemetery on the set of a horror film comedy called *Theatre of Blood*. They lived in Los Angeles. There were no children from either marriage. 'I've never seen myself as an old gran,' she once said.

31 May 1991

EVA BARTOK

Film actress more remarkable for her good looks and complicated private life than for her screen performances

*

Eva Bartok, who has died aged 72, had looks which won her parts in any number of forgettable films; her principal talent, however, was providing fodder for gossip columns. In her heyday in the Fifties and Sixties she was rarely out of the news, as she wafted between her penthouse in Rome and her flat in Mayfair. By the age of 32 she had been divorced and married four times, and she was no less profligate with lovers. Should her sex life fail to afford copy, there was her chocolate coloured Rolls-Royce, or her bucket-shaped hats, which set the fashion in both London and Paris.

The publicity surrounding Eva Bartok reached its zenith in 1957, when she gave birth to a daughter. Medically, she explained, this had been made possible by the ministrations of an Indonesian guru called Pak Sabu. The question remained: who was the father? The year before, Eva Bartok had married the German actor Curt Jurgens; soon afterwards, however, she had plunged into an affair with Frank Sinatra. Going to bed with the singer, she insisted, 'had been the most natural thing in the world'. Jurgens disagreed, and they were divorced immediately after her daughter's birth.

Rumour recalled that Eva Bartok had recently made a film, *Ten Thousand Bedrooms* (1957) with Dean Martin. Another putative father, much touted in the press, was the 3rd Marquess of Milford Haven, with whom her name had been linked for years. For once Eva Bartok was divulging nothing, save that the father of her child had not 'grown' sufficiently to be married.

As an actress she was given to bemoaning that her fatal beauty had prevented a proper appreciation of her talent. 'I've been thinking of having the opposite of a nose job,' she said, 'to make myself look unattractive.'

But in 1965, when Eva Bartok appeared in *Winter in Ischia*, a television play by Robin Maugham, Philip Purser observed in the *Daily Telegraph* that her performance was so awful that it should be preserved in the National Film Archive. In that same year she appeared in the West End in a play called *Paint Myself Black*. She looked prettier than ever, Bernard Levin thought, 'and acts even worse'. But Eva Bartok's courage was always a match for the vicissitudes of her career.

She was born Eva Martha Sjoke in Budapest, on 18 June 1926, the daughter of a journalist and an actress. Though she began her acting career with the Budapest Children's Theatre, the advent of the Second World War, and the death of her father, left her struggling for survival. Security of a kind came in the form of an SS officer, who announced his intention of marrying her immediately. 'But she is not yet 16,' her mother interposed. 'If she does not do what I say,' returned the Nazi, 'she will never be 16.'

After the war Eva Sjoke obtained an annulment on grounds of coercion. She resumed her acting career, appearing in a Hungarian film called *Prophet of the Fields*. Her ambition now fired, she wrote to the Hungarian producer Alexander Paal in Hollywood, asking for an American visa. 'Can't be done,' Paal wrote back, 'but when I come to Budapest I will marry you.' And so, in 1948, he did. Later that year she arrived in Britain, where Sir Alexander Korda changed her name to Eva Bartok.

Subsequently she went to Hollywood, where she made her

debut, appropriately enough as a Hungarian refugee, in *Tale of Five Cities* (1951). Later that year she was in *The Crimson Pirate*, a spoof pirate film which gave Burt Lancaster plenty of opportunity to display his acrobatic skill. In Britain, Eva Bartok had a part in *The Assassin* (1952), helping to hunt down Richard Todd in Venice. She also appeared in *Front Page Story* (1954), with Jack Hawkins; joined Leslie Phillips to foil a mad scientist in *The Gamma People* (1955); and survived an air crash in *SOS Pacific* (1959), only to discover that the island on which they had landed was about to be used to test a hydrogen bomb. In *Operation Amsterdam* (1960) she and Peter Finch saved industrial diamonds from the advancing Nazis.

Meanwhile in 1951 Eva Bartok had divorced Paal and married William Wordsworth, great great grandson of the poet. A publicity agent, he was given to having her photographed with lions and elephants. This did not prevent the marriage failing within four years, after which Eva Bartok plunged into the unhappy episode with Curt Jurgens. After the birth of her daughter, Eva remained under the influence of her Indonesian guru. 'First you have the experience,' she instructed reporters, 'and then you have the explanation.' In the sixties and seventies her experience consisted of sticking her daughter in international schools, and travelling in Indonesia and India (where she had an affair with the Shiv of Palitana). She also spent some time in Bolivia. 'To withdraw is not to run away,' she assured the press.

Her film career petered out with a role in *Pele, King of Football* (1974). In 1983 she was again in London, expressing enthusiasm for Lady Olga Maitland's Women for Peace. She also hinted darkly at a fifth marriage and divorce – 'but why should I make him famous?'

Eva Bartok dabbled in painting and in sculpture, and in the early Nineties was involved with an art gallery in San Francisco.

A few years ago she returned to Britain and set up in an hotel in west London. In 1997 she was found wandering the streets, and taken into hospital. 'I've made a mess of my life,' she confessed. 'I have been a sentimental fool.' But she remained undaunted. 'Maybe I'll find a flat in Park Lane like in the old days,' she told reporters.

5 August 1998

UPSTAIRS, DOWNSTAIRS

*

NESTA COX

*British 'Nanny of Nanteuil' who spoke nursery Franglais and
served through the German occupation of France*

*

Nesta Cox, known as 'the Nanny of Nanteuil', who has died at
Blois in France aged 92, was brought up to believe in the inde-
structibility of the British Empire, although in the event she herself proved the more indestructible. 'Nanny' Cox lived her life to
standards of service, devotion and loyalty which she never questioned and which saw her safely though the German occupation
of France and membership of the French Resistance.

Nesta Ellen Cox was born at Thetford, Norfolk, on 19
December 1899. She had no brothers or sisters and when she was
orphaned at the age of three she was taken in by the family of
an Anglican clergyman at Farnham. After her training she started
work as a 15-year-old nurserymaid but her exceptional gift for
looking after children soon secured her an appointment as nanny.
She spent four years with the family of a Royal Indian Navy captain in Ceylon, where there was a white Rolls-Royce for the use
of herself and the children.

Then, after an appointment in Gloucestershire, she moved to
the house which was to become her home for the rest of her life,
Château Nanteuil, near Huisseau-sur-Cosson in the Loir et
Cher. She was issued with her *carte d'identité* in 1925, and became
one of the legion of British nannies employed to bring up
French children between the wars. The house belonged to
William Gardnor-Beard, a member of a prosperous family of
mine owners, who had married Anne-Marie Denisane, great-
niece of the Marquise de Perrigny. Mme Gardnor-Beard, a
spirited young Frenchwoman, earned some notoriety on her
honeymoon in Arcachon by publicly slapping the face of Mme

Joseph Caillaux (the wife of Poincaré's finance minister and herself notorious for shooting dead the editor of *Le Figaro* after he had suggested that Caillaux was unpatriotic). Mme Gardnor-Beard and Nanny Cox were both strong characters, but after a difficult few weeks they became firm friends and everyone in Nanteuil soon grew to love 'N'neee'.

Rather in the manner of the establishments portrayed in Anthony Powell's novel *A Question of Upbringing* and Terence Rattigan's play *French Without Tears*, the Gardnor-Beards had set up an informal tutoring course which attracted English boys, and later girls, who were filling in time before university, the Army or the Diplomatic Service.

Among those who stayed at Nanteuil were Valerian Wellesley (later the 8th Duke of Wellington) and Jeremy Hutchinson (later Lord Hutchinson of Lullington, QC). It became one of the traditions of the house that anyone arriving from England should bring Nanny some tea, good tea in those days being unobtainable in the Loir et Cher.

The use of English was strictly forbidden at Nanteuil, except of course in the nursery. But since Nanny invited Gardnor-Beard's pupils to nursery tea, there was one period in the day when the rule could be broken. As time passed, however, Nanny abandoned conventional English and tended to address all nationalities in a nursery 'Franglais' of her own invention, which was spoken with little attempt at a French accent but which – thanks to her magical powers of communication – everyone understood. In return she had no trouble in understanding even Parisian argot when it came her way.

After the death of William Gardnor-Beard his widow married Comte Pierre de Bernard. On the outbreak of war in 1939 the majority of English nannies working in France returned to England but Nanny Cox refused to abandon her post. The Gardnor-Beards and their children had become her family and Nanteuil her home. After the fall of France in 1940 the house stood just north of the demarcation line and within the occupied zone.

Shortly after Dunkirk a message arrived that somebody outside wished to speak to Mme de Bernard. She and Nanny went out to find a former pupil, William Bradford, now an officer in the Black Watch, who had escaped capture and was trying to make his way back to England. He had swum the River Loire in the mistaken belief that Nanteuil was in the Vichy zone. There were German troops quartered on the house at the time but the de Bernards managed to help Bradford on his way. He later rose to command the 51st Highland Division.

It was in this manner that the de Bernards joined the Sologne Resistance. They, and Nanny, were recruited by Colonel Buckmaster's *Reseau Adolphe* which later became part of the much larger 'Prosper Network'.

Nanny's first task was to help Anne-Marie de Bernard interview the often dubious 'English' men or women, who claimed to have been sent from London. The network eventually received Yvonne Rudellat, the first woman agent sent by Special Operations Executive into occupied territory.

Despite the proximity of German troops, the park of Nanteuil was used to conceal arms and radio transmitters parachuted by the RAF. On one occasion the RAF even parachuted supplies of tea for Nanny, who regularly assisted the de Bernards in supporting sabotage and passing on RAF aircrew. When the Prosper Network was broken by the Abwehr in June 1943, the de Bernards were arrested by the Gestapo at Orleans and subsequently deported.

Nanny Cox was left in sole charge of the children and the house. It was a difficult as well as a frightening time for her, but she made as little of it as anyone possibly could – only saying later that she had always kept a copy of the New Testament with her in case she, too, was picked up.

After the War both Pierre and Anne-Marie de Bernard

returned from the concentration camps, although with their health broken. Mme de Bernard re-opened the school at Nanteuil and the English pupils re-appeared, still bearing their packets of tea. Nanny Cox, though entitled to hold the *carte de résistance*, never applied for one; she never considered that she had done anything worth remarking, nor did she bear ill-will towards the Germans, remembering that many of the ordinary soldiers had behaved correctly. She regarded the war and the occupation of France as an episode of extremely bad behaviour which was now closed.

Nanny Cox enjoyed occasional visits to England but otherwise never left Nanteuil. She lived to look after the children of her original children and then the children of those children. It was not uncommon for visitors to see old – sometimes very old – pupils of the school at Nanteuil returning to the house and being moved to tears on finding Nanny Cox still there, largely unchanged.

If, for the first time in 67 years, tea is not served at 4 o'clock sharp at Nanteuil this week, Nanny's spirit still watches over the house. At her request her ashes have been scattered beneath an oak tree in the park.

2 March 1992

HERMIONE, COUNTESS OF RANFURLY

Author of To War With Whitaker, *her memoir of life in Cairo with Eisenhower, SOE and the family retainer*

*

Hermione, Countess of Ranfurly, who has died aged 87, was the author of one of the most delightful memoirs of recent times, *To War With Whitaker* (1994), and the kind of woman for whom words such as pluck and spirit might have been invented. Exuberant, witty and vigorously outspoken, the book, based on her wartime diaries, told how as a bride of eight months she had broken every rule in the Army to be near her husband after he was posted to Palestine with his faithful cook–butler, Whitaker.

The newly married Ranfurlys had been on a stalking holiday in Scotland when the news came through that the Germans were invading Poland. Awaiting them when they returned to London was a telegram from Lord Ranfurly's Yeomanry regiment, the Sherwood Rangers, telling him to report immediately to Nottinghamshire. He turned to Whitaker to ask if he was coming too. 'Whitaker sat there looking fat and rather red,' Lady Ranfurly recorded, 'and he said, "To the war my Lord?" and Dan said "Yes". And Whitaker said: "Very good, my Lord," as though Dan had asked for a cup of coffee.'

Even as they left for Palestine, Lady Ranfurly was plotting to join them. In 1940, the military authorities tried to ship her back to England, but within a year she was confidential secretary to the head of Special Operations Executive in Cairo. By the end of the war she probably knew more secrets than any civilian in the region, and had managed, as one senior officer put it, to 'out-manoeuvre every general in the Middle East'.

The Countess read secret telegrams to and from Churchill, heard all the gossip and watched the famous faces come and go. Her acquaintances included Lady Diana Cooper, Sir Walter Monckton, Anthony Eden (whom she extracted from an ambas-sadorial lunch to complain about the financial chaos that SOE was in) and Gaston Palewski, Nancy Mitford's great love, who, true to form, also pursued her. She dined with General Eisenhower and Douglas Fairbanks Jr. She met Noël Coward and Evelyn Waugh, befriended the kings of Greece, Egypt and Yugoslavia, and chatted to Antoine de Saint-Exupéry and Freya Stark ('a very brave lady with an iron will hidden under the hats she wears more often than not'). General Patton gave her silk stockings for Christmas; Marshal Tito came for tea with her ('he was short and stocky and dressed to kill'); she helped to glue up the lining of General Montgomery's beret and taught Admiral Hewitt how to dance the Boomps-a-Daisy.

She was born Hermione Llewellyn on 13 November 1913. 'I started life as a disappointment – because I wasn't a boy,' she recalled. 'I continued being a disappointment – because I was ugly. Instead of minding, I determined to ride better, run faster, be funnier and give more generous presents than the rest of the family.'

Her grandfather had inherited two estates in South Wales: Cwrt Colman, near Cardiff; and Baglan, halfway between Briton Ferry and Aberavon; but Hermione was born at Postlipp Hall, a large Elizabethan house in the Cotswolds which her father rented. In May 1914 the family moved to a cottage on the Baglan estate, but life remained comfortable until she was 13, when 'we became poor very quickly' – her father had squandered all his money on houses and horses. A series of disasters then ensued. Her parents separated; her mother, a manic depressive, suffered a nervous breakdown; and her elder brother, whom she adored, was killed in an air crash.

Hermione's first job was selling cookers for the Gas Light & Coke Company. After a secretarial course, she went to Australia in 1937 to become personal assistant to the Governor of New South Wales. There she met her future husband, Daniel Knox, 6th Earl of Ranfurly, who was ADC to Lord Gowrie, the Governor-General. They met again back in Britain and were married in 1939, both aged 25.

When news of war interrupted their holiday beside Loch Torridon, the Ranfurlys drove south the next day. 'As we stacked our guns, golf clubs and fishing rods into the back of our Buick,' Hermione Ranfurly wrote in her diary, 'fear pinched my heart: those are the toys of yesterday I thought; they belong to another world.' Ignoring regulations barring civilian wives from joining soldiers at the front, Hermione Ranfurly obtained a passage to

Egypt from a shady travel agent with a brother in the Passport Office, and in February 1940 set off for the Middle East, taking her husband's shotguns with her. With her shorthand and typing, she imagined it would be easy to make herself useful. But after a year searching for a job, she was forcibly expelled by an indignant, one-eyed brigadier. She jumped ship at Cape Town, which was fortunate since the vessel was sunk soon after it left port. She got an aeroplane ticket back to Egypt by telling Thomas Cook she was on a secret mission.

In April 1941, Lord Ranfurly was reported missing in the Western Desert after the Battle of Tobruk. His wife did not know if he was alive until she received a letter from him five months later. She finally heard that he was in good health in a PoW camp in Italy, but it was three years before he escaped and they could be reunited.

Meanwhile, she grew dissatisfied with SOE, which seemed to her to be working 'across, if not against, the war effort'. With her striking dark looks and potent social connections, she charmed her way into a series of jobs as a personal assistant to the top brass. 'It helped that you knew how to write an invitation properly, and how to arrange a bowl of flowers,' she remembered. 'It helped that you knew how to get on with the staff – I mean, my Spaniards wouldn't have been with me for 30 years if I treated servants like the *nouveaux riches* do.'

Whitaker stayed with her until the end of the war and then returned with the Ranfurlys when they went back to England. He followed them when they moved to the country, but was 'absolutely appalled' by cowpats and wet grass. He retreated back to London and 'must have been dead by 1950 – we cried like children.'

After the war, Lord Ranfurly worked in insurance at Lloyd's and later farmed in Buckinghamshire. Lady Ranfurly set about trying to sort her wartime letters and diaries into some kind of order on the sitting room floor. In 1953, her husband was appointed Governor of the Bahamas. Lady Ranfurly took an interest in every aspect of Bahamian life and was horrified by much of what she saw. In response to the lack of books in schools and libraries, she asked her friends in London to send out unwanted volumes, and soon the Ranfurly Library Service in Nassau was flourishing. When the couple returned to London in 1957, Lady Ranfurly set to work to extend the library service to all parts of the world short of English books. By the time she finally retired in the late 1980s, more than half a million books were being sent abroad each year. The organisation is now known as Book Aid International.

She was appointed OBE in 1970.

After Lord Ranfurly's death in 1988, his Countess went back to working on her diaries. She kept horses in her stables, family portraits in the hall and 'my two fat Spaniards' to cook and clean. She chain-smoked into her eighties, and liked old age because 'you have so many more memories than when you are young'. Spurred on by the success of *To War With Whitaker* she wrote a memoir of her childhood, *The Ugly One*, in 1998.

She is survived by her daughter, Lady Caroline Simmonds.

13 February 2001

SHEILA MINTO

Secretary to eight prime ministers who stood up to
Winston Churchill

*

Sheila Minto, who has died aged 86, joined the staff at 10 Downing Street in 1935 and remained there for 33 years, serving eight prime ministers. As a neophyte she typed Stanley Baldwin's letters from his longhand drafts, and before long she graduated to improving Neville Chamberlain's English – 'to make the sense clear'. During the Second World War she learnt to cope with Winston Churchill's eccentric working habits, though she found it difficult to make coherent shorthand notes with an incontinent budgerigar liable to settle on her head. Gradually, as Minto served successive prime ministers up to and including Harold Wilson, she acquired the status of a matriarch. But she was respected and enjoyed rather than feared. Her colleagues at No. 10 found her a benign presence; and Lord Home of the Hirsel, one of the masters she loved best, summed her up as 'a most friendly person, and a great companion to all at No. 10 – a splendid organiser, with a wonderful sense of humour'.

Sheila Allison Minto was born at Highgate on 19 September 1908, the youngest of the seven children of a sugar buyer. The family moved to Scotland when she was still a child, and she grew up near Dunoon. In 1929 she returned to London, and joined the secretarial staff at the War Office. She enjoyed herself enormously – young officers, tennis club, dramatic society – and was not at all pleased to be sent for an interview at No. 10 in 1935. She thought it would be dull and 'political'. Dull, though, was the last epithet applicable to the job, while the first lesson she learnt was that the permanent staff must never have political views. The secretaries had to work in the nooks and corners, attics and basements of No. 10 – and especially in the garden rooms, on ground level at the back of the house, below the Private Office and the Cabinet Room at Downing Street level. The rooms overlook the back gate from Horse Guards Parade, through which Minto watched many public figures slip quietly in. Among the first she saw were King Edward VIII and the Duke of York – the latter 'pale and worried' at the prospect of succeeding his brother.

Minto soon learnt the cardinal rule of her job – 'to keep quiet and look rather stupid' when political events were being discussed outside the office. With the advent of Neville Chamberlain, and the deterioration of the situation in Europe, she was again involved in dramatic events. She made her first-ever trip across the Channel (and the first of many high-level missions) accompanying Chamberlain and Halifax to meet Mussolini and Ciano. It was at this period, too, that she met the young Lord Dunglass, Chamberlain's Parliamentary Private Secretary, whom she was to welcome back to No. 10 25 years later as Sir Alec Douglas-Home.

Minto was only a few feet away from Neville Chamberlain when he broadcast his announcement of the outbreak of war. Only then did No. 10 adopt the round-the-clock staffing which has been maintained ever since. Fortunately Minto was robust enough to stand up to Winston Churchill, though feebler souls might have categorised his behaviour as bullying. She became and remained devoted to the great man. Working with him throughout the war (despite personal bereavement) tempered her courage, resilience and humour into a formidable combination. Minto became the senior clerical member of staff, and recruited and organised her secretarial successors.

The 1945 general election result was a shock to all who had lived on close terms with Churchill, but Clement Attlee was a familiar and trusted figure who earned the liking and respect of his office staff. In any case, Minto observed: 'It doesn't matter what he is – or indeed what his politics are.' This principle was strictly adhered to, and reinforced by the endemic tendency among the staff at No. 10 to regard the place as a cut above the sordid realities of the hustings. So it was galling for Minto, later in her career, to encounter accusations of political bias.

The post-war period proved a happy one, as Minto built up a loyal and varied team – contrary to the view advanced by Harold Wilson in the 1964 election campaign that the office at No. 10 was staffed by 'a bunch of Tory debs'. Minto knew that 'happiness makes people efficient'. She could enjoy a hilarious anecdote without in any way undermining her effortless natural authority.

One of her chief responsibilities was to organise the administration of the Honours Lists. This meant a huge correspondence, ranging from members of the general public to Buckingham Palace, and demanded a meticulous system. It was only just that Sheila Minto herself should three times have appeared in the list – no doubt through elaborate machinations behind her back. She was appointed MBE in Churchill's 1945 Resignation Honours, OBE in 1961 and – the honour she treasured most – to the Royal Victorian Order (now the LVO) in 1966.

When Harold Wilson became Prime Minister in 1964 the staff looked forward to showing him how misplaced his criticisms of the Downing Street office had been. But the last four years of Minto's life at No. 10 were a long struggle to maintain the morale of her staff and to fight their battles on several fronts. She was not once mentioned in *Inside No. 10* (1972), by Harold Wilson's political secretary, Marcia Williams.

Sadly, retirement, when it came in 1968, was not altogether unwelcome. But Minto was not made for inaction, and for some years her gifts were put to excellent use as personal secretary to Lord Diplock, the senior Law Lord.

In later life Sheila Minto achieved a modest prominence as a public figure, even appearing on the Wogan show. Freed from years of total discretion, she gossiped gently to press and television interviewers about her memories, and was able, with an infectious chuckle, to shed a human light on the history through which she had lived.

25 October 1994

BINDY LAMBTON

*Wife of Lord Lambton with a genius for entertaining guests, who
sometimes found lions in the bedrooms*

*

'Bindy' Lambton, who has died aged 81, was the wife of Lord
Lambton, the former Conservative Minister, and a favourite
subject, because of her large-boned and angular beauty, for portraits by her friend Lucian Freud.

Born Belinda Blew-Jones on 23 December 1921, Bindy – as she
was always known – was the daughter of Major Douglas Holden
Blew-Jones, of Westward Ho, a tall, handsome officer in the Life
Guards with size 24 feet. Her mother, Violet Birkin, was one of
three daughters of the Nottingham lace king, Sir Charles Birkin.

Bindy dearly loved her father, but her relationship with her
mother was never close. Violet Blew-Jones drank too much and
proved a bad mother. She abandoned the infant Bindy to the care
of her beloved aunt, Mrs Freda Dudley Ward, who was shortly
to become engaged in a secret romance, conducted throughout
with the utmost discretion, with the then Prince of Wales (a
lesson which Bindy never forgot). As well as being passionately
fond of her Aunt Freda, Bindy idealised Freda's daughters, Angie
and Pempie Dudley Ward, and strove to be as beautiful and popular as these two dazzling paragons; Angie married Major-
General Sir Robert Laycock, the Second World War commando
leader, while Pempie went on to become a famous actress and
the wife of Sir Carol Reed, the film director.

Bindy had no education, since she was expelled from 11
schools for various wildnesses, only one of which is recorded –
that of putting a bell-shaped impediment under the headmistress's piano pedal. Right from the start, however, Bindy's
extraordinary individuality, handsome good looks, high spirits

and original wit began to attract an army of life-long admirers. When she was 18 she met and married Tony Lambton, son of the 5th Earl of Durham, and embarked enthusiastically on married life. After producing her first daughter, Lucinda, she was told by many eminent doctors on no account to have more children; but Bindy bravely produced four more daughters, and the family moved to Biddick Hall, a perfect red brick Queen Anne house on the Lambton estate in County Durham.

Having endured a rather sad, precarious childhood, Bindy Lambton was determined that her own children should enjoy a perfect idyll. All her fantasies of the ideal were brought into play, with lavish Christmases, birthday parties, ponies and horse shows; later there were trips around Britain and the Continent in a 50ft caravan, drawn by a Land Rover with Bindy Lambton at the wheel, and often Lady Diana Cooper as second driver. Blackpool illuminations were an annual treat, and to ensure privacy at beauty spots she trained her army of children to fight and be naughty, to see off the other tourists. Stately mansions, unused to caravans, were not spared these visitations; but, because it was Bindy Lambton, all gates were opened and all arms outstretched.

In the early 1950s Lord Lambton entered politics, as MP for Berwick-upon-Tweed, with the backing and encouragement of Bindy. They acquired a haunted Georgian house in Mayfair, 11 South Audley Street, which Bindy furnished with notable good taste, and where the couple led a glamorous life, providing her with the opportunity to give free rein to her genius for lavish entertainment. Never a martyr to the humdrum, Bindy created a fairyland of joyousness which few could resist. The list of friends and admirers was endless: Ari Onassis, Judy Montagu, Nancy Mitford (who described Bindy as 'blissful'), David Somerset, Jai and Ayesha Jaipur, Richard Sykes and also such American illuminati as Jock and Betsy Whitney, Babe and Bill Paley, Stash and Lee Radziwill, David O. Selznick and his wife

Irene, Jack and Drue Heinz, Paul Getty and even Bing Crosby. All fell under her spell.

It was at this time, too, that she posed for the famous portraits by Lucian Freud, with whom she watched the racing every afternoon on a flickering black and white television set. She also entertained generously at Biddick Hall, with a famous shoot and wonderful food prepared by Berta, the cook, while lions and leopards which the local butcher kept in the gardens roamed the bedrooms. Then, in 1961, the longed-for son and heir Ned arrived.

Shortly thereafter the shadows began to fall. First there was Bindy Lambton's go-karting accident, resulting in badly shattered legs which had to be pinned together bone by bone by a ground-breaking surgeon who was so frowned upon by the British medical establishment that Bindy Lambton had to discharge herself from hospital to be treated by him at the Dorchester Hotel. Then, just as her legs healed, she drove into the path of a lorry on the A1. This time virtually every bone in her body was broken, and she was not expected to survive. But with characteristic fortitude she pulled through. Encased in plaster like an Egyptian mummy – in which state she was affectionately sketched by the great *New Yorker* cartoonist Charles Addams – Bindy Lambton was confined to a wheelchair for almost two years, which probably laid the foundations for her arthritis and extreme lameness in later life.

In 1966 she bought 58 Hamilton Terrace, a house suggestive of an Odeon cinema built by Aunt Freda in the 1930s. Here Bindy installed a butterfly-shaped swimming pool and created a beautiful garden. But the family was never happy in this house. Her marriage to Tony, perhaps under extreme pressure from the years of infirmity, was beginning to disintegrate. For a while it looked as if Bindy Lambton might follow in her mother's footsteps, but her strength of character, unquenchable high spirits and zest for life pulled her through, and she moved on to the final phase.

In 1970 her husband, who had succeeded as the 6th Earl of Durham, gave up the peerage to retain his Commons seat. But two years later he resigned as Under-Secretary for Defence in the Heath Government following a call-girl scandal, and went to live in Italy. Bindy Lambton moved to 213 Kings Road, formerly the home of her cousin Pempie Reed. Here she found a new lease of life, attracting legions of friends and admirers from new generations: Shimi Lovat, Leigh Bowery, Mick Jagger and Jerry Hall, and, most importantly of all, in her later years, the musician Jools Holland and his entire big band.

She also became adept at deep sea diving, initiated into that dangerous sport by the Olympic medallist, Vane Ivanovic. After watching her diving off the Barrier Reef, the American conservative publicist, William F. Buckley Jnr, wrote: 'I have never met a braver man than Bindy Lambton acting as bait for sharks.'

In her last years, almost entirely blind and totally crippled, Bindy Lambton's *joie de vivre* remained undimmed. So assiduous was her attendance at Jools Holland's concerts that, at one point, he invited her in her wheelchair to sit next to the guitarist on the stage at Newcastle City Hall – for all the world as if she were a paid-up member of the band.

Although her attendances at Durham Cathedral services were less frequent, these too could be notable. One recent Bishop is unlikely to forget how, after an Easter Sunday service, Bindy Lambton followed him down the aisle in her wheelchair, with headlights blazing, cheerfully proclaiming 'Christ is risen'.

Bindy never wished to be thought of as 'eccentric', for she always strove to be – and imagined herself to be – a pillar of respectable society. Her cheerfulness survived to the end. In hospital on the day of her death, just before being given a morphine injection, she amazed both the doctor and nurses by singing and acting out a favourite 1940s song:

> *Cocaine Bill and Morphine Sue*
> *Strolling down the avenue two by two.*
> *O honey*
> *Won't you have a little sniff on me,*
> *Have a sniff on me.*

Those were her last words.

19 February 2003

BETTY KENWARD

*Social columnist whose 'Jennifer's Diary' chronicled the activities
of the English upper classes for half a century*

*

Betty Kenward, who has died aged 94, was better known as the columnist 'Jennifer' whose 'Diary' indefatigably chronicled the social activities of the English upper classes for almost half a century. 'Jennifer's Diary' appeared first in *Tatler*, then *Queen* and then *Harpers & Queen*. In tone it was somewhat suggestive of the ramblings of a retired nanny obsessed with 'Society' – and indeed at one stage Mrs Kenward, who came from minor landed stock, had worked as a 'dame' (or house matron) at Eton. Her claimed advantage over her competitors was her entrée into exclusive parties, which she achieved mainly because of her fathomless discretion and her determination never to speak ill of anyone – save only, perhaps, of her avowed enemy Margaret, Duchess of Argyll.

Heavily powdered and immaculate in pearl choker and kid gloves, her lacquered honey-coloured hair drawn back into a stiff bouffant held in place with a distinctive velvet bow, Betty Kenward would sail through social gatherings like a pocket battleship, never missing anyone she considered important. 'I have long believed Mrs Kenward to be the second finest reporter in

Britain after Max Hastings,' a *Daily Express* columnist once wrote. Her unorthodox punctuation and bland reportage may have attracted a certain ridicule, but her persistence and accuracy always won a degree of admiration.

Celebrated for her claim on *Desert Island Discs*, 'I am a true Cockney, I was born in Cadogan Gardens', she was born Elizabeth Kemp-Welch on 14 July 1906, the only daughter of Brian Kemp-Welch of Kineton, Warwickshire, from a family noted in *Burke's Landed Gentry*. Her father insisted that young Betty be educated by a governess, and she later attended a finishing school at Les Tourelles, Brussels. She did not have an easy childhood; in her memoirs published in 1992, she revealed that her mother had had many affairs, the dire social consequences of which had become apparent to Betty during her third term at finishing school. She had become friends with a girl called Bunty with whom she hoped to share a room the next term; but when Bunty arrived back 'she told me very sweetly that her aunt would not let her share a room with me as my mother was living with a man who was not her husband'. Betty was 'shattered, but it made me realise early on what a lot high standards mean in life'.

In 1932, Betty married, at St Margaret's, Westminster, Captain Peter Kenward of the 14/20th Hussars. The next day the wedding received 106 lines in the social page of the *Daily Telegraph*. Divorced in 1942, Betty Kenward was left to bring up her nine-year-old son, Jim. With no obvious career prospects, she secured Jim's schooling at Winchester by working first, it is said, in a munitions factory, and later as a dame for the Eton housemaster Cyril Butterwick.

Jim Kenward, who would qualify as a chartered accountant and later move to Canada, was to prove a constant source of inspiration for Jennifer's Christmastide greetings, though she admitted that his children were less than enthusiastic about visits from strict 'Granny London'.

During the Second World War, Betty Kenward began writing a social column for *Tatler* after it had paid her 10s 6d for her account of a local flower show. Initially entitled 'On and Off Duty in Town and Country', the column changed its name in 1945 to 'Jennifer's Diary' because the editor thought Betty Kenward 'looked like a Jennifer'. In 1959 Jennifer moved to Jocelyn Stevens's rejuvenated *Queen* magazine which in 1970 was amalgamated with *Harpers Bazaar*. She continued writing for *Harpers & Queen* until her retirement, aged 84, in 1991.

'Sometimes I wonder whether she keeps a tape-recorder hidden behind that bow of hers,' the party-planner Lady Elizabeth Anson once remarked. In fact, Betty Kenward would not even use a notebook but relied on her memory to produce lengthy lists of the previous day's engagements. Her memory, as well as being efficient, was carefully selective; scandal had no place in 'Jennifer's Diary'. 'If Betty wanted to be a different kind of reporter, by God she could write a column,' observed Jocelyn Stevens, her proprietor at Queen – though he recognised that 'she knows it all in order not to print it'.

Remorselessly, she stuck to an all but vanished view of the social order. Arrivistes – journalists, politicians (except Sir Ian Gilmour, Bt), writers (except John Julius Norwich), advertisers and publishers – had no place in her column. While the land-owning classes capitulated to upwardly mobile executives and debutantes gave way to night-clubbing nymphettes, 'Jennifer's Diary' remained the last bastion of the structured pre-war class system. The shires were Jennifer's spiritual heartland; county families would invite her to their weddings if for no other reason than that she had dutifully written up their parents' marriage ceremony a quarter of a century before. It was from these county families that Jennifer drew most of her 'dear friends', that privileged few granted the special dignity of remaining nameless in her column. How close these friends were is a matter of some doubt. 'Although one reads of the dear friends,' a colleague observed, 'they don't really exist. She's not a very friendly person.'

Certainly, Betty could prove insufferably snobbish and crochetty. Her telephone manner could be brusque towards anyone she judged her social inferior, and she was prone to long-running feuds. Her notorious distaste for Margaret, Duchess of Argyll dated from 1963 when the judge presiding over the Duchess's divorce case branded her 'wholly immoral' and 'completely promiscuous'. The Duchess sullied 'Jennifer's Diary' no more. Less easily explicable was Betty's grievance against Peter Townend, the social editor of *Tatler* from the late 1960s. Whenever she found herself attending the same party as Mr Townend, it was a matter of some principle that she must be placed on the top table while he sat with the press. Least auspicious of Mrs Kenward's rows was that with Antony Armstrong-Jones. When working as society photographer on *Queen* magazine, he once made the mistake of approaching her at a function. 'My photographers never speak to me at parties,' Mrs Kenward insisted testily. A year later, Mr Armstrong-Jones (now the Earl of Snowdon) became engaged to Princess Margaret. On hearing the news, Betty Kenward is said to have spent the afternoon in her office, kicking her waste paper basket disconsolately and intoning: 'What a turn up this is.'

Her column proved the ideal means of revenge. For many years, she described the royal couple's presence at parties without mentioning Lord Snowdon's name; for example: 'Princess Margaret; her husband,' and then the name of some eligible male. She was also notably prickly when dealing with young staff; few of her secretaries lasted longer than four months. Her ideal secretary had to be smart enough to know what Jennifer was talking about, but not so smart that she would appear at the same parties. Clergymen's daughters were ideal, but by the mid-1980s the right sort were in short supply. Betty Kenward's requirements for her secretaries were strict; they must write with pens, not ball-points; they should not have red hair or smoke, and they should not be Irish – unless, of course, they hailed from the Ascendancy. One advertisement sought a girl with 'no, repeat no, ambitions to write'. There were, though, some perks. Secretaries were released from their duties at lunchtime every Friday, to ensure that they arrived at country house parties before nightfall. Secretaries quickly learned that 'Mrs K' always travelled first-class by train and insisted on travelling with her back to the engine because, oblivious to the end of the steam era, she explained, 'otherwise one gets so dirty'.

The key to Betty Kenward's extraordinary mental processes lay in her writings. They were ostensibly a dull catalogue of names and places, as for instance in an extract from a description of the aftermath of a Harrow School Songs concert at the Albert Hall:

> 'I stayed on for supper in the Boissier box, where, besides Mr and Mrs Roger Boissier, I met his brother and sister-in-law Mr and Mrs Martin Boissier, and their attractive daughter Miss Susan Boissier; their cousins Mr and Mrs Peter Boissier, and their sons Commander Paul Boissier, who commands a submarine, with his wife Susie; and Mr John Boissier, and his wife Annie. Also Roger and Bridget Boissier's son Mr Rupert Boissier, and Miss Isabelle Barratt. Sadly Roger and Bridget Boissier's daughter Miss Clare Boissier was not present as she is in New Zealand.'

But behind such bathos lay a secret code full of prejudices, careful omissions and damning phrases which only the keen student of her column could ever hope to comprehend.

Another feature of Betty Kenward's copy was the idiosyncratic system of punctuation she developed, in particular her pointed use of the semi-colon and the comma. In lists of those who attended a party, the Royal Family and others of special importance would be cordoned off from the lowly with a semi-colon, and even in mid-sentence the Queen, received an honorary comma.

Adjectives were carefully graded. Party hostesses were always 'generous', 'tireless' and 'extremely pretty'. Anyone vaguely pul-chritudinous was 'pretty'; plain debutantes and ugly brides were 'radiant' or at least 'spirited'; in the most desperate cases, Jennifer would describe their 'beautiful dress' instead.

In the open-plan *Harpers & Queen* office, only Betty Kenward and her two assistants were graced with a special room, which looked like a Wendy House, with a curtained port-hole. Driven to work by her indulgent chauffeur – 'dear Peter' – Betty Kenward would make a brief appearance before lunching at Claridge's. After spending an afternoon filing her copy for the previous evening, she would generally go on to attend a nightly average of two cocktail parties and one formal dinner. Although she was only paid a small retainer by her employers, she enjoyed an impressive expense account. Her clothes, her food, her travel and even her *pied-à-terre* in Hill Street, Mayfair, were for many years provided and maintained for her. Even when quite seri-ously ill, Mrs Kenward never failed to produce her copy. She would write from her hospital bed about her 'tireless' nurses and would attend functions a day after enduring painful surgery.

Betty Kenward was appointed MBE in 1986. She never mar-ried again, though she claimed that 'three kind gentlemen' had asked for her hand in marriage. Her son survives her.

26 January 2001

LADY DOROTHY HEBER PERCY

Youngest of the Lygon sisters whose family inspired the Flytes in Evelyn Waugh's novel Brideshead Revisited

*

Lady Dorothy Heber Percy, known to her friends as 'Coote', who has died aged 89, was the youngest and cosiest of the Lygon sisters.

She was born Lady Dorothy Lygon on 22 February 1912, the fourth daughter of the 7th Earl Beauchamp, KG, who, after acts unpardonable, was obliged to leave the country and settled on the Continent. The story goes that Lady Beauchamp received a visit from her brother, the Duke of Westminster, who explained the reason for this precipitate departure, the full horror of which she did not entirely digest. 'Bend d'Or tells me that Beauchamp is a bugler,' she said. While Lord Beauchamp was still at Madresfield, the family seat near Malvern, his daughters used to urge the male house guests to lock their doors at night against the nocturnal prowlings of their father. One morning the peer told his third daughter, Mary: 'He's a nice young man, your friend, but he's damned uncivil.'

Evelyn Waugh's novel *Brideshead Revisited* clearly owed much inspiration to the Lygon family, though in conversation with Lady Dorothy, Waugh went to some pains to claim that they were only partly the inspiration and that all the ages and details were different. Nevertheless, Lord Beauchamp was, in certain respects, the model for Waugh's Lord Marchmain, living in exile in Venice with his mistress, and Madresfield was the inspiration for Brideshead. Lady Dorothy claimed that the only connection between Brideshead and Madresfield was the art nouveau chapel, while Waugh's biographer Christopher Sykes saw some parallels with the much grander Castle Howard, which was used in the Granada television film. 'Coote', or 'Pollen', or even 'Poll' as she was called, was an early friend of Evelyn Waugh and, according to Waugh's wife Laura, 'the nicest of all your friends'. It is tempting to suggest that she might have been, in part, the inspiration for Lady Cordelia Flyte, the precocious, but devoutly Roman Catholic younger sister in *Brideshead Revisited*. Waugh had met her brothers at Oxford, and was soon a frequent visitor to Madresfield.

After Lord Beauchamp left England in 1931, the family was divided, Lady Beauchamp departing with one son, while Coote's eldest brother, Lord Elmley, and Hugh Lygon (the more wayward brother to whom Waugh's character Lord Sebastian Flyte owed much) took over the house with the three unmarried sisters, Sibell, Mary ('Maimie') and Dorothy. Of these sisters, the elder two were beauties, particularly the blonde Maimie, while Coote had, in the words of Selina Hastings, another of Waugh's biographers, 'a large, plain face and wore spectacles', a look she carried into grown-up life.

Evelyn Waugh was a welcome diversion in the household. He would often be writing while staying with them, though the sisters frequently dragged him from his desk to partake in some amusement. Despite this, he dedicated *Black Mischief* jointly to Mary and Dorothy in 1932. Waugh once ran across Coote's childish diary and could not resist adding pornographic passages about participation in orgies to the young girl's script, and he appended to her innocent drawing of a cart horse a giant penis. 'It was like having Puck as a member of the household,' she recalled later.

In the Second World War, Coote served as a Flight Officer in the WAAF, and was posted to Italy working on photographic interpretation. After the war she took up farming in Gloucestershire. In the 1950s, she worked as social secretary at the British Embassy in Athens, and in 1956 spent six months in Istanbul, working as a governess, before going to live on the Greek island of Hydra. She returned to England in the 1960s and for many years worked as an archivist at Christie's. She settled near Faringdon, the eccentric Oxfordshire home of Lord Berners, the inspiration for Nancy Mitford's 'Lord Merlin'. Berners dyed his doves a variety of colours and summoned guests to dinner with a music box. Penelope Betjeman once rode her horse into the drawing room for tea.

Coote – who all this time had remained a spinster – knew Lord Berners well and was a witness to his tempestuous relationship with Robert Heber Percy, the young man nicknamed 'Mad Boy', who lived there with him. Berners died in 1950, and Heber Percy inherited the estate, which he ran with supreme efficiency, maintaining the Berners eccentricities, and adding follies of his own, most notably two enormous griffins that presided over a swimming pool. A wild and pugnacious character, Robert Heber Percy also enjoyed running an undertakers' business, and relished their annual conferences, which invariably provided him with a fund of good stories. He had married Jennifer Fry for a time and produced a beautiful daughter, Victoria. But more usually his stable-mate was Hugh Cruddas ('The Captain'), though eventually they fell out. Evelyn Waugh wrote to Diana Mosley: 'The Mad Boy has installed a Mad Boy of his own. Has there ever been a property in history that has devolved from catamite to catamite for any length of time?' Coote and her sister Maimie were regular visitors over the years. While Coote remained alert, brisk, and full of stories, Maimie, her beauty faded and her spirit dimmed by drink, would sit gazing mute into space, stroking her little dog.

As the years passed, and Robert Heber Percy became frailer, though no less volatile, Coote unwisely accepted a proposal of marriage from him, and, excited as any young bride, became the mistress of Faringdon in 1985. This caused a good deal of disruption in the domestic arrangements; the faithful Rosa, Heber Percy's cook, departing in high dudgeon, and there was antipathy from some of Heber Percy's regular lady guests who had come to treat Faringdon as their own patch. But this phase was of short duration and Coote soon retreated to a nearby bungalow, where she was much happier. Robert Heber Percy died in 1987, leaving Faringdon to his daughter.

Lately, Lady Dorothy assisted John Byrne in a stylish re-issue of Lord Berners's most elusive book, *The Girls of Radcliff Hall* (Cygnet Press, 2000), a mischievous fictional evocation of life at Faringdon, in which all the boys (including Heber Percy) become girls at a boarding school, with Lord Berners as the headmistress.

17 November 2001

DIANA, LADY DELAMERE

Femme fatale of Happy Valley who took the secret of a murder to her grave

*

Diana, Lady Delamere, who has died aged 74, became the central figure in what has popularly been portrayed as one of the *crimes passionel* of the century when her elderly second husband Sir 'Jock' Delves Broughton, 11th Bt, was tried in Kenya for the murder of her lover, the 22nd Earl of Erroll, in 1941. Broughton was acquitted at the trial, which caused a major sensation even though it took place in the middle of the 1939–45 war, but committed suicide the following year. His widow, who subsequently married twice more, is thought to have taken to her grave the full story of who was responsible for the body in the Buick on the Nairobi Road.

The case inspired James Fox's riveting book *White Mischief*, later to be released as a feature film, and also the television play *The Happy Valley*. Fox's fellow sleuth into the mystery, Cyril Connolly, who had been at Eton with the dashing 'Joss' Erroll, described Lady Delamere as 'one of those creamy ash blondes of the period with a passion for clothes and jewels, both worn to perfection, and for enjoying herself and bringing out enjoyment in others'.

Quite apart from her familiar role as the *femme fatale* of the Erroll case, Diana Delamere was a woman of considerable fascination. She rode fearlessly to hounds, flew with Amy Johnson, fished the sea for marlin, owned a string of racehorses, shrewdly managed vast estates and eventually became the doyenne of white Kenyan Society.

Born in 1913, she was the daughter of Seymour Caldwell, of The Red House, Hove, an Old Etonian gambler. Following a brief marriage to Vernon Motion, who played second piano in the Savoy Orpheans, she ran a cocktail club in Mayfair called The Blue Goose. In November 1940, at Durban Register Office, South Africa, she married Sir Henry John ('Jock') Delves Broughton, a Cheshire baronet 30 years her senior with whom she had emigrated from England. Immediately afterwards they settled in the so-called 'White Highlands' of Kenya, where she soon met the 22nd Earl of Erroll, Hereditary Lord High Constable of Scotland, Chief of the Hays, Military Secretary of the East Africa Command and a philanderer notorious even by the louche standards of 'Happy Valley'. By Christmas Lord Erroll and Lady Broughton were embroiled in a passionate love affair.

On 18 January, Lady Broughton's lover and husband confronted one another. 'Diana tells me she is in love with you,' was the Baronet's opening gambit according to the evidence of Lord Erroll's garden boy. 'Well, she has never told me that but I am frightfully in love with her,' replied the Earl. On 23 January Broughton dined with his wife and Erroll at the Muthaiga Club, and, in the course of a bizarre evening, proposed a toast: 'I wish them every happiness and may their union be blessed with an heir. To Diana and Joss.' In the early hours of the following morning two African milk boys discovered Erroll's corpse. The following month Lady Broughton and her husband went off on a shooting safari into the Southern Masai Reserve.

On the first day of Broughton's trial for murder in May 1941, his wife made a memorable entrance into the court attired in an elegant widow's ensemble of black hat, veil and a profusion of diamonds. She left the court only once in the three-week trial, when Erroll's ear, preserved in a jar, was handed round as an exhibit.

Following Broughton's acquittal and suicide, she married for the third time, in 1943, Gilbert Colvile, an extensive cattle-rancher at Naivasha, Kenya. They were divorced in 1955 and later that year she married, fourthly and finally, the 4th Lord Delamere, who died in 1979.

Lady Delamere continued to live in semi-regal state at Soysambu, Elementeita, where her father-in-law, the 3rd Lord Delamere, had pioneered the gilded exodus to the heady freedom of the White Highlands.

7 September 1987

JEAN SMITH

Nanny whose loving advice on bringing up children led her to become a television star and Daily Telegraph columnist

*

Jean Smith, who has died aged 82, was a family nanny of the old school whose untypically liberal approach to childcare led her to become an unlikely celebrity in her seventies. She was persuaded by one of her former charges to collaborate on a child-care manual, *Nanny Knows Best*, which was made into a BBC television series in 1993. In it Nanny Smith visited three families each week, dispensing expert reassurance to parents despairing over sleepless nights or – in one case – a small boy who would eat only food that was dyed blue. With her white hair, beady eye and warm smile, she was a sort of cross between John Harvey-Jones and Miss Marple.

Some progressive-minded writers claimed to see in her a 'smug absolutism'. But the book was a bestseller, and Miss Smith became probably the best-known nanny since 'Crawfie', the royal servant who caused a scandal when she spilt the beans in 1949. She enjoyed her moment of fame and was often recognised by strangers as she went shopping near her flat in Victoria.

Later she had a column in the *Daily* and *Sunday Telegraphs*, dispensing advice on nappies, sleeping and how to achieve a peaceful Sunday lunch; there was also a set of spin-off books. But by

1999 she had begun to show signs of forgetfulness and after a fall she was diagnosed with Alzheimer's disease. She moved into a nursing home in Hammersmith, Nazareth House, where the staff invariably addressed her as Nanny. She received a steady stream of visits from the children she had brought up, by now aged 25 to 65, who formed an email group to exchange news of her welfare. In 43 years as a live-in nanny, she had worked for only five families, bringing up ten children and showing rare devotion. She was on duty round the clock, apart from on Thursdays, when she swapped her navy nurse's uniform for a smart suit and went into the West End to meet other nannies for shopping, lunch at Lyons' Corner House or an exhibition. She would often return with a present for the children.

Nanny Smith was a traditionalist on many fronts, imposing a firm routine, eschewing demand feeding, pushing a pram the size of a small car, and dressing children in smock dresses, white leggings and stiff coats with velvet collars. Yet behind the starched exterior she was ahead of her time with an easy-going outlook which was a reaction to her own upbringing. In her book she wrote that her childhood had been happy and secure though her admired mother was strict. 'Ever since I was 12, still smarting from one of my mother's tellings-off,' she said, 'I decided that when I grew up I would be involved with children and that I would look at each and every situation through their eyes.'

Jean Smith was born on 5 May 1922 at Ilkley, Yorkshire, the eldest of three children. She grew up in the mining community of Treeton, where her father was the village policeman. In 1938, young Jean saw an advertisement for girls to train as nursery nurses. 'It seemed like the answer to a prayer,' she said. She took a one-year course at St Monica's, a Church home in Bradford which took in unmarried mothers. After qualifying, she stayed on as a member of staff before leaving to become a family nanny in Derbyshire. Always a sociable person, she fell in love with a young man who was serving in the Far East. When he was killed, his loss made a deep impression, and she went to the Cenotaph every year to remember him. Later in the War, she became engaged to a Belgian refugee, but broke off the relationship after taking a temporary job with a new baby. 'When it came to the crunch,' she said, 'I had become so attached to the baby I did not want to leave.'

That baby grew up to become a teacher of dyslexic children. Nanny Smith's other charges included a physiotherapist, a fashion stylist, a sculptor and four journalists. She taught them to read and write herself; encouraged creativity and caring; and banned fighting. The nursery was a haven of calm, in which there were baths every night at 6 pm since playing with water was therapeutic. She never made her charges eat food they disliked and felt there were no bad children, only bad parents. One father she worked for went home each night and asked if his children had been good; Nanny replied, pointedly, that they had been happy. She had moved to London after the war and spent the rest of her life there. She remained proud of her roots and returned to Yorkshire for her holidays. After retiring she was in demand as a maternity nurse. A former charge, the writer Nina Grunfeld, asked for help with her newborn son and spotted that Nanny's store of know-how, assembled over 50 years, could benefit parents if captured in a book.

Jean Smith died in her sleep, holding her teddy. She leaves a sister.

18 May 2004

WRITERS AND ARTISTS
*

NORA BELOFF

Combative and litigious foreign correspondent who brooked no contradiction

*

Nora Beloff, who has died aged 78, was for 30 years a dedicated and combative journalist on the *Observer*, during that time she became the first woman foreign correspondent in Washington, and also broke new ground as the paper's political editor. She wrote with great authority and fierce conviction, though her ferocity could sometimes spill over. She did not take kindly to contradiction; tended to feel that anyone who disagreed with her was either a fool or a knave – probably both; and often took the trouble to let the offender know in person what she thought of him.

In a profession rife with jesters and jests, Nora Beloff conspic-uously lacked a sense of humour. In 1969 Auberon Waugh, giving free rein to his fancy in a *Private Eye* column, suggested that she was frequently to be found in bed with Harold Wilson and other members of his Cabinet. Nothing improper occurred, he said. 'That suggests,' Waugh volunteered, 'she is a woman with whom sexual relationships would not be desired.' Nora sued for libel and in 1972 was awarded £3,000. This was some compensation for the loss of another action she had brought against *Private Eye*, in which she charged the journal with print-ing a memorandum about Reginald Maudling she had circulated within the *Observer*. The costs, estimated at £10,000, were awarded against her.

This litigiousness did not make Nora Beloff popular in Fleet Street – but then she never imagined it was her job to be popu-lar. It says much for her talent and professionalism that, notwith-standing the conservatism of her own instincts, she held senior posts for so many years at such a determinedly progressive news-paper. She might have lasted even longer but for an untoward incident. In 1978 she was plotting to unseat Donald Trelford, who had succeeded David Astor as editor three years before, when a letter she wrote to a would-be conspirator found its way to Trelford's desk.

Nora Beloff was born on 24 January 1919 into a prosperous and cultivated Latvian Jewish family which made its home in London. The historian Lord Beloff is her brother. Another brother was professor of parapsychology at Edinburgh, while a sister, a biochemist, was married to Sir Boris Chain, who won the Nobel Prize for his part in the development of penicillin. It is possible that Nora's grim determination to succeed in what was then very much the male section of journalism sprang from her anxiety to keep up with her siblings. At all events, she unde-niably achieved recognition in her chosen field: David Astor, the editor of the *Observer* from 1948 to 1975, described her as one of his most valued colleagues.

Nora Beloff was educated at King Alfred School and read his-tory at Lady Margaret Hall, Oxford. From 1941 to 1944 she served in the Political Intelligence Department of the Foreign Office, and then worked for two years at the embassy in Paris. She began her career as a journalist at Reuter's News Agency, before joining the *Economist* in Paris in 1946. Two years later she found her life's work at the *Observer*. David Astor surrounded himself with a rich array of talent, including Edward Crankshaw, Sebastian Haffner, Arthur Koestler, Isaac Deuscher and Lajos Lederer. It was difficult to shine in such company, but Nora Beloff managed to make her mark – first as correspondent in Paris, Washington, Moscow and Brussels, then from 1964 to 1976 as political correspondent, and finally in a roving capacity from 1976 to 1978.

Her years as political correspondent took in Harold Wilson's first two periods in office. The Prime Minister became convinced that she was conspiring with younger Labour MPs to undermine him, and tried to get her sacked; Nora Beloff's main concern, though, was that the Labour movement was being infiltrated and to an extent taken over by Trotskyites. Her colleagues thought her fears far-fetched, but on this issue she was proved right. She also believed that Michael Foot, one of the idols of the *Observer*, was a sinister influence, and said as much in a hard-hitting book, *Freedom Under Foot* (1976). Nora Beloff disliked the way in which the lobby system worked as a conduit for leaks and was the first person to expose it. She was also to the fore in exposing the political influence of Marcia Williams.

She was particularly well informed about Eastern Europe and the Balkans; and in this respect too her views sometimes brought her into conflict with her colleagues. Lajos Lederer, for example, was a friend and admirer of Tito; Nora Beloff was neither. She was outraged when the *Observer* sent a wreath to Tito's funeral in 1980, and when she wrote *Tito's False Legacy* in 1985 she noted in her preface that the book was 'in part, a penance for unquestionably accepting the Titoist bias shared by most of my countrymen.' Always a fearless reporter, Nora so irritated the authorities during her years in Paris that the French Minister of Defence refused her permission to attend press conferences. In 1979 she was arrested on the border of the Soviet Union and Hungary, held for 24 hours and accused of 'spreading hostile propaganda'. In 1984 she was expelled from Yugoslavia.

She had good contacts, intense application, a faultless eye for the heart of a situation, and a lively provocative style. The author of several controversial books, she latterly stood forth as an impassioned defender of the Serbian cause in the Yugoslavian conflict. For all her prickliness, Nora Beloff could be a stimulating companion; certainly she was a tireless conversationalist, quite unabashed by awkward situations. One evening she was in full flow at a grand dinner party when she suddenly felt sick. Without rising from the table she vomited into her handbag, wiped her mouth and, after an apology to her hostess – 'no reflection on your food, my dear' – continued with her conversation.

Nora Beloff had many friends and admirers, of whom Lord Goodman was among the closest. In 1977, when she was 58, she married Clifford Makins, the sports editor of the *Observer*. He died in 1990.

15 February 1997

MARY WESLEY

Novelist who embarked on her career at the age of 70 and rebelled against the 'hypocrisy' of her background

*

Mary Wesley, the writer who has died aged 90, defied literary convention by becoming a best-selling novelist at the age of 70, and social convention by writing explicitly about sex; her best known books, *Jumping the Queue* (1982) and *The Camomile Lawn* (1984), were both successfully adapted for television.

Mary Wesley's books were generally set in the West Country, in the war or pre-war period, and peopled by upper-middle class characters with names such as Piers, Calypso and Cosmo. Her skill at organising interconnected lives and loves, and her meticulous rendering of clipped drawing room chit-chat tempted some reviewers to make fanciful comparisons to writers such as Jane Austen. But there was a darker side to her writing. For though she wrote within the conventions of the traditional English novel, beneath the comedy of manners and the inconsequential and dispassionate style, there lay a tangled web of brutality, incest, homosexuality, murder, suicide, cruelty and illegitimacy. Mary Wesley refused to make any concessions to the sort of harmless narrative that might be expected from someone of her age, and her books were explicit in their sexual content and language: 'The young always think that they invented sex and somehow hold full literary rights on the subject,' she once observed.

On one occasion she was interviewed by the BBC about the language in *The Camomile Lawn*: 'Well,' she said, 'fuck is an Old English word, and is quite appropriate in certain contexts.' The next thing she knew, the interviewer had rung her editor and told him that he could not possibly use the interview because he was interviewing the Duke of Edinburgh on the same programme.

Mary Wesley always denied that her books were autobiographical, though her stories often featured a young female character resembling herself as a girl, one who feels herself to be a shy misfit in a hostile world. Moreover, the theme of superficial good manners cloaking moral corruption arose out of her bitter resentment of the family which had turned its back on her, and the Edwardian values they upheld: 'I write about the world I was brought up in, a world where snobbery, hypocrisy and unquestioned conservatism are the norm. I just try and show it like it is, and, God knows, that's damning enough.' Her subversive social views were seemingly at odds with her rather chilly aristocratic manner, and she had her detractors: she was famously rubbished by Anita Brookner, while some of her fellow Socialists felt that her claims to have rejected her upper-middle-class upbringing rang false. Her books sold, according to a reviewer in the *New Statesman*, only because 'so many people in this country not only believe in the class system but aspire to rise in it. What irritates is that she runs with the hare and hunts with the hounds, pretending to satirise what she actually glorifies.'

The youngest of three children, she was born Mary Aline Farmar in Berkshire on 24 June 1912. Her father was an Army officer; her mother was a descendant of the first Duke of Wellington's elder brother, an ancestry which explains why, when looking for a pen name, Mary chose first Wellesley, and then Wesley, as the family had earlier been known. As a child, Mary felt rejected and unloved. She positively loathed her mother who, she felt, crushed her every initiative. She was three years old when she first came into contact with her father, when he sent a message to her in her bath ordering her to stop screaming; she was screaming because her beloved Scottish nanny had been sacked to make way for a governess. As the family moved around Europe, Mary endured a succession of 'governesses' – in reality untrained *au pairs* – who taught her nothing, but spoke in their own languages; as a result, she grew up ignorant of the world but fluent in French, Italian and German.

Deprived of friends of her own age (her isolation compounded by continually moving house), she became a keen gardener and an avid reader of whatever books she could find. She would explore her feelings of loneliness and rejection as a child in *A Sensible Life* (1991), of which the heroine, Flora Trevelyan, is a 10-year-old misfit whose parents hate her but who finds hope in the kindness of strangers.

When Mary was 14 her mother decided the time had come to take her older daughter to join her father in India. Mary, meanwhile, was sent to schools in England where she was desperately unhappy. After attending a finishing school in Paris and a domestic science course in London, she was presented at Court and launched herself on London society. Dark, petite and beautiful, Mary Wesley made up for lost time, catching up on friendships and taking lovers. In a reaction against her parents' respectable conservatism, she took a course in International Politics at the LSE, worked in a canteen for down-and-outs, and attended Communist Party meetings.

But in 1937, to the surprise of her left-wing friends, she married the 2nd Lord Swinfen, a peer ten years her senior with a house in Ovington Square, Knightsbridge. As Lady Swinfen, she attended the Coronation of George VI and had two sons. But her husband proved as stuffy and conventional as the parents she had tried to escape, and when he refused her permission to model hats for *Vogue*, because he thought it unseemly, it was clear their relationship could not last. In 1940 she took her two sons to their house in Cornwall, and rang her husband to say she would not be coming back. During the War she was one of the pretty girls recruited by John Bolitho for the War Office, and was involved in reading decoded German ciphers. Once she noticed a build-up of German troops in Schleswig Holstein: 'It looks as if they are going to invade Denmark,' she said. Back came the response, 'Oh Mary, what a lot of balls.' The next day the invasion took place.

This was a period which she brought to life in her novels, notably in *The Camomile Lawn*, which chronicles the experience of an extended upper-middle-class family during the Blitz. 'Many women my age will tell you how much they enjoyed that time,' she explained, 'because it was so liberating. They'd escaped from home, got jobs, lived absolutely for the moment, slept with their lovers – because the next day they might be dead.'

In 1934 she met Eric Siepmann, a foreign correspondent for the *Manchester Guardian*. She was dining at the Ritz with another man when she was handed a note which read, 'You can't stay with that old bore. Come dancing at the Ambassadors'; two days later they became lovers. After they had gone on a prolonged walking expedition together, Siepmann recorded her effect on him with a simple list in his journal: 'Campion, ragged robin, thistle, dog rose, cow parsley, honeydew, purple and yellow vetch, Michaelmas daisies, thrift, meadowsweet.'

After the war, Mary Wesley obtained accreditation as a journalist with *Twentieth Century Magazine* and followed Siepmann to Berlin, where he was working for the *Sunday Times*. Her articles for the magazine were not used because she wrote that she hated the English, American and French occupying forces having servants, cars and plenty to eat while the Germans were still starving in holes in the ground. Siepmann had already been married twice, and her relationship with him met with disapproval from her family – especially since it took several years to track down his second wife to get the divorce papers signed. Her parents refused to meet him, and all but cut out Mary from their wills. She and Siepmann finally married in 1952, and had a son. It was a happy, if not always comfortable, relationship. Siepmann was a great quitter of jobs, so Mary had to get used to being hard up. He encouraged her to write, and she wrote some of his articles and reviews when he faced too many deadlines; yet, apart from two children's books published in America, she never found the confidence to approach a publisher of her own. Most of her literary efforts went straight into the wastepaper bin.

When Siepmann died of Parkinson's Disease in 1970, Mary Wesley found herself virtually penniless with a teenager to support. She scrimped and saved to make ends meet, working in an antique shop, teaching French (until the school discovered she was not qualified), and even sold some of her possessions. Eventually, she was forced to sell her cottage on Dartmoor, moving to more modest premises at Totnes. Four years after her husband's death she began to write novels; but it was not until the writer Antonia White caught her in the act of throwing away a manuscript that she began to think seriously of having her work published. Still in the depths of grief, she wrote a distinctly autobiographical novel about a woman who, devastated by the sudden death of her husband, undergoes a series of painful revelations about the true nature of her relationship with him and with her children.

Joining the Queue was rejected by seven publishers before Macmillan spotted her 'very strong individual voice'. She was so short of money by this time that Macmillans had to send her money for the train fare to London. The book sold 100,000 copies, but left her family in a state of shock: 'How could you write such a dreadful book about such awful people?' her brother asked. Over the next 15 years Mary Wesley produced ten best-sellers which sold more than three million copies. After *The Camomile Lawn* (1984) came *Harnessing Peacocks* (1985); *The Vacillations of Polly Carew* (1986); *Not that Sort of Girl* (1987); and *Second Fiddle* (1988). She continued writing well into the 1990s, producing such works as *A Sensible Life* (1991); *A Dubious Legacy* (1993); *An Imaginative Experience* (1994); and *Part of the Furniture* (1997). She also published three children's books: *Speaking Terms* (1968); *The Sixth Seal* (1968); and *Haphazard House* (1983).

With six-figure advances for her books, television series and foreign sales, Mary Wesley became a rich woman. She was eagerly sought by journalists intrigued by the combination of great age and sexual licence which was her unique selling point. Those who got behind her formidable icy reserve discovered a woman of forceful opinions, sharp intellect and a waspish sense of humour.

Left-wing in her political views, she gave generously to charities such as Amnesty and Prisoners of Conscience. Her opinion of Mrs Thatcher was best summed up by the fact that she carried a note about with her 'to the effect that, if I am ever involved in a disaster, I do not wish to be visited by Mrs Thatcher'.

She and her husband had converted to Roman Catholicism in 1960, though she confessed to being in a state of rage 'because they've rewritten the Bible and done away with Latin'; she had 'no time at all' for Pope John Paul II.

Mary Wesley is survived by her three sons.

1 January 2003

BARBARA WACE

Journalist who covered the invasion of France and became a busy freelance while living close to Fleet Street

*

Barbara Wace, who has died aged 95, was one of the first female journalists to land in France after the Allied invasion in 1944. Nothing was said about Reuters sending a one-handed reporter (Doon Campbell), or Associated Press a one-eyed correspondent (Roger Greene); but the idea of women in the field seemed highly unsuitable until some male correspondents' girlfriends, themselves reporters, appeared in Brussels.

Barbara Wace was assigned by the American news agency Associated Press to cover the arrival of the first members of the American Women's Army Corps on Omaha Beach 40 days after the first landings. Given special protective underwear, she received a cable saying 'KEEP OUT OF DANGER SPOTS THIS IS AN ORDER' from her bureau chief. She filed five stories, which were eagerly devoured by newspapers throughout the United States. However, the American Women's Army Corps was none too pleased when she reported how they had received wolf whistles while being carried in the back of a lorry.

After returning to Britain, Barbara Wace was sent to cover the siege of Brest, where she fitted in with her male colleagues – subject to certain difficulties, such as how to find a suitable lavatory when there was only a 40-seater available for soldiers. At AP's London office she caused much merriment by sending a message 'LOST SKIRT BREST FALLEN', and eventually was exasperated to find her dispatch appear under the byline of a male correspondent sent out to replace her. However, this did not stop the agency later sending Barbara Wace to cover the return to Oslo of the Norwegian government, and then the return of King Haakon VII from exile.

After the War, Barbara Wace joined the Kemsley news service in New York, then embarked on a freelance career as a writer and photographer, beginning with the then-novel assignment of a 14,000-mile journey around America in a Greyhound bus for the *Reader's Digest*. After that she had such diverse paymasters as the National Geographic, the BBC World Service and the *New York Times* (for whom she covered the Coronation) while travelling the world like an intrepid English spinster of the 19th century.

Unlike most London journalists, Barbara Wace actually lived, for 40 years, just off Fleet Street. She had a small, book-jammed, fifth-floor flat above the Clachan pub at Old Mitre Court, which she had taken because it could be reached with ease during the Blitz. Towards the end of her stay there she watched the crowd waiting for two days for the marriage of the Prince of Wales.

Barbara Wace was born at Gillingham, Kent, on 4 September 1907, the second daughter of Brigadier-General 'Gerth' Wace, CB, DSO. She went to the Royal School, Bath, and spent part of her childhood in Saarbrucken, where her father was vice-president of the Saar Boundary Commission.

During the 1930s she became secretary at the Foreign Office to Viscount Cranborne, the Parliamentary Under-Secretary; then to Anthony Eden, the Foreign Secretary, with whom she went to the League of Nations Assembly in Geneva. From 1935 to 1936 she was at the Berlin embassy. 'It was clear to our people there, if not in Whitehall, what the Nazis were all about,' she recalled. In the embassy box at the Berlin Olympics in 1936, Barbara Wace sat a few feet from Hitler as Jessie Owens, the black American sprinter, won the 100 yards dash. She never forgot the look on Hitler's face at the time, nor the mesmeric effect of the mob chanting 'Heil Hitler' at Nazi rallies. 'One recognised with horror the power of the shrieking adulation,' she remembered.

'At moments one felt close to being drawn in, to leaping up and joining the frantic saluting.'

Barbara next joined the public relations department of the Savoy, then rejoined the Foreign Office, which sent her to help set up the British Information Service in Washington, with the brief of persuading the Americans that Britain would win the war. On returning to London in late 1943, she joined Associated Press, which first sent her to cover a basketball game between two American army teams at the Albert Hall. As she did not know anything about the sport she began her story: 'Queen Victoria would turn in her grave at the idea of those half-naked youths from the New World throwing a huge ball about in the place named after her dear Albert.'

In all her travels, whether scuba diving off the Andaman Islands or becoming separated from a dog-sled on Baffin Island, she kept the enthusiasm of a girl on her first day trip to Calais. Her work was enriched by a sense for colours and customs and she wrote observant, low-key pieces about some of the world's odder places. She went to Albania with the first small party of tourists in 20 years in 1957, and found peasants 'living in conditions of Biblical antiquity'. In the Pescadores, off Taiwan, she discovered that an exciting evening out was a 'long glass of sparkling well water in the hotel lounge'. In Muscat, His Highness Said bin Tamur assured her, speaking of his ambitions for his country after the discovery of oil: 'Money is the buttress of hope.' Barbara Wace remembered sitting exchanging pleasantries with Omani chieftains in the sand, wondering what topics it would be polite to broach, and discovering that 'in Oman silence is perfectly polite'. Then, like any proper English lady in the desert, she joined her hosts dining on locusts roasted on a stick over the campfire.

She continued to write into her eighties, contributing a large number of travel articles to the *Daily Telegraph*. In 1990 she sponsored research into the work of the Master Wace, a neglected medieval chronicler who wrote a verse narrative of the Norman invasion in the 12th century, and from whom she might have been descended.

Barbara Wace was unmarried.

21 January 2003

FIORE DE HENRIQUEZ

Sculptress whose work was informed by her hermaphrodism, and included public commissions and many portraits of celebrities

*

Fiore de Henriquez, who has died aged 82, was one of the most respected and prolific figures in post-war sculpture; she ranged from portrait busts to crucifixions and pietas, and from semi-abstract and mythical figures to life-sized statues and monumental public commissions.

Her work revealed an intuitive grasp of plastic form and a keen eye for expression and character, yet she herself remained something of an enigma, and it was only in the last few years that she revealed to the writer Jan Marsh (whose biography of Fiore de Henriquez is to be published shortly), that she was, in fact, a hermaphrodite. Brought up as a girl in pre-war Italy, Fiore discovered her androgyny at puberty when, as well as beginning menstruation and developing breasts, she discovered that she also had male genitalia. She kept this secret from family and friends and, though she always felt more male than female (she was attracted to women, never to men), she always referred to herself as a 'sculptress', channelling her prodigious energies into her art.

She saw the creative process as a metaphor for her own duality: 'I begin to embrace a piece of clay; it is soft and pliable, all feminine,' she told Jan Marsh. 'Then it goes hard, terracotta, and is cast in plaster, pure gesso, virile and rigid, that I carve with a knife. Next it is made all feminine in wax, all pliable once more, to be caressed and stroked. Then masculine again in bronze, hard amd solid. All the time, you must think: will you leave something feminine, or make it more masculine; how will you shape and finish it?' It was possibly this struggle between the warring sides of her nature that gave Fiore de Henriquez's art its vitality and extraordinary diversity. Even in portrait sculpture, she could range from craggy vividness – as in her bust of Augustus John – to classical sensitivity – as in her head of Odette Churchill.

Some found her androgyny repellent – there were not very subtly coded references in the press to her 'mannish' appearance, 'broad shoulders', 'beetling eyebrows', and 'hefty shoes'. But others found her compelling and she formed deep friendships with people of both sexes. One to come under her spell was the painter Augustus John, who met her at a London dinner party in the early 1950s. 'Her dark, savage but eminently attractive features under a mop of coal-black hair, might have deserved the epithet "saturnine",' John recalled, 'but for the geniality and high spirits which animated her flashing Adriatic eyes. Her stalwart legs were encased in black velvet breeches ornamented with pearl buttons, with white stockings and buckled shoes. A regular Macaroni!' They became great friends and she encouraged him to try his hand at sculpting. 'A whole new phase in my history opened up,' he recalled. 'Provided by Fiore with everything I needed, I set to work to produce a head of W.B. Yeats from memory. I bless the day I met Fiore.'

Although she executed thousands of commissions, Fiore de Henriquez, possibly out of fear of the hostility which her appearance often provoked, never tried to establish a reputation and suffered from critical neglect. It was only in later life that she began to exhibit regularly and attracted some of the recognition that was her due.

Maria Fiore de Henriquez was born at Trieste on 20 June

1921 into a family of complex ancestry. On her father's side she was descended from Spanish noblemen of the Habsburg court in Vienna; her grandfather and great uncles had served as vice-admirals in the Austro-Hungarian navy. Her mother was of Turkish-Russian origin. It was always clear that Fiore was different. She adored her father and elder brother, but her mother was always angry with her. A few minutes after Fiore was born, she thrust her into cold water to see if she would survive. She insisted on dressing her in frocks and ribbons, which Fiore detested. 'Why have you such a beautiful daughter,' her mother asked Margot Fonteyn's mother, 'when I have this monster?' As a child in Mussolini's Italy, Fiore joined the Fascist youth movement, becoming leader of its girls' gymnastic team. But in 1935 her beloved father was denounced as an anti-fascist and sent into internal exile for refusing to Italianise his name.

Fiore had no particular interest in art but, while studying languages and philosophy in Venice, she saw someone working in clay and found her vocation. After briefly studying at the Accademia under Arturo Martini, she moved during the War to the Dolomite resort of Cortina d'Ampezzo. There she began to sculpt for some of the wealthier residents and did clandestine work helping partisans and Jewish refugees fleeing from Nazi occupation. Towards the end of the War she was captured and interrogated by the occupying Nazi forces, but managed to escape by jumping from the window of an upstairs lavatory.

After the War, Fiore moved to Florence where she became studio assistant to the sculptor Antonio Berti, who helped her to arrange her first exhibition, in 1947. It was a sell-out. She then moved south to Positano on the Amalfi coast, where the wheel-chair-bound German painter Kurt Kramer asked her to marry him. She was fond of him and briefly considered the matter before dismissing it as impossible.

In 1949 she won her first major public commission, for the main square of Salerno. But when her identity was revealed at the unveiling, rival artists conspired to destroy her figure because she was a woman and an outsider. Deeply upset, she decided to move to London. Her first commission, a portrait of the Royal sculptor Sir William Reid Dick, brought her immediate recognition at the Royal Academy – she had two heads in the 1950 summer show – and in 1951 Jacob Epstein invited her to create three enormous figures for the Festival of Britain, for which she negotiated a then astronomical fee of £4,000. Meanwhile society hostesses with bohemian tastes competed to secure her exotic presence at their tables.

From then on she was deluged with commissions – in 1954, she was reported to have completed no fewer than 500 portrait busts in four years. Her sitters included the Queen Mother, Odette Churchill, Alicia Markova, Laurence Olivier, Igor Stravinsky, Peter Ustinov and Margot Fonteyn. 'For a new person I always wear a skirt when I visit their homes for the first time,' she explained. 'Afterwards they understand me better in trousers.' She took British citizenship in 1957.

In 1955 she travelled to America to work with the architect Claude Phillimore on an abortive design for a civic centre in Hollywood for the millionaire Huntingdon Hartford. From then on she travelled widely, flitting between London, Italy, Japan, Hong Kong and America, where, for 20 years, she undertook an annual two-month tour demonstrating her art (in the early days, Jennifer Paterson of *Two Fat Ladies* worked as her administrative assistant).

In 1963 she was commissioned to do a bust of President Kennedy, a project which had to be completed posthumously from photographs. Later commissions included 20 life-sized bronzes of racehorses and their jockeys for a race course in New York. American modernism inspired her to experiment with looser forms and she developed new motifs, often involving conjoined figures which seemed to represent the duality of her nature. In the early 1960s she found a new mentor in the cubist sculptor Jacques Lipchitz, whom she introduced to the bronze foundries of Pietrasanta, in Italy.

It was on a visit to Italy in 1968 that she discovered and later bought the ruined hamlet of Peralta, north of Lucca, which became her base. She restored the buildings, creating a haven where artists could come to write, sculpt or simply walk in the hills. But during the mid-1960s, she suffered some kind of mental breakdown after undergoing surgery to remove her male reproductive organs. While physiologically the operation was a success, it did nothing to remove her feelings of duality, and she produced a series of tortured pieces inspired by mythological creatures – half beast, half human. But she eventually recovered and in 1985 she built a tower in Peralta to celebrate its resurrection, and possibly her own recovery.

11 June 2004

JILL TWEEDIE

Feminist writer and controversialist who loved tilting at conventional wisdom and shattering taboos

*

Jill Tweedie, the writer who has died aged 57 (four months after learning she was suffering from motor neurone disease), championed feminist causes with passion, but also with humour and sexual candour.

At the height of her success as a columnist, in the 1970s, her readers would seize the *Guardian* each week to see what taboos she had shattered this time. No received opinion or conventional wisdom was safe from her. English public-school men she condemned as dirty and untrained in the ways of personal cleanliness. As 'a gauche Republican' she found curtseying to royalty was 'an odd and atavistic ritual'. She resented being 'prayed at' and being forced to stand for grace: 'too many Christians are tactless and impolite, assuming my acceptance of that which I – and others like me – have carefully and thoughtfully rejected.'

Such feminist causes, such as better treatment of women in childbirth and the principle that rape can exist within marriage, were taken up with a commitment which made her immensely readable. But it also made her the butt of other journalists who did not share her views. She was a constant critic of the Conservative government, but when the Tories came to power in 1979 and Margaret Thatcher became Europe's first woman Prime Minister, Tweedie said that she could not help feeling a thrill.

Indeed her radical *Guardian* readers were probably unaware that Jill Tweedie had been given her first chance in journalism on the *Sunday Telegraph*. Tweedie herself later recalled her years on the *Telegraph* as the happiest days of her life: 'There was a wonderful woman called Winefride Jackson who was just like a mummy to us. I felt like I'd gone back to school and I just loved it. Then one day she came sweeping into the room and called out "I say, girls, Yoko Ono has said women are the niggers of the world. Does anyone know what she means?" I did. And I knew then I had to move on.' She found herself as a columnist on the *Guardian* from 1969 to 1988, and was named 'Woman Journalist of the Year' in 1971 and 1972.

Jill Sheila Tweedie was born in Egypt in 1936. She was the daughter of a conventional Scottish father – whom she detested and called 'The Cleft', although she later admitted that she felt lost when he died and was no longer there to rebel against – and a repining mother of Turkish extraction. In her autobiography, *Eating Children*, Jill Tweedie described her childhood notion that she was a changeling. This feeling grew into the unhappy impression that she was large, gawky and a disappointment to her parents. Her height meant that she could not realise her ambition to be a dancer. At 16 she was sent to a Swiss finishing school, where the pleasures of speculating about men and sex and talking franglais were brought to a sudden halt by the death of a beautiful American called Carla, who dived into shallow water on a swimming expedition: 'She looked like a sleeping mermaid, her long hair floating out on the lazy lap of the waves. I watched until the skin on my body became suddenly much too tight.' In her autobiography, this event seems to portend a tragic vein which ran through her life.

At 18 – after a courtship in which her future husband stubbed out cigarettes on either his or her hands, and burst into her apartment with a pick-axe – she married Bela Cziraky, a Hungarian count ('Istvan the Mad Magyar'). She was devastated when their first son died a 'cot death' at five months. They later had a daughter, Ilona, and a second son, Adam. There was a disastrous end to the marriage.

'Obsessive love is terrible,' she later recalled to the journalist Valerie Grove. 'People think it is enviable, but it's a kind of torture. If it was manifested in any other way, people would call it hostility. When the demon lover is male it usually resolves itself in murder. The ideal marriage is much closer to friendship.' The Count took the two children away, and for three years Tweedie knew nothing about where or how they were. Mary Stott, former woman's editor of the *Guardian*, remembers Tweedie telling her about a recurrent nightmare in which she saw little, bloody footprints going down the road.

In 1965 Tweedie had a third child, Luke, by a Dutch lover, Bob d'Ancona, with whom she lived in what she described as a kind of commune. Lasting happiness came with her marriage to the journalist Alan Brien, whom she met on a press trip. They were married in 1973.

Jill Tweedie's books included *In the Name of Love* (1979), *It's Only Me* (1980), *Letters from a Faint-hearted Feminist* (published in 1982, and later made into a television series) and *More from*

Martha (1983). She also published two novels, *Bliss* (1983) and *Internal Affairs* (1986).

Tweedie characteristically decided to share with the news-paper-reading public the news that she had been diagnosed as having motor neurone disease. She did so through Polly Toynbee, her *Guardian* colleague, because she felt she could not write the piece herself without sounding either flippant and plucky or self-pitying. 'Goddammit,' Toynbee wrote, 'she has been plunged into a grotesque mental torture chamber, she says, without hope or light.' In the view of Peter Cardy, director of the Motor Neurone Disease Association, Jill Tweedie 'performed a great service by making her anger and wretchedness public. There is so much pressure to put up with and shut up about a fatal illness. She dra-matically made it clear you don't have to pretend to be a hero.'

13 November 1993

KAY THOMPSON

Comedy revue star surprised by the success of Eloise, her children's book anti-heroine

*

Kay Thompson, who has died aged 85, was best known for creating the children's character Eloise, the spoiled and deter-mined six-year-old who lives in and terrorises the Plaza Hotel in New York. Neglected by her socialite mother, Eloise is left to her own devices, and rockets round the hotel's thickly-carpeted corridors with her pug dog in search of entertainment. This she finds in such exercises as pouring water down the mail chutes ('Just zippety jingle and skibble away zap!') and torment-ing the beleaguered porter. Brought to life in crisp line draw-ings by Hilary Knight, the haughty but lovable Eloise introduces the reader to her various enemies and accomplices among the hotel staff and clientele.

The success of the *Eloise* books lay in Kay Thompson's placing her heroine in the setting of a grand hotel, the epitome of a grown up's world, but a place where a child – especially a naughty one – could run wild. *Eloise*, the first book, appeared in 1955; by the time *Eloise in Paris* appeared two years later, the first had sold 150,000 copies. Next came *Eloise at Christmastime* (1958), and then *Eloise in Moscow* (1959). The untidy little girl in the grand hotel rapidly became something of an industry. Thompson formed Eloise Ltd to take care of her, with headquarters appropriately located at the Plaza Hotel, and built up a catalogue of spin-off products which included a record, *Absolutely Christmas Time*, a set of French postcards, Eloise dolls and an Emergency Hotel Kit for itinerant six year olds.

But for Kay Thompson, Eloise was merely one detour in an unusually multifarious career. She was, variously, a singer, dancer, actress, songwriter, composer and arranger, clothes designer, and businesswoman; all of which demanded, she said, 'just a matter of constant adjustment of one's heads'.

Kay Thompson was born on 9 November 1912 in St Louis, Missouri, the daughter of a jewel merchant. She began to play the piano when she was four, and at 15 played Liszt with the St Louis Symphony Orchestra.

Two years later she went to California in pursuit of fame, and after a brief spell as a diving instructor found work as a vocal arranger and singer for radio, with Bing Crosby and the Mills Brothers among others. She found similar work in New York, before being given her own radio show, Kay Thompson and Company, co-starring the comedian Jim Backus. The rapid demise of the show determined her to head West again, and she returned to Hollywood with plans to become an actress. She found work, though, as an arranger and composer, and was soon active during one of Hollywood's most productive periods for musicals. She worked on such films as *The Ziegfeld Follies* (1946), *The Harvey Girls* (1946) and *The Kid From Brooklyn* (1946), with stars including Lena Horne and Judy Garland. Garland became a life-long friend, and appointed Kay Thompson godmother to her daughter Liza Minnelli.

In 1947, with her studio contract up, Kay Thompson formed a night club act, consisting of herself backed by the Williams Brothers (one of whom, Andy, would later have a successful solo career of his own). Their first show, at Ciro's in Hollywood, brought the house down. They went on the road, and by February the next year Kay Thompson was performing in Miami for $15,000 a week. Her act was structured like a revue in miniature, designed to make the most of her talents both as singer and as comedienne. Her sleek figure and parodic skills were well-matched by the energetic chorus of the Williams Brothers behind her, and by a series of routines which were fast and funny, described by one reviewer as 'a combination of ballet, barber shop, roughhouse and penthouse'. For the next six years the act travelled the world. When it disbanded in 1953, Kay Thompson, in typically adroit manner, branched out into designing, for long-legged women, the 'Kay Thompson Fancy Pants'.

In early 1954 she opened a one-woman show at the Plaza Hotel, playing the role of a blasé society hostess entertaining a cocktail party. This, though successful, was not destined for the long run of its predecessor.

Eloise was born of Kay Thompson's extensive travelling and performing experiences. The character first appeared when one day Kay – normally punctual – arrived late for a rehearsal. After the Williams brothers shouted their disapproval, she spontaneously replied in a high, child's voice: 'All right, all right, I'm late. I'm Eloise and af'r all, I'm only six.' The character stuck, and thereafter would enliven rehearsals.

Meanwhile Kay Thompson continued to act and write. In

1957 she was well cast as the fashion magazine editor in *Funny Face*, alongside Fred Astaire and Audrey Hepburn. She shone in several of the film's musical numbers, including the opening song, *Think Pink*, and *Bonjour Paris*, with both leads. Kay made one more film, Otto Preminger's *Tell Me That You Love Me, Junie Moon* (1970), after which she became increasingly reclusive. She lived with Liza Minnelli on the Upper East Side in Manhattan.

Today the *Eloise* books continue to sell in large numbers.

Kay Thompson married twice, first to Jack Jenney and secondly to Bill Spier; both marriages were dissolved.

9 July 1998

ROSAMOND LEHMANN

Rediscovered novelist who gave up writing after the break up of her affair with Cecil Day Lewis

*

Rosamond Lehmann, the novelist who has died aged 89, had the unusual experience for a writer of seeing her work eclipsed and forgotten, then rediscovered within her lifetime – a curious example, as she wryly expressed it, of posthumous fame that was not in fact posthumous.

When her first novel, *Dusty Answer*, was published in 1927, she achieved the kind of instant celebrity of which most writers can only dream. Other and better novels followed in the 1930s and 1940s, and by the time *The Echoing Grove* appeared in 1953, Rosamond Lehmann was a household name in literary circles. But although *The Echoing Grove* was widely acclaimed, it was followed by 23 years of silence, when the sources of creation appeared to fail, until the publication of *A Sea-Grape Tree*, which was generally judged disappointing.

Speculation on why Rosamond Lehmann abandoned fiction for so many years has been abundant and frequently foolish. The popular theory that she was too devastated by the desertion of her lover, the poet Cecil Day-Lewis, is groundless, since *The Echoing Grove* itself was written after the relationship ended, and carries clear traces of that crisis in the author's life.

It would, however, be true to say that Miss Lehmann never entirely recovered from the cruel breaking-off of that affair, and for the rest of her life reacted to any mention of it with bitterness. Another explanation advanced for the decline in her literary output was the death from polio in 1958 of her daughter, Sally. Certainly, this tragedy led Miss Lehmann into a set of beliefs which most people would categorise as spiritualism. But Sally's death hardly stopped her writing – it did not occur until some half-dozen years after *The Echoing Grove* was written. Rosamond Lehmann's own account of her creative silence is perhaps nearest to the truth: that the central themes of her novels – love, betrayal, family rivalries, sexual passion – were not of a kind to inspire indefinitely.

Meanwhile a generation grew up which had never heard of Rosamond Lehmann. Only in the 1980s, when Virago Press began reissuing her novels, did she regain her true place, no longer as a fashionable woman novelist, but as an example of some of the most subtle and enduring qualities in English 20th-century fiction.

Rosamond Nina Lehmann was born in a large, comfortable house on the Thames at Bourne End, Bucks, in 1901, and educated at Girton College, Cambridge. This was achieved largely under the influence of her American mother, Alice Davis, who was descended from Robert Chambers – of the *Encyclopaedia*. Her father was R.C. Lehmann, Cambridge scholar – and founder of *Granta* – celebrated oarsman, one-time editor of the *Daily News* and a distinguished member of the *Punch* round table.

The Lehmanns were Jews, a cosmopolitan and talented family

of musicians and painters who came originally from Hamburg. Once settled in England, they chose to disregard their roots, and Rosamond remained all her life part proud and part embarrassed by any mention of her Jewish heritage. Along with her brother, John Lehmann the writer, and her two sisters – of whom Beatrix achieved fame as an actress – Rosamond grew up in the pleasant, sheltered world of the English upper-middle class. Among the most vivid memories of Rosamond's early years were the splendid children's parties given by Lady Desborough at nearby Taplow, where for the first time the impressionable little girl caught sight of those golden and unattainable young men who were later to play so romantic a part in her novels.

It was at Cambridge that Rosamond met her first husband, Leslie (later Lord) Runciman. The marriage was not a success, and in 1928 she married Wogan Philipps, eldest son of the first Lord Milford, the shipping magnate. That marriage too was dissolved in 1944 and Philipps subsequently succeeded to the Barony of Milford, becoming well-known as the 'Communist peer'. The Philipps had two children, Hugo and Sally.

The 1930s, when Rosamond Lehmann was bearing her children, were also her most fertile creative years, during which she wrote her two best loved books, *Invitation to the Waltz* and *The Weather in the Streets*. The latter book in particular, a heart-rending evocation of a young woman's unhappy love affair with a married man, has become a classic of its genre. Daring in its day (many people were shocked by the harrowingly explicit description of an abortion), it now seems simply timeless.

The War brought a series of unforgettable short stories, mostly produced for John Lehmann's *New Writing*. Then followed *The Ballad and the Source* – a more opulently romantic and uneven work – before *The Echoing Grove* brought, in the writer's own words, 'some cycle to a close'. Between this and her final novel, *A Sea-Grape Tree*, Rosamond Lehmann wrote in 1967 a marvellous short autobiographical work, *The Swan in the*

Evening, in which she movingly described her discovery, after Sally's death, of the spirit world. For many of her later years she was Vice-President of the College of Psychic Studies. Sally's death also inspired her husband, the poet P.J. Kavanagh, to write *The Perfect Stranger*, a haunting evocation of their love affair.

Sensitive to a fault and emotionally demanding in all her relationships, Rosamond craved admiration and was never wholly satisfied with any of her remarkable achievements. She was never convinced that her novels had received the recognition they deserved, nor her physical loveliness the homage that was its due. But this apart, she had many exceptional qualities: she was warm, highly intelligent, generous, and often very perceptive where others were concerned. A famous beauty in her youth, she never became reconciled to old age, although she took pleasure in her late renaissance, and continued to the last to extend friendship to people young enough to be her own lost daughter – her granddaughter Anna, Hugo's child, remaining her especial favourite.

When Rosamond Lehmann became blind in her last years, many friends would go and read to her. In the final analysis, despite her apparent vulnerability, she was, as she herself once said, 'a great survivor'.

In 1982 she was awarded the CBE.

14 March 1990

SARAH KANE

Playwright whose works created a sensation with scenes of unbridled brutality

*

Sarah Kane, the playwright who has committed suicide aged 28, made a controversial debut with *Blasted*, which opened in 1995 at the Royal Court Theatre Upstairs. The play, about the nature of violence and war, was set in a Leeds hotel room that erupts into a Bosnian battlefield. In what the *Daily Mail* critic Jack Tinker described as 'a disgusting feast of filth', it featured, among other atrocities, scenes of masturbation, fellatio, micturation, frottage, defecation, homosexual rape, eye-gouging, tongue-munching and baby-eating.

As furious headlines demanded the play should be banned, Sarah Kane found herself catapulted from nowhere to instant notoriety. The critics were bitterly divided: some declared themselves physically sickened by the gratuitous violence and depravity; others hailed her as a new and original talent. Her work, her supporters argued, was a magnificent dark vision of the late 20th century, and an honest and brave portrayal of human brutality. According to the playwright Harold Pinter, Sarah Kane 'was facing something actual and true and ugly and painful'. Sarah Kane herself declared that *Blasted* was 'quite a peaceful play about hope'.

The attendant publicity ensured that *Blasted* played to capacity houses for the remainder of its run. It was later performed all over the Continent, where there was an extraordinary curiosity about Sarah Kane's work and what it said about contemporary Britain. Success brought her immediate commissions for further works in a similar vein. Her next play *Phaedra's Love* (Gate Theatre, 1996) was billed as a modern version of the Greek tragedy of *Phaedra*, who conceived a violent passion for her stepson Hippolytus and committed suicide when he rejected her. Euripides, Seneca and Racine had all told the story, though in their versions the violence and the gore had been kept off the stage. Sarah made her own additions to the original. Hippolytus was presented as a terminal depressive who eats burgers and masturbates into his socks; Theseus rapes his daughter to enthusiastic cheers; Hippolytus has his penis cut off and grilled on a barbecue. Throats are slit with playful abandon; blood spurts all over the place. Yet *Phaedra's Love* failed to inspire even those critics who had been impressed by *Blasted*. 'It's not a theatre critic that's required here,' wrote the *Daily Telegraph*'s critic Charles Spencer, 'it's a psychiatrist.'

Sarah Kane again inspired critical acclaim with *Cleansed*, (Royal Court, 1998), a play apparently inspired by Roland Barthes's assertion: 'When one is in love, one is in Dachau.' The play, if anything more extreme than *Blasted*, featured sex changes, rats, the injection of heroin into an eyeball, violent amputations and suicide.

Sarah Kane claimed that the violence of her writing derived from her religious upbringing; the Bible, she noted, 'is full of rape, mutilation, war and pestilence. I think because of the way I was brought up it has created a dilemma in my head about when life begins and ends, and what hope really is.' Before her death, however, Sarah Kane had been attempting to acquire a truer classical sensibility. Her last play, *Crave*, first seen at the Traverse Theatre during last year's Edinburgh Festival, moved away from the stage violence of her earlier efforts. In its exploration of humanity and man's relentless need for love, she converted previously hostile critics with the tender and lyrical quality of her writing.

Sarah Kane was born on 3 February 1971 in Essex, where her father was East Anglian correspondent for the *Daily Mirror*. At seven she was writing a short story about a man who met a violent end. Her interest in the theatre began at school, where she directed productions of Chekhov and *Oh! What a Lovely War*. For a short time in her teens, she came under the influence of her family's born-again Christianity. But by the time she arrived at Bristol University to study drama, she had abandoned her faith and turned against the values of her upbringing. At first, she had imagined she would become a theatre director, but, finding there was nothing she wanted to direct, she turned her talents instead to writing plays. An early effort, a monologue written while she was still an undergraduate, was performed first at

Bristol, then at the Edinburgh Festival. After graduating with a First, she moved to London, where she wrote two further monologues before *Blasted* catapulted her to fame.

Though deeply disturbed by the reaction to her earlier plays, she remained unrepentent: 'If you want to write about extreme love, you can only write about it in an extreme way. Otherwise it doesn't mean anything.'

At the end of her life, she derived no pleasure from the more favourable critical reception given to *Crave*. 'Some people seem to find release at the end of it,' she said, 'but I think it's only the release of death. In my other plays, it was the release of deciding to go on living despite the fact that it's terrible.'

She never married.

24 February 1999

PATRICIA HIGHSMITH

Thriller writer who confronted her own demons by creating the amoral anti-hero Tom Ripley

*

Patricia Highsmith, the American-born thriller writer who has died aged 74, created the character Tom Ripley, among the most convincing literary portrayals of a psychopath and the protagonist of five successful novels beginning with *The Talented Mr Ripley* (1957) and concluding with *Ripley Under Water* (1991).

An amoral pragmatist, the charming Ripley comes from America to Europe, ruthlessly addresses himself to acquiring riches through selling forged works of art, and obtains – over several dead bodies – a beautiful wife and a splendid French property. He has no qualms ('Never kick a man when he's down, Tom thought, and gave Pritchard another kick, hard, in the midriff'), and the conventional denouements of what the thriller trade terms the 'English cosies' were flouted. Indeed, controlling intelligence and occasional killings are all that Highsmith had in common with the detective stories of Agatha Christie or P.D. James. 'Ripley doesn't suffer as much as the rest of us do from the knowledge that he has done something wrong,' remarked Highsmith. 'Maybe I have a certain contempt for justice.'

Highsmith's well-meaning characters fared badly; but Ripley was consistently permitted a happy ending, and the books were certainly not to everyone's taste. While the moral ambiguity of *The Talented Mr Ripley* earned Highsmith the admiration of Graham Greene, it also caused one distinguished member of the Crime Writers' Association critics' panel to threaten resignation if it were given an award.

As a child Highsmith devoured the texts on psychiatry she found on her parents' shelves, in particular Karl Menninger's *The Human Mind*, a rich source of case studies of schizophrenia, paranoia, kleptomania and pederasty. In her 20 novels and various collections of short stories, her enthusiasts maintained that she assiduously mapped the potential violence and callousness of the human psyche; her critics opined that she simply over-cultivated neurosis. Though she claimed never to think about style Highsmith used words to seduce readers into a sense of uneasy security through a meticulous attention to the dull minutiae of life. She was never more dangerous than when describing a man mowing the lawn, since murder was almost certainly on his mind.

Her first novel, *Strangers on a Train* (1950), survived rejection by six publishers and was immediately filmed by Alfred Hitchcock. On the Continent her existential bleakness attracted French and German intellectuals and film-makers; the first *Ripley* novel was filmed with Alain Delon, whom Highsmith afterwards considered her model for the urbane and chilly murderer. *Ripley's Game* was also filmed, by the German Wim Wenders, as *The American*

Friend (1977). 'I do not understand people who make a noise,' said Highsmith. 'Consequently I fear them. And since I fear them, I hate them.' She had a curious fascination for snails, and said writers were born with too little shell. Though she denied being a misanthrope, she abhorred crowds. She avoided society, and was never lured by a name (she was 'too busy' to meet Hitchcock). Her writing was in opposition to the world: 'You can't do both,' she said, citing the example of her friend Truman Capote, whom she thought had been destroyed by cocktail parties.

In 1953 Highsmith published *The Price of Salt* (under the pseudonym Claire Morgan) about a lesbian affair; it was re-published in 1990 as *Carol*. Regardless of the book's literary merits, its treatment of the subject was revolutionary. 'Prior to this book,' noted Highsmith, 'homosexuals in American novels had to pay for their deviancy by cutting their throats . . . or by switching to heterosexuality.'

But Highsmith's personal life was inscrutable; she thought that emotional attachments were accidental, and 'nothing to do with orgasms'. She insisted she had affairs with men as well as women, but none lasted. In later years she was happiest living with her cats, first in rural France, then in Switzerland, in a small village outside Lugano. Thither travelled many journalists, all determined to extract a little more from her than their predecessors; all returned with much the same interview. 'My idea of a good time,' she said, 'is to buy enough food and milk and catfood and beer to last for ten days without needing to go out again.'

She was politically disengaged and could be disparaging of others' charitable efforts, though she did dedicate *People Who Knock on the Door* (1983) to the Palestinian cause. 'If I saw a kitten and a little human baby sitting on the curb starving,' she said, 'I would feed the kitten first, if nobody was looking.'

Patricia Highsmith was born at Fort Worth, Texas, on 1 January 1921. Her father, Jay Bernard Plangman, was a commercial artist, but her parents had separated, and she was adopted by her mother's second husband. The family moved to New York, to a claustrophobic apartment which she recalled as chaotic and echoing with quarrels (which left her with a strong distaste for family life). She thought that the books about psychiatry which she found on her parents' shelves must have had an effect on her imagination 'because I started writing these weirdo stories when I was 15 or 16.' She wrote a story for her school magazine, about a pyromaniac nanny, which was refused as too unpleasant. At Barnard College she studied English composition, but, being also a capable artist, was undecided whether she really wanted to be an author or a painter. Having graduated in 1942, she worked as a script writer for comic books. Finally determined to be a writer, she went to Mexico, where, after a false start with a gothic novel, she wrote *Strangers on a Train*.

Highsmith was urged to follow *Strangers on a Train* with something similar, but instead she wrote *The Price of Salt*, pseudonymously. 'I'm not afraid of the labels now,' she explained when the book was reprinted, 'but then it would have been "Lesbian Writer of Books". People would have gone around saying "queer, queer, queer".'

In contrast to the *Ripley* books, *Deep Water* (1957), *The Glass Cell* (1965), *A Dog's Ransom* (1972) and *Found in the Streets* (1986) feature characters drawn into criminality and destroyed by accident or by others' corruption. Less gloomy but typically oblique was *The Tremor of Forgery* (1969) in which an American abroad is never quite certain whether or not he has killed somebody. Among her volumes of short stories were *Little Tales of Misogyny* (1977), mostly about weak husbands who killed disagreeable wives, and *The Animal Lover's Book of Beastly Murder* (1975), typified by the tale of a man suffocated by fast-breeding snails.

After spending a little time in Europe during the 1950s, Highsmith returned to America. Still restless, she came to England and set up in Suffolk in 1962. Five years later she moved to France, and then to Switzerland.

Highsmith was a talented painter of surprisingly cheerful subject matter.

6 February 1995

OLIVIA GOLDSMITH

Author of The First Wives Club who took revenge on her former husband by writing a blockbuster novel

*

Olivia Goldsmith, who has died in New York aged 54 after complications following plastic surgery, was the author of the best-selling novel *The First Wives Club* (1992), the tale of ex-wives wreaking revenge on their rich husbands; in 1996 it became a hit film starring Goldie Hawn, Diane Keaton and Bette Midler as the vengeful trio. Olivia Goldsmith had been inspired to write the book when her own 'extremely nasty' divorce left her broke and bitter. Her husband had come away from the marriage with an apartment in Manhattan, a beach house in the Hamptons and a Jaguar; she received $300,000 and spent the entire sum on lawyers. 'I hate divorce lawyers and judges more than I ever did my ex,' she said in 1996, adding, 'no, that's not right. I hate them all, and I want them dead.'

But although attracted by the idea of both murder and castration, she decided that her revenge would be sweeter (and more protracted) if she wrote a blockbuster book inspired by her experiences. Struck by an article in *Fortune*, a glossy financial magazine, describing how rich older businessmen swapped their ageing spouses for young, sleek and beautiful 'trophy wives', she created Anna, Brenda and Elise, three well-heeled New York ladies who find themselves unceremoniously dumped by their ghastly husbands. Unlike the murderous heroines of classical literature, Olivia Goldsmith's protagonists plot a more modern revenge and go for their menfolk where it will hurt most: 'the ego and the wallet'. After almost 500 pages of energetic plot twists which begin with a suicide and weave in alcoholism, obesity, handicapped children, lesbianism, trips to Japan and countless New York society balls, the three women triumph and their ex-husbands are left bankrupt, humiliated and abandoned.

After the book had been rejected a number of times, Olivia Goldsmith, a diminutive and slightly plump brunette, took to donning high heels and a long blonde wig to convince potential publishers that she was a marketable author. But it was not until three (female) Hollywood producers took an interest in the story that she eventually found a publisher. The presentation of the book made it as sellable as possible. The cover featured a woman's hand, immaculately manicured, holding two golf balls in such a tight grip that they are beginning to crack; the author's biographical blurb included the line 'Olivia Goldsmith is a first wife'. It became a best-seller, described by one critic as 'an exquisite tale of retribution'.

The film, a crude, cruel and more slapstick version of the book, was equally successful, and although lacking in substance and subtlety, it had its moments, as when Bette Midler's character meets her husband's thin and beautiful mistress, and remarks that 'the bulimia has finally paid off'.

The success of *The First Wives Club* and subsequent books earned Olivia Goldsmith some $4.5 million in royalties and, having acquired houses, cars, money and even affairs with younger men, she vowed never to marry again. As Ivana Trump, making her cameo appearance as the patron of The First Wives Club, explained: 'Don't get mad – get everything.'

Olivia Goldsmith was born Randy Goldfield in New York in 1949. One of three daughters of a civil servant and a teacher, she grew up in Dumont, New Jersey, and attended New York University. Having changed her name to Justine Olivia Rendal, she became a successful businesswoman and was one of the first women to be a partner at the management consultant firm Booz Allen Hamilton before she married and decided to write children's books. But the marriage collapsed after five years and she found herself homeless and jobless.

After the success of *The First Wives Club*, she wrote *Flavour of the Month* (1993) and *Fashionably Late* (1994), satires on the film and fashion world respectively, before turning her pen on the publishing world with *Bestseller* (1996). Subsequent publications included *Marrying Mom* (1996), the story of a widow whose children attempt to marry her off in order to get rid of her. *Switcheroo* was the tale of a wife who agrees to swap places with her husband's mistress.

Olivia Goldsmith described her books as 'cabin-class Dickens', and with their brightly coloured covers and liberal doses of sex, money and glamour they definitely belonged to the 'holiday read' genre. But her work had more edge, humour and satire than many of her peers and it was not without some merit; she never failed to include her own moral convictions and was outspoken about the issues close to her heart. 'It's a terrible shame that after all these years of feminism, women should be back in the place where they are regarded as expendable,' she said when *The First Wives Club* was published. She also lamented an increasingly ageist and sexist society. 'The stereotypes presented to women are more tyrannical than ever. While the median age of women in America is rising each year,' she explained, 'fashion models are becoming statistically younger and thinner than ever.'

She was appalled that Hillary Clinton stood by her husband after the Monica Lewinsky affair. 'I am desolated,' she said, 'that the American people didn't want a stronger image for Hillary Clinton; that her popularity went up as she was more victimised.'

Charismatic and witty ('I make my living writing cheery little comedies about women who get shafted by men'), her only regret was that she had spent many of her child-bearing years dealing with her divorce and by the time she was free again, she was not able to conceive. But she lavished affection on her cats and dogs and cited her favourite hobbies as 'reading, sex and sleeping'. 'Living well,' she once declared, echoing the words from *The First Wives Club*, 'is the best revenge.'

In a recent interview Olivia Goldsmith joked that after her death she would have cosmetic surgery so that her friends would be able to say that she 'never looked better'. She died after falling into a coma following a face-lift operation.

17 January 2004

RUMER GODDEN

Novelist who excelled at writing about children and nuns but hated the film of Black Narcissus

✳

Rumer Godden, who has died aged 90, was a novelist of many gifts: she could see the world through the eyes of children with a vivid and sometimes uncomfortable realism; she excelled at portraying the sensuous atmosphere and contradictions of India in the last days of the Raj; and she was deeply interested in the religious and contemplative life. *Black Narcissus* (1938), for instance, deals with the struggle of a group of nuns to maintain their convent in a disused Indian palace. The heady 'pagan' atmosphere of the subcontinent prevails, while the deeply felt ideals of each nun are, in turn, eroded and overthrown. In the 60 years since its first publication, the book has never been out of print.

The Greengage Summer (1958), by contrast, is set in France, where four children are left virtually alone in a château-hotel after their mother is taken ill, and rudely thrust into the adult world. The English paramour of the hotel's proprietress falls in love with the 16-year-old; her 13-year-old sister sits on the side-lines, teetering on the brink of womanhood; and their brother, aged eight, passes his time in a fantasy of couture, obsessed by *Vogue*, and dressing up his dolls with false bosoms.

Both these books became successful films. But Rumer Godden hated Michael Powell and Emeric Pressburger's version of *Black Narcissus* (1947), which starred Deborah Kerr and David Farrar. 'Everything about it was phoney,' she complained. 'The outside shots were done in a Surrey garden and the Himalayas were just muslin mounted on poles.' *The Greengage Summer* (1961), with Kenneth More and the young Susannah York, was a solid if uninspired reproduction of the book. The best film of Rumer Godden's work was Jean Renoir's *The River* (1951), based on a novel which she had published in 1946. Set in India, and concerned with her perennial theme of the tran-sition from childhood to adolescence, the book was perhaps the most autobiographical of all her novels. But her early years did not merely afford material for her books; they gave her the urge to write them.

Margaret Rumer (the family name of her maternal grand-mother) Godden was born at Eastbourne – 'the most dreadful place', as she later came to think – on 10 December 1907. At six months she was taken by her parents to India, where her father ran a steamship company in the Bengal delta. Superficially she and her three sisters led a blissful existence, far removed from the horrors that Europe was enduring in the First World War. But Rumer Godden, cursed with a nose that resembled the Duke of Wellington's, was the only plain daughter. She was especially jealous of her elder sister Jon, who was as talented as she was beautiful. 'Everything she did was marvellous,' Rumer recalled at the end of her life, 'and nobody took any notice of me, which was very healthy. To be ignored is the best possible thing for a writer. My writing was an effort to outdo Jon.'

Rumer Godden was turning out poetry at the age of five, and embarked upon her first autobiography two years later. When asked if she would like a dog, she replied that she wanted a unicorn. Her entire life would be a flight from the commonplace. Her childhood was certainly eclectic. At the Goddens' house in Narayangunj the servants at table were Muslims; the valet and the nanny were Christians from Madras; another valet was a Buddhist from Nepal. The gardeners were Brahmins and the sweepers Untouchables. When Rumer Godden swore at a Brahmin gardener, her father made her apologise and touch the man's feet. But later, after reading E. M. Forster's *A Passage to India* (1924), Rumer Godden came to regard her parents' attitudes as totally hidebound, 'oblivious to everything Indian except their servants'.

In 1920 she and her sisters were sent to school in England. With their wild, precocious ways, and their sing-song Eurasian accents, they were ridiculed by teachers and fellow pupils alike. Rumer and Jon changed schools five times in as many years, only settling down when they were sent to a permissive establishment called Moira House.

Rumer Godden trained in ballet, and back in India in 1925 opened a multi-racial dance school in Calcutta, which she ran successfully for eight years. But in 1934 she became pregnant as a result of a liaison with the dashing Laurence Sinclair Foster, 'one of the Worcester Fosters', a stockbroker who thought that Omar Khayyam was a kind of curry. 'You'll just have to marry me and pretend you like it,' he told her. So the knot was tied; the baby, however, died four days after birth. Rumer Godden's first novel, *Chinese Puzzle*, was published the next year.

Two further daughters survived, but the marriage did not prosper. When she sat silent and icy at cocktail parties, Foster would say: 'Can't you be more chatty?' In 1941 he left to join the Army, leaving her encumbered with debts which mopped up the proceeds of *Black Narcissus*. She retreated to Kashmir, and moved into a cottage high in the mountains with no electricity or running water – 'the most beautiful place you could imagine', as she thought. To support her girls she got up at 4 am to write, and returned to her desk when they had gone to bed until 11 pm.

It was while they were living in Kashmir that a cook attempted to poison them by mixing powdered glass, opium and marijuana with the lunchtime fare of dahl and rice. 'It's gritty,' her elder girl complained. In consequence, none but the dog perished.

In 1949 Rumer Godden married a civil servant called James Haynes Dixon, who looked after her devotedly, leaving her free to produce a steady stream of books in the 1950s and 1960s. 'A nice, ugly man,' she described him. 'He would do anything for me, but it was not the other way round.' Her heart, she claimed, had been given to Jane Austen's Mr Darcy: 'I loved him far more than my own husbands.'

Back in Britain they lived in style at Lamb House in Rye, once home to Henry James, and at the Old Hall in Highgate, where Margaret Rutherford lived upstairs, and the essayist Francis Bacon had died. James Dixon expired in 1975. 'I never want to be consoled,' Rumer Godden wrote in her diary; 'I never want another man in my life.'

Meanwhile her books were gaining increasing acclaim. She continued to approach her writing with iron discipline, and when she had finished a book would read it to a 'victim' over three days. 'It's very tiring for them,' she admitted, 'but I ply them with food and drink.'

Altogether she published 24 novels, the last one, *Cromartie v The God Shiva, Acting Through the Government of India*, appearing only last year, to excellent reviews. Other novels were *Kingfishers Catch Fire* (1953), *An Episode of Sparrows* (1955), *Two Under the Indian Sun* (1966), *Shiva's Pigeons* (1972), *The Peacock Spring* (1975, televised 1995), *Five For Sorrow, Ten For Joy* (1979), *The Dark Horse* (1981) and *Coromandel Sea Change* (1991). Rumer Godden also published poetry, translations, a biography of Hans

Christian Andersen and two volumes of autobiography: *A Time to Dance, No Time To Weep* (1987) and *A House with Four Rooms* (1989). She has been translated into 12 languages.

She also wrote books for children, including *The Doll's House* (1947), *The Mousewife* (1951) and *Miss Happiness and Miss Flower* (1961). In 1972 she won the Whitbread Award for *The Diddakoi*; Kingsley Amis called it 'the sort of book children had to fight for to get it from adults'. 'There are several things children will not put up with in a book,' she reflected. 'You have to have a proper beginning and an end; you cannot have flashbacks. Then you can't have a lot of description: keep it to a minimum. And you must be very careful with words. I find I use fewer, and they have to fit the case exactly and be chosen with extreme care.'

Rumer Godden converted to Roman Catholicism in 1968. 'I like the way everything is clear and concise,' she remarked apropos her new religion. 'You'll always be forgiven but you must know the rules.'

In preparation for *In This House of Breda* (1969), about life in a Benedictine convent, she lived for three years at the gate of an English abbey. But she remained prickly, and enjoyed recounting her reply to an American who asked for her autograph. 'Thank you for your autograph. We have had your handwriting analysed. You are mean, petty, selfish and greedy.'

Rumer Godden earned plenty of money, and knew how to spend it. From her seventies she lived with her daughter in Dumfriesshire. She was devoted to her pekinese, the last of a line of 35 of that breed she had owned since buying herself a puppy on her 16th birthday.

Rumer Godden was appointed OBE in 1993.

11 November 1998

JANET FRAME

Writer who took alienation for her theme and whose
autobiography inspired the film An Angel at My Table

*

Janet Frame, who has died aged 79, was a novelist, poet, essayist and short story writer; in her homeland of New Zealand she was regarded as one of the country's most distinguished literary figures, but she achieved international recognition only after her three-volume autobiography inspired Jane Campion's acclaimed film *An Angel at My Table* (1990).

Janet Frame's life and work were inextricably linked; much of her fiction dwelt at length on insanity, breakdown and death – all of which featured in her own life. Her autobiography, however, revealed these horrors with such lightness of touch – and even humour – that for many it was her most accessible work. The memoir chronicled a strange and chaotic childhood, her misdiagnosis as a schizophrenic and the eight years spent in an institution before she was able to follow her dream of becoming a writer. Yet Janet Frame's transformation from a painfully shy and introspective child into a celebrated author was not one with which she was comfortable; up until her death she remained a recluse, living under an assumed name and going to considerable lengths to avoid publicity.

The third of five children, Janet Paterson Frame was born on 28 August 1924 at Dunedin, in New Zealand. Her father was an impoverished railway worker whose job forced the family to move many times before they finally settled in Oamaru in 1930. Her mother, a former housemaid who had, for a time, worked for the family of Katherine Mansfield, had been born into the Christadelphian faith, which invested everyday objects with religious significance. Janet Frame wrote: 'She had only to say of any commonplace object, "Look, kiddies, a stone", to fill that stone with wonder as if it were a holy object.'

In many ways, Janet Frame's childhood was a catalogue of poverty, debt, illness and tragedy: her older brother was severely epileptic, and was regularly beaten by their father; Myrtle, her eldest sister, drowned in a local swimming pool when Janet was 13; and ten years later her younger sister, Isabel, also drowned. But the family had a rich literary life, and although the children ran wild they were passionate about poetry and fascinated by language; Janet read voraciously, comparing herself and her sisters to the Brontës. She was also timid, and her shyness was exacerbated by her embarrassment at her unruly red hair and decayed teeth. Her awkwardness only increased with puberty (when she entered what she described as 'the adolescent homelessness of self'), and she immersed herself in a world of imagination and literature in order to escape from reality.

She was, however, an exemplary pupil, and, after attending Oamaru North School and Waitaki Girls' High School, she won a place at Dunedin Teacher Training School and Otago University. In 1945 a school inspector came to visit her as she was teaching a class and, terrified of being judged, she walked out, never to return. Although she continued to study Psychology at the university, she became increasingly lonely and withdrawn, and in her lodgings one night she took a quantity of aspirin. She awoke the next morning with nothing worse than a headache and relief that she was alive, and thought nothing of referring to the 'suicide attempt' in an autobiographical essay written for a psychology class. Within days, however, her tutors suggested to her that she might 'need a little rest', and she was committed to a mental hospital; she later admitted that an innocent crush on a tutor who had compared her to van Gogh had led her to romanticise the notion of being schizophrenic.

Janet Frame spent the next eight years in a series of psychiatric institutions, 'a concentrated course in the horrors of insanity and the dwelling-place of those judged insane'. Her second novel, *Faces in the Water* (1961), described her journey through 'madness'. 'I was put in hospital because a great gap opened in the ice floe between myself and the other people whom I watched with their world, drifting away . . .' During her years of incarceration, and despite the shrieks and moans of her fellow inmates, the sadism of the nurses and the effects of ECT, which was administered 200 times, Janet Frame managed to write *The Lagoon*, a collection of short stories. In 1954 she was about to undergo a frontal lobotomy when one of the doctors who was to perform the operation happened to read that her book had won a literary prize. 'I've decided,' he told her, 'that you should remain as you are.' As Janet Frame herself wrote more than once in her autobiography: 'My writing saved me.' She was released from hospital and, still fragile, was taken in by the New Zealand author Frank Sargeson, who encouraged her to write and allowed her to live in an old army hut in his garden. During this period she worked on *Owls Do Cry* (1961), a strongly autobiographical account of four children from an impoverished family.

In 1956 Janet Frame won a literary travel scholarship and sailed to Europe. A spell in Ibiza (during which she had a love affair with an American whose child she miscarried) was followed by seven years in Britain. In London, where the diagnosis of schizophrenia was formally rejected by the Maudsley hospital, she wrote extensively, producing *The Edge of the Alphabet* (1962) and *Scented Gardens for the Blind* (1963). The *Daily Telegraph*, reviewing *Scented Gardens*, described her as 'a specialist in depicting mental anguish and unbalance' with her 'intense, nervous, witty euphonious prose that seems to come direct from the experience she is dealing with'.

On the death of her father in 1963, Janet Frame returned to New Zealand. In 1965 *The Adaptable Man* was published, followed by *A State of Siege* (1967). *The Rainbirds* (1968) was about a young man who awakes from a coma to find that everyone had expected him to die; rather than being overjoyed at his recovery, they are merely miserably disorientated. Like much of her work, its theme was alienation. Her writing often pitted misfits against the repressive puritanism and philistinism of conformist society. *Daughter Buffalo* (1972) was written during a period when Janet Frame was travelling between New Zealand and America. But in 1972 she moved to the Whangaparaoa Peninsula (north of Auckland), and produced no work until *Living in the Manioto* (1981), described by the *Daily Telegraph* as 'probably as near as a masterpiece as we are likely to see this year'.

The three volumes of her autobiography, *To the Is-Land*, *The Envoy from Mirror City* and *An Angel at My Table*, were published in Britain in 1983, 1984 and 1985. In 1990, the publication of all three in a single volume prompted Michael Holroyd, writing in the *Sunday Times*, to describe it as 'one of the greatest autobiographies written this century'.

Janet Frame received many honours. She was a Burns Scholar, a Sargeson Fellow and was awarded the New Zealand Scholarship in Letters. A later book, *The Carpathians* (1989), won the Commonwealth Literature Prize. In 1983 she was appointed CBE. Last year she was shortlisted for the Nobel Prize for Literature.

Although she wrote under her own name, for much of her later life she lived under the pseudonym Janet Clutha. After the release of the film of *An Angel at My Table*, there were many attempts to interview her, but few were successful. She greeted the many accolades she received with a modesty bordering on disbelief. 'I am not really a writer,' she explained. 'I am just someone who is haunted, and I will write the hauntings down.' She had written her autobiography, she would say, only as an attempt to set the record straight after so many critics had identified autobiographical truths in her fiction.

In 2003 Janet Frame was diagnosed with terminal cancer. 'The prospect of having one's tomorrows cut off,' she said, 'at first it was quite alarming but I've got used to it now.'

She was unmarried.

30 January 2004

ANGELA CARTER

Novelist of exuberant invention with a taste for fairytales and sceptical, musical, politicised comedy

*

Angela Carter, the novelist, who has died aged 51, was one of the most important writers at work in the English language. She was often described – at a time when the term was being bandied freely about – as a 'magic realist'.

The writers of this school – Gunter Grass, Gabriel Garcia Marquez, Salman Rushdie among them – combined exuberant fantasy and a chiselled clarity of depiction to write realistically about unrealistic events. At a time when serious fiction seemed to suffer from anaemia and timidity they re-emphasised the importance of storytelling and of the fact that literature should be exuberant and enjoyable to read. Although the movement has had its excesses and backslidings – from the occasional over-rating of its minor practitioners to Mario Vargas Llosa's failed campaign for the presidency of Peru – the global success of 'magic realism' is largely responsible for the decline in once-fashionable discussions about 'the death of the novel'.

Carter's *Nights at the Circus* (1984, which jointly won the James Tait Black Memorial Prize) is a classic of this genre. In the novel *Fevvers*, a 6ft tall Cockney trapeze artiste with wings comes to fascinate a sceptical American called James Walser. His obsession with whether Fevvers is or is not an impostor – which stands in for the reader's interest in the same question – is exposed by the book as too narrowly reasoned and he ends up in Siberia, drinking hallucinogenic reindeer urine in a shamanistic initiation ceremony.

Carter's interest in the farther shores of the imagination, in fantasy, and most specifically in fairytales, was lifelong. Their presence informs her novels from *The Magic Toyshop* (1967) to *Wise Children* (1991). In 1990 Carter edited *The Virago Book of Fairy Tales*. *The Bloody Chamber* (1979), a collection of re-worked, re-imagined classic tales – one of which was later made into the film *The Company of Wolves* – shows Carter taking the opportunity to give her own particular twist of sexual unease to the vivid, cruel world of the fairy story. The result is perhaps her most flawless book, as surprising and disconcerting as the original unbowdlerised Grimm. At the same time, however, there is a strong vein of Englishness in Carter's work – an Englishness apparent in her earthy, cheerfully vulgar humour and in the distinctive flavour of her sceptical, irreverent feminism.

George Steiner remarked that no other language has an equivalent phrase to the English 'come off it'. Carter often said 'come off it', particularly in her lucid, funny debunking journalism for the *Guardian* and *New Society* as collected in the volume *Nothing Sacred*. Her description of the domestic life of the Wordsworths, living in a stultifying atmosphere of electric sexual tension and drug abuse, is a wonderfully vivid comic corrective to the received image of the Westmorland sage.

These three strands of Carter's work – the exuberant fantastic invention, the interest in archetypal fairytale patterns, and her taste for sceptical, musical, politicised comedy – come together in her best and last novel, *Wise Children*. The twins Nora and Dora Chance, the illegitimate daughters of celebrated Shakespearean actor Sir Melchior Hazard, live a rackety theatrical life from Brixton in the Twenties through to New York, Hollywood (where they live at a hotel called 'The Forest of

Arden') and back again to retirement in Brixton. Full of magnificently quirky imagery – 'the lights of Electric Avenue glowing like bad fish through a good old London fog' – *Wise Children* is a warm, funny, brilliant novel which also constitutes a cruel reminder of what we have been deprived of by its author's death.

She was born Angela Stalker at Eastbourne in 1940. Her father (who 'wore glamorous Edgar Wallace hats and smoked a pipe which he kept in the pocket of his jacket, which occasionally caught fire') was a journalist of Scots descent; her mother was a cashier at Selfridges. Angela Carter recalled that she 'had a core of iron built into me by my grandmother'. An impressive matriarch 'who looked like the Giles granny', she came from a mining family in South Yorkshire and decided the family would be safer during the War in the South Yorkshire coalfields.

After the War young Angela was educated at a direct-grant school in Balham and experienced a pre-television childhood in which she read omnivorously. She also ate copiously and at school, she recalled, she spent much of her time 'brooding fatly alone'. Her nickname was 'Tub'. She subsequently developed full-blown anorexia – 'long before the condition had been properly invented'.

Despite her wide reading she did not do well enough in examinations at school to win a place at university, and her father fixed her up with a job as a journalist. She was apprenticed to the *Croydon Advertiser*, where she turned out to be 'not too good on facts – already the writer of fiction was showing through'. But she turned out to be adept at talking to people in shock; she was so ashamed of asking questions that she was gentler than the average journalist. At 18, she recalled, 'I looked like a 30-year old divorcée. I was shy, immature, insensitive, selfish, pain-in-the-neck, way-out and terribly unhappy. I didn't even have the self-confidence to get away with being a pain-in-the-neck. In my condition then, being a reporter was a contradiction in terms.'

In 1960 she married Paul Carter, an industrial chemist from

Cheam who took her on 'Ban the Bomb' marches and introduced her to jazz. The next year she followed him to Bristol where she failed to land a job on the *Bristol Evening Post*. Instead she entered Bristol University to read for a degree in English. She specialised in the medieval period to avoid Leavisite dogma, and also to avoid the risk of having her pleasure in modern writing ruined by the obligations to have opinions about it.

Her first novel, *Shadow Dance* – a peculiar, violent thriller about which she was later rather embarrassed – was published in 1966. The next year her second, *The Magic Toyshop*, was much more successful, and won the John Llewellyn Rhys Memorial Award. It told the story of a newly orphaned 15-year-old, innocent if narcissistic, who is sent to live in a bizarre south London toyshop with a tyrannical uncle; it was later made into a film starring Tom Bell.

Several Pleasures (1968) won the Somerset Maugham Award, the money from which enabled her to leave her husband. 'I'm sure Somerset Maugham would have been very pleased,' she said. The couple separated at San Francisco airport. Carter flew to Japan where she was to spend the next two years. The first fruit of her time in Japan was the novel *The Infernal Desire Machine of Dr Hoffman* (1972) which she wrote in three months. The novel, an energetic but not entirely successful evocation of a phantasmagoric 'disruption of the reality principle', marked a new ambition in her work. Carter's time in Japan was also crucial in giving a new impetus to her feminism. 'Feminists accuse me of being an "Uncle Tom",' she would say, 'but I don't think I'd be the person I am if it weren't for the women's movement in the Sixties.'

This new impetus was apparent in the baroque power of *The Passion of New Eve* (1977) and her entertaining, challenging essay on the Marquis de Sade, *The Sadeian Woman* (1979). In her ingeniously argued thesis she sought to rehabilitate him as the Enlightenment thinker who 'put pornography in the service of women'; in other words, he employed that elaborate edifice of sexual fantasy partly to demonstrate that women should be as free as men to do what takes their fancy. In 1979 she also published her first masterpiece, *The Bloody Chamber*. *Black Venus* (1986) took its title from one of Carter's most affectionately demystifying stories, concerning Jeanne Duval, the black prostitute who was Baudelaire's mistress and muse.

Angela Carter was one of the most stylish English prose writers of the age. Some found her language almost too perfect: John Mortimer, for instance, remarked that a prolonged submission to it was apt to leave the reader in a somewhat heady condition. David Holloway, the former literary editor of the *Daily Telegraph*, called Carter 'the Salvador Dali of English letters. Her draughtsmanship is as clear, her colours as bright and her intentions as obscure'. Noting that she taught creative writing at American universities, he observed that it was impossible not to feel that she was too consciously crafting her work – 'but there is wonderful sensual flow to her writing'.

Besides teaching stints in Australia, Texas and Iowa, she was a Fellow in Creative Writing at Sheffield University from 1976 to 1978. Throughout the productive years in which she wrote her major work, Angela Carter was living with her partner, Mark Pearce, a potter. Their son, Alexander, was born in 1984 – the same year which saw the publication of *Nights at the Circus*.

17 February 1992

LOWLIFE AND THE AFTERLIFE

*

HENRIETTA MORAES

Soho beauty who was painted by Bacon and Freud, lived fast,
married thrice and sought a new start

*

Henrietta Moraes, who has died aged 67, found her home in Soho and was painted by Francis Bacon, Lucian Freud and, much later, Maggi Hambling.

When she arrived in London aged 18, she went under the name of Wendy Welling, her mother's surname. She at once took to the bohemian life of Soho, drinking in the York Minster in Dean Street, known as the French Pub, and, in the afternoons when pubs were closed, in the Colony Room Club. She was not unlike other habitués of Soho in her heroic drinking, but she was distinguished by her beauty, wit and surface toughness. It was the world described by Julian Maclaren Ross in *Soho in the Forties* and by Daniel Farson in *Soho in the Fifties*, of macintoshes, men in hats, cigarette smoke, gangsters, tarts, petty criminals, cold nights, sailors and no money.

There was a rough and tumble in conversation, plenty of unconventional sexual liaisons, and a camaraderie between refugees from suburban conventions that sometimes developed into kindness or love. She embraced it all. At the Gargoyle nightclub she would meet the same crowd night after night: Brian Howard, Cyril Connolly, Philip Toynbee, Francis Bacon, Michael Wishart, Lucian Freud, John Minton, Robert Colquhoun and Robert MacBryde. At the beginning of the 1950s she met and fell in love with another Soho fixture, the film-maker Michael Law. It was he who suggested she find a better name, and for the rest of her life she was known as Henrietta. They married and in the early 1950s lived in a house in Dean Street.

Henrietta now sat for Lucian Freud, whose portrait of her she later put on the dustjacket of her memoirs. Soho life moved fast, from the Coach and Horses to an afternoon drinking club, to the French when it opened again for the evening, to a nightclub. All along the way were strange, witty, unreliable, dangerous and sexually active characters. 'In the Fifties, everyone was extremely rude to one another,' she remembered. All this time money was short, as it was for most Soho people.

Among her friends was John Minton, the painter. He had good looks, talent and friends, but was haunted by a melancholy streak and troubled by his homosexuality. She also fell in with Norman Bowler, who had been living in Minton's house in Apollo Place, Chelsea. She became pregnant by him and they married; they were to have a boy and a girl. Some time later, just before his 40th birthday, Minton committed suicide. Henrietta Bowler heard the news when she was in hospital, pregnant, and suffering from typhoid. Many had assumed that Minton would leave his house to Norman Bowler, whom he loved, but he left it to Henrietta.

During her marriage to Norman Bowler she took a job with David Archer, the unpractical patron of literary talents. He had just opened a new bookshop, in Greek Street, and Henrietta worked at the coffee bar inside the shop, making egg and water-cress rolls. 'All David Archer really wanted,' she recalled, 'was a sort of salon. Strangers would come in off the street, and he would not want them to buy a book. He'd say: "Hey, don't ask me. I mean, there's a very good bookshop up the road called Foyle's, go there."'

One of the writers that David Archer tried to help was Dom Moraes. He was a smooth-tongued Indian, a great young hope of Commonwealth poetry who later won the Hawthornden Prize. Henrietta was later to refer to him ambiguously as 'that 24-hour poet'. His first volume of poetry, *A Beginning*, was dedicated to her. Quite soon, in 1961, she married him. Dom Moraes spent three years at Oxford, which Henrietta enjoyed;

she made new friends such as Peter Levi, the poet. But settled back in London, Dom Moraes went out one day to buy some cigarettes and never returned.

About this time, Francis Bacon was painting her. He explained that he would like to paint her from photographs. These were supplied by John Deakin, an impossible friend of Archer's who managed to get sacked as a photographer by *Vogue* twice. He took a fine series of images of Henrietta Moraes lying naked on a bed, which Bacon used. But she was surprised to find that Deakin was soon offering spare prints for sale to sailors at 10 shillings each.

In the 1960s, as well as drinking hugely, Henrietta Moraes used drugs more and more. Though one of Bacon's paintings of her shows a naked body with a syringe stuck in one arm, she did not use heroin. But, along with the usual pills, she eventually took to LSD. Her life became increasingly ramshackle; the spell of Soho was broken.

Henrietta Moraes was born Audrey Wendy Abbott in Simla on 22 May 1931. Her father, whom she never knew, was an Indian Air Force officer nicknamed Ginger. When she was 18 months old her mother returned to England to work as a nurse; at three Audrey was sent to board at a convent. She remembered her childhood as cruelly unhappy. Her largely absent mother she called 'Mummy Judy'. When she was sick over her bed in the school dormitory she ate up every bit again lest she be detected. When staying with her grandmother at Bedford, taking dull walks beside the flooded Ouse, she would hear how her father was an 'absolute monster, a really wicked man'. She was shuttled from grandmother (who, she said, beat her with a strap) to schools. Always on the edge of expulsion, she eventually left to take a secretarial course in London, and her life in Soho began.

After the end of her marriage to Dom Moraes, drugs and drink drove her to burglary; she failed and went to prison. Once out she drifted away from Soho, and for four years travelled

Britain in a gipsy caravan. She had friends with country houses, many of whom, like her, were captivated by drugs. She drifted ever westward, via Hay-on-Wye and a job in a bookshop, to Ireland. By the end of the Eighties she was back in London, poor and sick from drink. She found a way out of the vicious cycle of drink through Alcoholics Anonymous.

At the end of her life, living in a room in Chelsea with her dachsund, Max, she sat for Maggi Hambling, who became a friend.

9 January 1999

DOREEN VALIENTE

*Prominent witch who compiled new pagan rituals but disliked
the sexual demands of some coven leaders*

*

Doreen Valiente, who has died aged 77, was one of Britain's most influential witches. Along with figures such as Aleister Crowley, Gerald Gardner and Cecil Williamson, she was responsible for the resurgence of witchcraft in the 20th century. Hailed by many practising pagans as the mother of modern witchcraft, or 'Wicca', she herself declined any such title, describing herself as a practitioner of the Old Religion.

An imposing figure, tall and dark with a penetrating eye, Doreen Valiente had a forthright character, an earthy sense of humour, and a raucous laugh. She brought a poetic kind of spirituality to the editing of Gerald Gardner's *Book of Shadows*, a hotchpotch of ancient ritual on which he based his new Wiccan cult in the early 1950s. When Doreen Valiente pointed out, to Gardner's intense embarrassment, that much of the ritual in his book seemed to be derived from Freemasonry, he admitted that he had originally received little more than a collection of 'fragments' from his initiator, the New Forest witch, Dorothy Clutterbuck. He went on to explain that he had added material piecemeal from Aleister Crowley, the Rosicrucians, Freemasonry, various friends and, more surprisingly, Rudyard Kipling, to 'strike the right chord'.

Doreen Valiente's own contribution to the body of Wiccan ritual cannot be overstated. She, perhaps more than Gardner, established the tone of modern witch rites. It amused her when she met people claiming to be 'hereditary witches' who quoted, as proof of their ancient lineage, rituals which she herself had written with Gardner in the 1950s.

She was born Doreen Dominy in 1922 in London. Her father's family came from Cerne Abbas in Dorset, home of the Giant, a priapic chalk man of enormous proportions. As a young child, Valiente claimed that she began to experience psychic episodes. By her late teens she was a practising clairvoyant. She worked as a secretary by day, and spent her evenings immersed in the esoteric works of the Golden Dawn, of ritual magicians such as Aleister Crowley and theosophists such as Madame Blavatsky.

In 1944 Doreen married Casimiro Valiente, a refugee from the Spanish Civil War who went on to fight for the Free French in the Second World War. The couple settled in Bournemouth, but the marriage was not a happy one. Casimiro was less enthused by the 'craft of the wise' than his spouse.

At the age of 30, Doreen Valiente contacted Cecil Williamson, then owner of the Witches' Mill Museum, for information on witchcraft. Williamson passed her letter to Gerald Gardner who, after the repeal of the Witchcraft Act in 1951, proclaimed himself to be the museum's 'resident witch'. She and Gardner met in 1952 in the New Forest home of Gardner's initiator Dorothy Clutterbuck. Doreen Valiente recalled that she had misgivings about initiation into witchcraft, fearing she would be required to sell her soul to the Devil. She decided to go ahead anyway. 'To be willing to sell one's soul to the Devil,' she said, 'was a state of mind that living in Bournemouth readily induced.' On being reassured that the 'Old Religion' admitted no devil-worship, Valiente joined Gardner's New Forest coven in 1953.

During the 1950s she worked with Gardner as the High Priestess of his coven. It was then that she reworked and created a large body of ritual material for Gardner's *Book of Shadows*. Valiente argued strongly against the inclusion of Aleister Crowley's poetry on the basis that it was 'too modern'. In her revision of the *Book of Shadows*, she based her new invocations on Charles Leland's *Gospel of the Witches* (1899). Given Gardner's taste for self-publicity, it was inevitable that he and Doreen Valiente would disagree. She maintained that secrecy was essential and that Gardner's 'going public' opened the way for 'undignified publicity antics which alienate intelligent people'. She had friends who had lost jobs and suffered physical attacks after it became public knowledge that they were witches.

Though she and Gardner were only intermittently on speaking terms, Doreen Valiente remained staunchly loyal to her initiator. She was never under any illusions about Gardner's sexual preferences, describing him on more than one occasion as 'a thoroughly kinky old goat who was into flagellation'. At the same time she defended Gardner, and pointed out that the lash was an integral part of many ancient mystery religions. While she admitted Gardner was a 'devious, manipulative old devil' she said his publicity-seeking was the action of 'someone who believed passionately that the craft of the wise should not be allowed to die'.

In 1957, after their disagreement over the issue of secrecy, Doreen Valiente left Gardner's coven. In 1964 she began working with the hereditary witch Robert Cochrane. Valiente approved of Cochrane's use of rhythmic poetry, dance and chanting, but had little time for his fondness for sexual liaisons with coven members. She later left the coven. In 1966 Cochrane committed suicide by taking an overdose of belladonna juice.

After the death of her husband in 1972, Doreen Valiente devoted herself full-time to writing about witchcraft. She corresponded on the subject in magazines such as *The Wiccan* and *The Cauldron*. Her best known work, *An ABC of Witchcraft*, was published in 1973. During the 1970s, she helped to establish the Pagan Federation. This organisation sought legislation which, members hoped, would enable pagans to worship freely without public opprobrium or discrimination.

In 1977 Doreen Valiente met Ron Cooke, a fellow witch whom she described as 'the love of my life'. They were to live together until his death in 1997. Throughout the 1980s and 1990s Doreen Valiente continued to practise magic as a 'solitary' with Ron Cooke, and to produce books on witchcraft. *The Rebirth of Witchcraft* was published in 1989, and in 1990 she edited Evan John Jones's book *Witchcraft: a Tradition Renewed*.

At the age of 75, she developed a penchant for 'skunk', a strong variety of cannabis, which she smoked in a newly acquired 'bong', a kind of hubble–bubble. She also indulged more freely her interest in tantric sex, with an emerging passion for black leather. But to the last, Doreen Valiente maintained she was nothing more than 'an old fashioned witch'.

10 September 1999

EILEEN FOX

Self-styled 'Queen of Soho' who sued British Airways claiming to have been bitten on the bottom by a flea

*

Eileen Fox, who has died aged 79, was a peripatetic bohemian and film extra, given to calling herself the 'Queen of Soho' in the 1960s and 1970s. As talkative as she was rotund, 'Foxy', as she was invariably known, was certainly hard to miss in the small knot of streets just to the north of London's Shaftesbury Avenue. If she felt that she was receiving insufficient attention she would remove her clothes in public view. Whether lunching at Jimmy the Greek's or devouring other customers' part-consumed cream buns at Patisserie Valerie, she made everyone else's business her own, often to their intense irritation.

The daughter of a prostitute and a father she never met, Eileen Daphne Fox was born of Jewish stock and brought up in east London in the 1920s. She was known from her early years simply as 'Foxy', a name that acknowledged both her easy informality and a natural cunning. It was not an easy childhood. Her mother had little money, and Foxy received a basic education, managing to master only capital letters. A flair for acting became apparent when she discarded her native Cockney accent in favour of something more refined. She worked as a telephone reception- ist at a West End law firm and impressed clients who, on being connected to the senior partner, would compliment him on employing such a high standard of switchboard operator. The object of their esteem, however, was not a pearled daughter of the shires but a plump, untidy woman who was seldom seen without several plastic bags full of possessions.

In Soho, Eileen Fox became acquainted with the set that included Francis Bacon and Jeffrey Bernard, though she disap- proved of their heavy drinking and always refused to buy alco- hol for friends. She herself preferred fizzy, soft drinks which soon rotted away her teeth. Eileen was a stranger to reticence. At the drop of a good polka she would seize the nearest man to give him a dance to remember. When short of money, which was often, she would approach strangers with the suggestion that she read their fortunes. Task done, she would insist that they cross her own palm with silver – preferably of a high denomination. She liked to strip, be it to enliven a party or to celebrate a rous- ing tune. A patriot, she could seldom hear 'Rule Britannia' without loosening her bra straps. In the late 1970s she became a regular visitor to Ibiza, though curiously she ignored the island's nudist beaches. As well as being a nude model for artists, Eileen undertook work as a film extra, specialising in crowd scenes that called for gummy medieval serfs. One of her last appearances was in Kevin Costner's *Robin Hood: Prince of Thieves* (1991).

In 1980 she took British Airways to the Court of Appeal, alleging that she had been bitten on the bottom while travelling on one of the company's Boeing 747s to the Seychelles. 'It was a jumbo jet and they must have been elephant fleas,' she told reporters afterwards. She claimed that the unsightly bites cost her professional earnings as a nude model. Lord Justice Megaw and his colleagues were not convinced. It transpired that Eileen Fox had earlier bounced a £500 cheque on British Airways and took exception when the airline sought recovery of the funds. After that case she refused to pay for air travel. Instead, she worked for an international courier firm, delivering parcels around the globe and frequently selling the return stub of her free ticket in order to explore countries at greater leisure. From Nepal to Nigeria, Peru to the Ukraine, Eileen could be found hitch-hiking well into her old age. British drivers, stopping to pick up a gnarled old peasant, were astonished to be addressed with a very English 'Cheers!' In Athens she spent several months working as a dishwasher, sleeping on the roof of a hotel near the airport while she earned her fare home. She was a frequent menace to British diplomats, who would find her on their embassy doorstep, demanding safe passage back to London. Although always claiming penury, she was a generous woman, fond of the young and earnest in her desire to help.

In the 1980s she took advantage of the Conservatives' right-to-buy policy and took a mortgage on her council house in Elspeth Road, Battersea. She later sold the house for a profit of £80,000 and used the money to become a landlord in the Balearics. She died in a nursing home on Ibiza, after a stroke. At her Anglican funeral the priest forwent traditional liturgy and instead invited congregants to tell their favourite Foxy memories.

To her own regret, she never married.

17 September 2002

ROSEMARY BROWN

Medium who claimed that Beethoven, Chopin and Liszt gave
her musical dictation from beyond the grave

*

Rosemary Brown, who has died aged 85, was a medium specialising in communication with dead composers; her clairvoyant contact with, among others, Liszt, Chopin, Beethoven, Schubert and Rachmaninov resulted in hundreds of piano miniatures which the composers 'dictated' to her.

In 1964, as a widow with two children, Rosemary Brown was working in a school kitchen at Balham, south London, when she was forced to take time off work after breaking two ribs in a fall. It was then that she was 'visited' by Liszt as she sat in front of a piano. 'I could stumble through an easy tune,' she said, 'but this was like automatic playing. I began to play virtuoso-style pieces, and it grew from there.' Liszt became her spiritual guide. He spoke English, but with a strong accent, so she took evening classes in German in order to communicate with him. He visited her often and even watched television with her. Through Liszt she claimed that she met Bach, Beethoven, Chopin and many others. Each composer would dictate to her, sometimes at the piano, sometimes preferring her to take musical notation.

Bach, she recalled, tended to be rather stern and impatient, and Beethoven was no longer deaf. Schubert was good humoured but 'still a little shy', had lost some weight, given up his spectacles and learned to speak English. The composers would also wear contemporary clothes. 'Debussy has wonderful things – sheepskin coats and so on. The others are more or less orthodox, though Liszt and Beethoven both have long hair.' Her composers did not confine themselves to purely musical messages. On one occasion, when her daughter had turned on the bath without Rosemary Brown's knowledge, Chopin came to the rescue: 'Suddenly he stopped giving me music and appeared to be quite agitated. He started speaking in French. Eventually I realised that he was saying "*Le bain va être englouti*".' She came to regard Liszt as a friend. 'He is,' she claimed, 'a very generous, very cultured, very devout man.'

Intrigued by her claims, numerous musicians, composers and critics clamoured to meet her and hear her work. In 1969 Richard Rodney Bennett interviewed her for BBC TV's *Music Now* programme, although he was non-committal as to the authenticity of the compositions. 'Whether she really has Debussy in her drawing room,' he said, 'I don't know.' A number of musical experts agreed that Rosemary Brown's music bore many similarities to the work of the composers she purported to represent, although many attributed this to a knack for musical mimicry; the tunes themselves, though recognisably influenced by individual composers, were somewhat slight. Some observed that if the great composers had wanted the world to hear them from the grave, they might have dictated music that was a little more inspirational. There was no doubt, however, as to Rosemary Brown's dedication and belief in her gift. A devout Christian, she made no money from her work, and sponsors helped to pay for records and recitals. 'Writing the music down takes hours,' she explained. 'It's very hard work, and I never know how it is going to sound until it is played. Don't think that it is easy going for me. I didn't ask to be chosen.'

She was born Rosemary Dickenson on 27 July 1916 at Stockwell, south London. She had ambitions to be a dancer but, after leaving school aged 15, she joined the Post Office and worked in various office jobs until her marriage. Throughout her youth she had experienced psychic phenomena, but did not become directly involved in spiritualism until 1961 after the deaths of both her mother and her husband.

She befriended a number of 'New Age' thinkers including Sir George Trevelyan, who, upon hearing of her musical discoveries, introduced her to George Firth, a former member of the Scottish Arts Council, and his wife Mary, a music teacher. In 1968 the Firths set up a charitable trust enabling Rosemary Brown to devote herself to her work as 'clerical assistant' to the spirits of dead musicians. She then appeared in a BBC TV news item and was catapulted into the public eye. In the early 1970s Rosemary Brown appeared regularly on television and in public. She played at the New York City Hall and appeared on the Johnny Carson Show in America, where her talents were embraced. In Britain, however, she had a mixed reception. In 1971 the first of a number of recordings of her work was made and a concert was given in which her 'dictations' were played alongside works written by the composers when they were alive. The reviews were scathing; the *Daily Telegraph* wrote that 'the superficial aspects of style, the mannerisms, were sometimes present, but what was missing in all cases was the hard creative thought that makes cogent syntax from vocabulary and that indicates the presence of a master.' However, Rosemary Brown maintained that the composers' intentions were only to prove the existence of an afterlife.

She gave a number of other recitals and there were further recordings in 1977 and 1988. However, by the 1980s poor health prevented her from continuing her work. Her publications included *Unfinished Symphonies* (1971), *Immortals at My Elbow* (1974) and *Look Beyond Today* (1986).

Rosemary Brown encountered many 'viperish attacks' on her credibility. She accepted that dishonest mediums had given spiritualism a bad press, but was adamant that clairvoyance was a genuine gift. 'I suspect,' she wrote in 1971, 'that many individuals highly gifted with extra sensory aptitudes keep silent about their abilities, fearing that to reveal them would invite persecution from religious bigots and otherwise biased people, as well as from the ill-disposed, envious and ignorant.'

She married Charles Brown, a government scientist, in 1952; he died in 1961. A son and a daughter survive her.

22 November 2001

Index

Abzug, Bella: feminist activist proud of her big hats, big mouth
and big ideas   81
Acton, Daphne, Lady: Catholic convert who built a church in
Africa and was described by Evelyn Waugh as 'the most
remarkable woman I know'   147

Bannister, Sybil: Englishwoman who spent the war in Germany
and was nearly burnt to death during the massed Allied
bombing of Wuppertal   23
Barnett, 'Sadie': last of the great Dickensian landladies   94
Bartok, Eva: film actress more remarkable for her good looks
and complicated private life than for her screen
performances   251
Beloff, Nora: combative and litigious foreign correspondent
who brooked no contradiction   289
Blankers-Koen, Fanny: Dutch sprinter, known as 'The Flying
Housewife', who was voted the greatest female athlete
of the last century   130
Borboni, Paola: actress known as 'Paola of the scandals' who
stunned 1920s Italy by baring her breasts on stage   245
Brown, Rosemary: medium who claimed that Beethoven,
Chopin and Liszt gave her musical dictation from beyond
the grave   350
Browne, Coral: actress who excelled at duchesses and dragons
and appeared in a film about her real life encounter in
Moscow with the spy Guy Burgess   247
Bullwinkel, Vivian: lone survivor of a massacre of young

Australian nurses by the Japanese on a tropical island
in 1942   9

Carter, Angela: novelist of exuberant invention with a taste for
fairytales and sceptical, musical, politicised comedy   333
Cartland, Dame Barbara: author of more than 700 romantic
novels who championed vitamins, honey, gypsies and the
colour pink   67
Cazalet-Keir, Thelma: Tory MP who championed women's
rights and initiated Churchill's only defeat in the
Commons   46
Cockburn, Patricia: Irish aristocrat who charmed tribes of
homicidal pygmies during her explorations in equatorial
Africa   172
Courtenay-Latimer, Marjorie: curator whose enthusiasm led
to the discovery of a prehistoric fish thought to be
extinct   212
Cox, Nesta: British 'Nanny of Nanteuil' who spoke nursery
Franglais and served through the German occupation   257
Cradock, Fanny: *grande dame* of the kitchen who appeared on
television in Norman Hartnell ballgowns   105
Cusack-Smith, Lady: fearless and colourful Master of
Foxhounds in County Galway who stood no nonsense
and loved to tango   125

D'Abo, Jennifer: entrepreneur driven by the thrill of the deal
who showed a talent for turning round moribund
companies   57
De Henriquez, Fiore: sculptress whose work was informed by
her hermaphrodism, and included public commissions
and many portraits of celebrities   301
Delamere, Diana, Lady: *femme fatale* of Happy Valley who took
the secret of a murder to her grave   281
Dickson, Dame Violet: *grande dame* of Kuwait who spent
60 years in Araby and held court over classic English
teas   89

Fox, Eileen: self-styled 'Queen of Soho' who sued British
    Airways claiming to have been bitten on the bottom
    by a flea   347
Frame, Janet: writer who took alienation for her theme and
    whose autobiography inspired the film *An Angel at My
    Table*   329
Furse, Elisabeth: one-time Communist whose bohemian bistro
    in London attracted politicians, diplomats and aristocrats   155

Gabor, Eva: starlet who specialised in jewels, mink and
    matrimony   242
Gibbs, Olive: formidable Labour *grande dame* and passionate
    campaigner for unilateral disarmament   61
Godden, Rumer: novelist who excelled at writing about
    children and nuns but hated the film of *Black
    Narcissus*   324
Goldsmith, Olivia: author of *The First Wives Club* who took
    revenge on her former husband by writing a blockbuster
    novel   321
Griffiths, Catherine: oldest survivor of the Welsh suffragettes
    who was jailed for breaking into the House of Lords   34
Grundy, Air Commodore Bridget: WAAF pioneer who began
    her wartime service by inspecting drains and ended up
    30 years later outranking rival men officers   53

Harriman, Pamela: English adventuress who set her cap at
    the rich and powerful and ended up as a millionairess
    and American ambassador in Paris   163
Hattersley, Enid: Lord Mayor of Sheffield who transformed
    the cultural life of the city and inspired her son's career   137
Heber Percy, Lady Dorothy: youngest of the Lygon sisters
    whose family inspired the Flytes in Evelyn Waugh's
    novel *Brideshead Revisited*   277
Highsmith, Patricia: thriller writer who confronted her
    own demons by creating the amoral anti-hero Tom
    Ripley   317

Hill, Pamela: a life dominated by a love that withstood war, separation and madness, only to be tested by a diary in code   15

Hopper, Rear-Admiral Grace: American computer expert who coined the term 'bug' and was known as the 'first lady of Software'   193

Hunter Cowan, Major Betty: Army major and member of a long-standing female partnership known as 'the Cavewomen'   99

Kane, Sarah: playwright whose works created a sensation with scenes of unbridled brutality   314

Kenward, Betty: social columnist whose 'Jennifer's Diary' chronicled the activities of the English upper classes for half a century   272

Kingsley, Victoria: collector of songs who could chant in Gaelic and accompany herself on an instrument made from the carapace of the hairy armadillo   239

Lambton, Bindy: wife of Lord Lambton with a genius for entertaining guests, who sometimes found lions in the bedrooms   268

Lehmann, Rosamond: rediscovered novelist who gave up writing after the break up of her affair with Cecil Day Lewis   311

Lillie, Beatrice: theatrical comedienne who delighted in comic chaos both on and off the stage   235

Lindell, Mary: head of the French Resistance at Lyons where she ran an escape route out of occupied France   18

Littlewood, Joan: visionary director whose Theatre Workshop for the working-class was hijacked by West End audiences   49

Longfield, Cynthia: intrepid traveller and naturalist who searched the world for dragonflies   196

Louden, Margaret: surgeon whose pioneering treatment saved people crushed by buildings in the Blitz   43

Mann Borgese, Elisabeth: intellectual who taught a dog to play
the piano   74

Markus, Rixi: first woman bridge grandmaster and member of a
partnership known as 'Frisky and Bitchy'   113

Mason, Portland: film star's daughter said to have smoked when
she was only three and to have had a couture dress at four   233

Mee, Margaret: botanical artist and traveller who braved snakes,
spiders and cannibals in her pursuit of rare species   36

Minto, Sheila: secretary to eight prime ministers who stood up
to Winston Churchill   264

Moraes, Henrietta: Soho beauty who was painted by Bacon and
Freud, lived fast, married thrice and sought a new start   341

Morphew, Patricia: fire-service driver in the Blitz who kept
driving after her car was holed by a bomb   20

Newcastle, Diana, Duchess of: fearless promoter of women's
racing who held a jockey's licence in four countries and
once competed in the Monte Carlo Rally   116

Paterson, Jennifer: eccentric but much-loved cook who latterly
achieved recognition as one of television's Two Fat Ladies   76

Pearson GC, Daphne: WAAF who won the George Cross for
dragging a pilot from a blazing aircraft loaded with bombs   12

Pushnik, Frieda: freak-show artiste with Barnum and Bailey   228

Ranfurly, Hermione Countess of: author of *To War With
Whitaker*, her memoir of life in Cairo with Eisenhower,
SOE and the family retainer   260

Reid, Beryl: comic actress who spent 30 years in variety before
hitting the big time   219

Ridley, Cressida: Asquith's granddaughter who turned her sharp
intellect not to Liberal politics but to neolithic archaeology
and made notable discoveries in Greece   207

Robertson, Barbara: stalwart of the Bath Music Festival who
organised a Roman orgy at which guests consumed fried
dormice   84

Sage, Lorna: writer and professor of English Literature whose
memoir of a bleak childhood in post-war provincial Britain
brought comparisons with the Brontës   205

Salaman, Peggy: aviatrix who beat the London to Cape Town
flying record with a couple of lion cubs   31

Sherlock, Dame Sheila: the world's foremost authority on the
liver and the first woman in Britain to become a Professor
of Medicine   29

Shilling, Beatrice 'Tilly': engineer and racing motor-cyclist
described as 'a flaming pathfinder of women's lib'   119

Smith, Jean: nanny whose loving advice on bringing up children
led her to become a television star and *Telegraph*
columnist   283

Smith, Julia: creator of *EastEnders*, the soap that gripped the
nation   86

Sutherland Pilch, Mervyn: elder of the golfing Barton girls
who vied with her sister for domination of the English
game in the 1930s   122

Tantri, K'tut: Scots-born writer and broadcaster who operated
under various pseudonyms, fell for a Balinese prince, and
as Surabaya Sue broadcast propaganda for Indonesian
guerrillas fighting the Dutch   168

Taylor, Shoe: butcher's daughter who sought, and found,
adventure as a hippy before becoming the devoted mistress
of Jonathan Guinness   176

Thomas, Irene: former chorus girl and pub pianist who became
BBC Brain of Britain and a mainstay of *Round Britain
Quiz*   223

Thompson, Doris: 'Queen Mother of Blackpool' who was c
hairman of the Pleasure Beach and rode its roller-coasters
aged 100   40

Thompson, Kay: comedy revue star surprised by the success of
Eloise, her children's book anti-heroine   308

Travers, Susan: Englishwoman who abandoned life as a socialite
to become the first female member of the Foreign Legion   182

Tweedie, Jill: feminist writer and controversialist who loved
    tilting at conventional wisdom and shattering taboos   305

Uvarov, Dame Olga: Russian child refugee who became the first
    woman president of the Royal College of Veterinary
    Surgeons   202

Valentine, Greta: beautiful bohemian mystic whose charms
    mesmerised Aleister Crowley, the black magician, in the
    1930s   151
Valiente, Doreen: prominent witch who compiled new pagan
    rituals but disliked the sexual demands of some coven
    leaders   344
Vayne, Kyra: soprano who performed with Gigli and Gobbi in
    the 1950s but then endured 40 years of obscurity before
    finding fresh celebrity   230

Wace, Barbara: journalist who covered the invasion of France
    and became a busy freelance while living close to Fleet
    Street   298
Waters, Elsie: partner in a famous sisterly comic double act   226
Webb, Violet: winner at the Los Angeles Games in 1932 of
    Britain's first Olympic medal for women's athletics   128
Wesley, Mary: novelist who embarked on her career at the age
    of 70 and rebelled against the 'hypocrisy' of her
    background   292
Widdowson, Elsie: nutritionist whose work on chemical
    composition of foodstuffs resulted in Britain's healthy
    wartime diet   198
Wilberforce, Marion: early aviatrix who flew a calf from Hungary
    and was one of only 11 women to fly a Lancaster bomber   186
Winch, Mary: veteran litigant who took on the English legal
    system and lost   102
Winchester, Bapsy Marchioness of: colourful Indian-born third
    wife of a marquess who sued Eve Fleming for 'enticing'
    her husband   179

Wishart, Lorna: femme fatale who was muse to both Laurie
Lee and Lucian Freud   144
Woodhouse, Barbara: dog trainer who could teach basic
obedience in less than six minutes   97
Wootton of Abinger, Baroness: socialist *grande dame* who
overcame wartime bereavement to become an academic
criminologist, writer and the first woman to sit on the
Woolsack   40